GARY WEST is a writer, musician and broadcaster based in Edinburgh, who has spent his professional life researching, teaching, performing and promoting the cultural and musical traditions of Scotland. A former professor and head of Celtic and Scottish Studies at the University of Edinburgh, he has published widely on the themes of music, heritage and folklore. He presented the specialist music programme *Pipeline* on BBC Radio Scotland for two decades before developing his own podcast, *Enjoy Your Piping*, which promotes bagpipe music on a weekly basis to over 100 nations worldwide. He serves as an external examiner at the Royal Conservatoire of Scotland and the University of the Highlands and Islands, and in 2020 was inducted into the Scottish Traditional Music Hall of Fame.

Brave New Music

The Martyn Bennett Story

GARY WEST

Luath Press Limited
EDINBURGH
www.luath.co.uk

First published 2025

ISBN: 978-1-80425-193-5 hardback
ISBN: 978-1-80425-211-6 paperback

The author's right to be identified as author of this book
under the Copyright, Designs and Patents Act 1988 has been asserted.

The paper used in this book is recyclable. It is made
from low-chlorine pulps produced in a low-energy,
low-emission manner from renewable forests.

Printed by
Robertson Printers, Forfar

Typeset in 11.5 point Sabon by
Main Point Books, Edinburgh.

© The Martyn Bennett Trust 2025

Contents

Overture ... 9

1. Beginnings ... 13
2. The Music Apprentice ... 38
3. Making a Name ... 76
4. First Born ... 109
5. Bellows Boy ... 131
6. Bothy Culture ... 155
7. Cuillin ... 177
8. Home ... 210
9. Glen Lyon ... 238
10. Grit ... 259
11. Blessed Warrior ... 298
12. Passing On ... 316
13. Liberation ... 337

Timeline ... 341
Author Acknowledgements ... 344
The Martyn Bennett Trust Acknowledgements ... 346
Photo Credits ... 347
Endnotes ... 348

> Dear Martyn
> I am delighted to hear about your new music (Brave new music!!). Davie Stewart would be proud to know his voice will be heard the world over.
> I give you my blessing to use my recordings!
>
> Love Hamish
>
> 19 Dec. 2001

Note to Martyn from Hamish Henderson.

Grit Orchestra, Playhouse, Edinburgh.

Overture

IT WAS THE most remarkable of standing ovations. All 3,000 of us sprung to our feet as a single, stamping mass. For the last two hours and more we had been immersed in music. Bold, brave, ballsy music. The man at the centre of things, baton in hand, all in black, was the epitome of cool. Facing him and us were around 80 of the Scottish nation's finest musicians, their usual labels of 'folk', 'jazz' or 'classical' cast aside in tribute to the eclectic soul of the music they had come to play: the music of Martyn Bennett.

In the summer of 2016 Greg Lawson had brought his Grit Orchestra to the Edinburgh International Festival. He had spent many months painstakingly reconstructing Martyn's final album, the one from which the orchestra had taken its name. Some 13 years earlier, *Grit* had been crafted almost entirely on a computer, for the cancer gradually taking hold in Martyn had also been disconnecting him from playing his beloved instruments. In fact, these instruments were no more – he had smashed them into pieces in a fit of frustrated, pain-induced rage. His bagpipes had made it through two world wars, he lamented, 'but they didn't make it through my war'.

What he did still have though was a deep love of the great voices of Scotland's past that had carried with them that vibrant, earthy song tradition into which he had been born and raised. And what's more, as he was always keen to point out, they were the voices of people he actually *knew*. Under them, over them, through them, all around them, he had draped a soundscape that drew on his long, intensive years of training as a piper, flute player, pianist, classical violinist, DJ, programmer, composer, producer, mountaineer and darling of the club dance floor. It was all in there: a love letter to the past, a celebration of the multi-cultural present, a glimpse, perhaps, of the future.

Grit, Martyn Bennett's fifth album, had been released in October 2003 to much acclaim. Tragically, he died 15 months later, on 30 January 2005. And so as we took to our feet in the Playhouse that evening, yes, we were acknowledging Greg Lawson's incredible achievement in reconstructing for the stage a musical creation that had only ever existed in a machine. And yes, we were cheering the 80 or so musicians whose skill had brought that score to life. Yet above all, I think, we were saluting the man who was no longer there in person, but whose presence and spirit I fancy we could all feel intensely that night.

The special atmosphere that was created by the Grit Orchestra mirrored Martyn Bennett's own live performances which could also be epic events. He knew how to put on a show for sure. They were often transformational for those who were there, creating indelible memories and a loyal fan base, as his wife Kirsten commented:

> There is so much written and remembered by folk whose lives were literally affected by the energy of these gigs whether they were early solo gigs or band gigs – it was Martyn who created that energy and whipped crowds of people into frenzied audiences all over the world. So many people would say that they came along to the gig because they couldn't understand the description of the music and they were intrigued. These people became really dedicated fans – it all made sense when you heard his music live.[1]

In the years since he died, Martyn's ability to inspire has shown no signs of diminishing: his music has filled concert halls and arenas, his story has been shared on the theatre stage, much of his other work also recast in full orchestral form, his memory toasted, and his name cited as their key inspiration by many young musicians who have followed in his wake. Martyn Bennett was a

OVERTURE

game-changer, but he never got the chance to write his own story, or not in book form at least, and I suspect he was not the kind of man who would ever have even contemplated doing so. His music did the talking. And so while researching and writing this book, I have continually wondered what he would make of the fact that someone is attempting to do it for him. He can't 'authorise' it, nor indeed can he specifically *un*authorise it. I have imagined how he might react to my words in different places – shake his head in disbelief, roll his eyes at my pompous pontificating, throw his head back in laughter, or simply get bored of reading about himself and take to the hills instead.

The last time I ever saw Martyn he was chatting to someone at a CD launch, and introduced me as being the 'slightly academic guy who presents the piping on the radio'. I remember the phrase precisely, not because I knew it would be the last I'd ever hear from him (of course I didn't) but because I was tickled by the 'slightly' qualifier. I mention this simply to point out that it may also be an accurate description of this book. It is slightly academic in that I have set out to assess Martyn's place in his world, to offer as balanced a view as I can of his contribution to the culture of his time, and to build some layers of context relating to what went before him and what he in turn has passed on. In the pages that follow I paint a picture of Martyn Bennett that draws on all of the varying versions of him shared with me by those who knew him best. Martyn lived in a world of sound, a good deal of which he created himself. However, my task here is to represent his extraordinary life in a world of words on the page. That has been tricky, for writing about music, as they say, is rather like dancing about architecture! So read on, but please do go and listen to his music for yourselves too. You will be marvellously rewarded, I assure you!

Gary West
Edinburgh,
November 2024

1

Beginnings

IT WAS A potent combination of geology and folklore that made Martyn Bennett. He was born in St John's, Newfoundland, Canada, on 17 February 1971, his parents, Ian Knight and Margaret Bennett, having met after each travelling to Memorial University to further their academic studies. As a promising young geologist, Ian was keen to explore the rock foundations of the west of the island, while as a folklorist, Margaret immersed herself in the cultural traditions that had evolved on its soils. Both were destined for successful careers in their respective fields, each gaining awards as well as wide recognition and professional respect from their peers. Later in life, Martyn reflected on his roots there:

> I don't know if anyone knows where Newfoundland is! Well, the reason I was born in Newfoundland is simple, because my mother, Margaret Bennett, is a fairly well-known folklorist nowadays and the reason for that is because she went there as a teenager to do a Master's degree with quite a famous folklorist called Herbert Halpert. She went to Newfoundland to study with him but at the same time she found a community in the west coast. A place called Codroy Valley where people were still speaking and singing songs in Gaelic and playing fiddle tunes and pipes and things and a lot of the stuff they

were doing had sort of died out in Scotland – well not
so much died out, it was like it had been preserved but
in Newfoundland it hadn't been preserved in a pickling
jar. It was actually part of everyday life and so that's how
she ended up there.[1] And then she met my father who is
Welsh and he was a fiddle player. And I transpired from
that![2]

The fact that Margaret's own father had moved to
Newfoundland some years before had created an initial close
connection there for her, but a further pull was the chance to
study under one of the most revered folklorists in the Western
world, Herbert Halpert (1911–2000). Her own immediate
roots were in Skye, where her mother's people, Stewarts, had
lived for many generations, and where Margaret and her three
sisters spent their formative years. With a singing mother and
piping father, music, song and story were a constant presence in
the family home on Skye, while spells on the Isle of Lewis and
in Shetland served only to broaden her cultural awareness and
to heighten her sensitivity to the nuances of localised tradition.[3]

Margaret's research in Newfoundland took her to the
Codroy Valley, a fertile estuary between the Anguille and
Long Range mountains on the south-western tip of the island, a
rich hunting ground for a youthful Highland folklorist. Settled
by Micmac, French, English, Irish and Scots, the rich cultural
layering to be found there was always likely to be a magnet
for her, but the fact that the Scots included several families of
Gaels proved to be an irresistible draw. As she was later to
explain in her book, *The Last Stronghold*, these were mainly
secondary migrants who had made the journey across from
Cape Breton in the mid-19th century, and who still retained
a strong oral tradition, carried by the Gaelic language, that
connected them directly back to the west Highlands of Scotland
that Margaret knew so well. Martyn was to come to spend

a good deal of time in his early years amongst these folk, retaining a lifelong fondness for them and a sense that he had been given an unusual outlook on the world by this start and a feeling of being an outsider:

> I still love to go over to Codroy Valley. I haven't been for quite a few years, but the people there are very interesting. They're from Moidart and Appin and they're French, French Canadian as well and they've been married into these big families, Cormies and MacArthurs and MacIsaacs, they've all intermarried and so they have a very strange view. My early childhood's a strange view of the world you know? So I started from a strange place.⁴

When Margaret made her fieldwork visits to the homes of these people she had 'a very young research assistant' who would crawl under tables to find sockets for the recording machine and regularly add in some questions of his own to the research encounter:

I'd always give him a role in the collecting trips, carrying a microphone stand, keeping an eye on the tape to make sure it didn't run out. During the recording session he listened intently, and I didn't realise until years later what a remarkably retentive memory he had. Not just for tunes, but for words too, and he remembered complete stories – some emerged years later on his albums. What goes into small minds?[5]

One thing that must have gone into Martyn's mind for sure was an appreciation that 'ordinary' people could have *extra*ordinary stories to tell, and that they themselves are the best placed folk to tell them. Allowing them to do so is what folklorists are all about, and Martyn was to witness many such collecting sessions throughout his childhood years. They had a significant influence on his thinking, his outlook and eventually, his work, and it seems to me that Martyn was to spend most of his life wrestling with that slippery concept which motivated so much of his mother's collecting: *tradition*. His relationship with it was intense and complex, yet it sits at the heart of so much of his creative output.

From early infancy Martyn was immersed in traditional music and culture simply by accompanying his mother. Her memories of these encounters and experiences also strongly suggest that Martyn was a remarkably curious and sensitive wee boy, especially when it came to understanding and experimenting with making sound. In a talk to students in the Royal Conservatoire of Scotland in 2023, she recounted an extraordinary occasion where she had confiscated the remote control from a toy car from Martyn, who was about five years old at the time, and had been told to stop driving it but had disobeyed. Margaret later discovered Martyn in the kitchen with a pair of spoons. It transpired that he was hitting them together in hopes that the soundwaves might move the car! This

early fascination with the technicalities of sound was evident, as his mother remembered, on another occasion, when Martyn climbed onto the knee of an Inuit throat singer at a folk festival in Mariposa, Ontario, and asked to see into her mouth in an attempt to work out how she made such an amazing sound![6]

Ian Knight was also drawn to the west coast of Newfoundland, but in his case it was the land itself that fascinated him rather than the ways of life that had developed upon it. From Cardiff in Wales, Ian initially moved to Newfoundland to undertake a graduate degree studying rocks in remote areas of Labrador. He later undertook research for the Newfoundland Geological Survey on the west of the island, including in the Codroy Valley and the neighbouring Anguille Mountains. Ian's research on the island was a key step in his development as a leading light of Canadian geology, as someone who, in the words of a colleague, 'reads rocks like a book, with a sharp eye for the smallest detail'.[7]

Ian and Margaret married in the spring of 1970, but went their separate ways in 1976, Margaret and Martyn moving briefly to Quebec and then on to Scotland. 'Looking back, I cannot help but see my role in his life as minor, as the time spent together after his mother and I split can be rolled up into not more than a year,' Ian reflected.[8] Living an ocean apart, of course, makes any relationship difficult and the combination of distance and circumstance led him to follow what he describes as a 'staccato life' with Martyn, and a relationship that was necessarily shaped by a different ethos. 'Although it is not widely known', he pointed out, 'we shared the same birthday yet were rarely – if ever – together on that day during his early years'. A mid-February birthday does not coincide with lengthy Scottish school holidays and it was only really in the summer and some Easter and Christmas breaks that Martyn was able to spend prolonged periods with his dad. At times they met up in Wales to stay with Ian's parents, heading out to the Brecon Beacons to climb Pen-y-Fan, or to the Gower Peninsula for cliff top walks. His Welsh grandparents loved him, but rarely saw him, and as Ian acknowledged, they were not closely involved in his life beyond the sending of a card or present at Christmas and on birthdays. When Martyn did visit, rugby matches at Cardiff Arms Park in his teen years were high on the agenda, at least for his grandfather who was an avid fan. On one of his trips to Wales in his early teens Martyn played his pipes on the front lawn of his grandparents' house dressed up in Highland gear, a sight and sound that the neighbours remembered for many years after.

In the early years following his separation from Margaret, Ian was heavily involved with a Wesleyan church in Mount Pearl, a town adjoining St John's in Newfoundland. The Church of the Nazarene took an evangelical approach to its teaching and practice, a legacy of the Holiness movement in the USA, and the much earlier teachings of John and Charles Wesley in Britain, and Martyn went with his dad to some of the camps they ran. Reflecting on that time now, Ian speaks perhaps with a hint of regret: 'I suspect that it was not that beneficial to either of us and it was only after my loss of belief in the early 1980s that we were able to enjoy visits as he grew older'. By his mid-teens, Martyn's trips to Newfoundland grew longer, and together father and son would head out on adventures west and north during Ian's summer geological fieldwork. Camping in the woods, they explored the coast of west Newfoundland bays and islands in zodiac and fishing boats, worked in canoes on lakes, flew in a helicopter and searched for rocks and fossils. While Martyn relished the adventure, Ian suspects that 'trailing around with a dad who is measuring strike and dip of rocks and rhapsodising lyrical about faults and sedimentary rocks was likely boring on many occasions', and Martyn was never beyond a bit of a lark should he spot the chance to have some fun. 'He found a grey, putty-like glacial mud in a karst hollow on a limestone island in Hare Bay, Great Northern Peninsula, when we were there on a bit of a dreary day and it wasn't too long before we were enjoying lobbing fists of sticky pudding at each other and smearing mud on our faces'. Yet boating close to whales and seals, glimpsing eider duck and tern colonies on rocky islands, and finding curious families of red fox cubs poking heads out of their many den burrows in an abandoned saw mill's slab and sawdust pile, were all part of the field work thrills. Encounters with beaver, otter, moose and caribou were by no means unknown either on these trips.

The mountain of Gros Morne in the National Park in western Newfoundland was a favourite for father and son to climb together or along with Ian's partner, Ruth, as Ian recalled:

> Rather than follow the marked route we most often went straight up the steepest slope to the bare summit and then found a moose trail to get lost on coming down the wooded back of the mountain. Other climbs over the Gros Morne

Tablelands, vast orange and yellow coloured ophiolitic slabs of ancient ocean floor saw us chased off the grass-tussocked mountain plateau by high winds driving low clouds and rain squalls that you could see coming from afar.

Martyn also had a remarkable head for heights and was able (and willing) to jump onto a grassy pedestal overlooking a sheer drop of a thousand feet 'without fear' as he did above the St Mary's bird sanctuary on the Avalon Peninsula. Ian still shudders when thinking about that! 'He'd climb rock faces without a second thought and would be with me one minute and waving from a cliff face the next. And don't give him an ATV (all-terrain vehicle) on a gravelled woods road: he was a wild demon, gone before I got my helmet on and could chase him!'

Despite Ian's suspicion that Martyn may have found the fieldtrip outings at times boring, the training seems to have stayed with him. When discussing his process of composing his final album, *Grit*, in 2003, it was a geological analogy that came to mind for Martyn. Instruments and electronics, he announced,

> are just tools for something I already can hear. It's like I can hear it and sometimes it's quite hard to actually get it out. You find sometimes it's like a bit of unhewn stone, you know. Sometimes the stone is kind of softer, it's limestone or soap stone even. It really just happens quick. It's done, you know. In a day or so you've got this track that you heard in your head that morning. But sometimes it can be a bit of granite, can't it? It can be hard, a bit of hard rock and you do it for ages and you just can't seem to get it.[9]

There was plenty of music in Martyn's life from the outset. In the early years in Mount Pearl before his parents separated, records of the Wombles, *Peter and the Wolf,* Gaelic singing, Cape Breton fiddlers, and a few classical albums such as *Pictures*

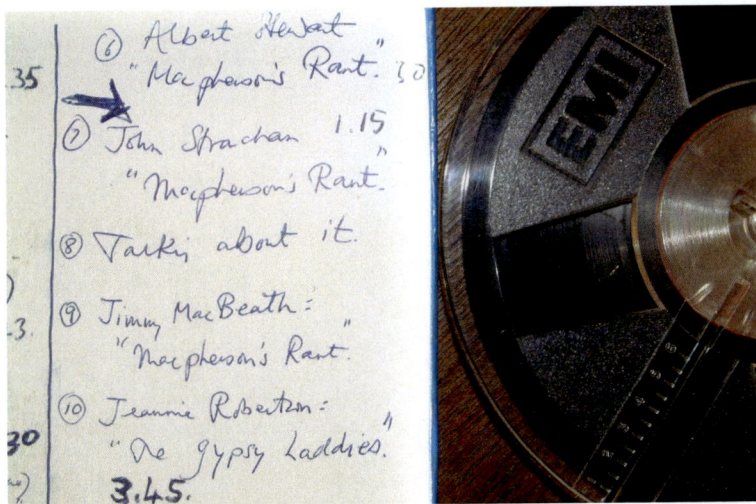

at an Exhibition, and Mozart's Horn Concertos were played on the little stereo system. And for Martyn, it wasn't just a case of listening, but often the stories behind the music had to be acted out too. 'There was an element of theatre to it all,' recalled Margaret, who in *Peter and the Wolf* invariably had to play the part of a bassoon![10] Martyn liked to be sung to by both his mum and dad – songs of the Beatles, Bob Dylan and Judy Collins as well as a few popular Welsh songs and hymns are the ones that stick in his father's mind. Ian had played violin in the Cardiff Schools Orchestra and tried to learn to play fiddle when he moved to Newfoundland as a graduate student in the early 1970s. Memorial University geology department was almost an amateur folk music school with both staff and graduate students who played instruments, as Ian reflected:

> I played the violin but not that well and I couldn't play fiddle tunes for the life of me, as hard as I tried. To play popular and Scottish fiddle tunes by ear, it took me many years and I only got to play reasonably with the help of a

tape of Aly Bain and the many Cape Breton fiddle records available at that time. It was a hard slog to change styles and play by ear, but eventually I got one tune and then others followed – but it was never fluent. Some of us grad students formed a small group called the CFA band, which stood for 'Come From Away'– a Newfoundland term for someone not born on the island. We played our gradually expanding repertoire of tunes at parties and winter carnival, meeting sometimes at our house. Margaret was to bring me into contact with Scottish Gaelic singing and fiddle playing which I loved.

One Irish tune that was popular in St John's and that was a favourite of Ian and his band mates was the 'Swallowtail Reel'. Martyn was familiar with the tune from the playing of the band, Ryan's Fancy, and it was also later to be a favourite of his when jamming with Edinburgh-based flute player, Cathal McConnell, but it is also a tune that has a lasting poignancy for Ian:

We were belting it out at a university winter carnival concert and were in full swing as were the rowdy students when my mind went blank. Luckily it was in a key that meant I could play two open strings imitating a pipe drone so kept fake fiddling until the tune came back. The students didn't seem to know or care as they kept clapping along and dancing their jig. It was a fellow geologist friend from the band, now living in North Carolina, that many years later pointed out after I sent him the CD after Martyn died that this opening tune on Martyn's first album was once a favourite tune of the band – I like to think that perhaps it was a quiet nod to the story and me that he opened the album with that tune.

Martyn was four years old when his parents went their separate ways, Margaret moving with her son to Quebec for a short stay to carry out more fieldwork amongst communities of Gaelic speakers there, and then on to Scotland where they eventually settled in Kingussie, while Ian remained in Newfoundland. While both live and recorded music in the house certainly formed a soundtrack to Martyn's early life, for Ian there was no hint that his son was any more musical than any other kids, and certainly there was no indication for him that it would be music that would shape his future. This is not a casual aside from Ian, but rather a strong and insistent conviction: 'I suppose my greatest fear', he explained, 'is that there will thrive a mythology about him that would be unfair to his memory and would make him unhappy'. The heart of the issue, in Ian's view, is that Martyn, like Mozart, was a child prodigy who was always destined for musical greatness. He saw no signs of this at all, in his recollection, and while their time spent together was limited, he felt sure that any deep interest or talent would surely have shown itself in their weeks together:

> If the relationship is good between a dad and his son, and I believe ours was, and you meet for only a short time during holidays, then an excited child wants to show you things that he knows and does – Martyn did none of this in musical terms and just enjoyed tussling on the rug, building models, fishing and other things that we did. There was a piano at my parents' house, sometimes I had my fiddle with me and sang and played at church and church camps including playing at a barn dance in the communal dining room of an old, majestic, monastic, English friary building, now a private school. Martyn had no interaction with the instruments and not a particularly favourable response to the dance even though it was a pretty wild and happy time.[11]

For Ian this is important, not only for our understanding of

Martyn, but because 'the sudden blossoming of his talent almost out of the blue' brings hope for children everywhere who do not seem to have much interest or direction. 'I hesitate to push my own ideas', his father explained, 'but I think that the musical evolution of Martyn reflects the talents and brain of a young, maturing, very talented, musically intelligent person rather than speculating on possible mysteries of an infant prodigy. It goes without saying that he benefited immensely from the advantages and encouragement of Margaret's guidance and immersion in the traditional music in Scotland with all the great players, singers and poets that he was able to hear and later honour in his music'.

Yet the music he was *hearing* in early childhood certainly stayed with Martyn all his days. In one of the interviews he gave late in his life as part of the making of a BBC Scotland *Grit* documentary, that was made very clear:

> The first song I ever remember would have to be 'Train on the Island'. Is that a Woody Guthrie song? Not sure if it is or not?[12] 'Train on the Island, hear the whistle blow, gone to visit my true love, I'm sick and I can't go', so that was the first song I ever learned was about being sick so that kind of sums up my life really! (laughs). Second song I remember – a song about a mother asking her son what he'd been eating in the woods.[13] He said 'snakes mother'. 'What colour were the snakes'? 'Green and yeller' (laughs). 'Mother be quick, I'm gonna be sick and lay me down to die' (laughs). They are all happy songs. When you are a kid every song is happy. And I loved eh, *Peter and the Wolf*. That was my favourite. *Peter and the Wolf*, Prokofiev. I think I've got one with – not sure if it is Alistair Cooke or if it was one with Sean Connery.[14] It might have been Sean's one. (In a Sean Connery accent) 'Peter said to the wolf'. And his grandfather. I loved the

grandfather tune (sings). Do you remember that one? It was great. The grandfather theme. (Sings again), that's Peter isn't it? I liked that one. Got it somewhere actually, *Peter and the Wolf* on vinyl. I have to do something with it. Yeah (sings). Mr Scruff version of *Peter and the Wolf*. Could be done! (laughs).[15]

Although Ian rejects the 'child prodigy' idea, once Martyn began to develop his piping, his father was indeed astounded at the rate of his progress. The first time he heard him play was soon after he had started lessons in Kingussie, and the two of them were on a train together, alone in one of the old-fashioned compartments. Exactly where this was Ian cannot recall, although he believes it may well have been in the area of the Welsh marches of Longmynd, travelling to South Wales to visit Martyn's grandparents. 'He pulled out a piping book and a chanter I believe his grandfather Bennett gave him, and just began to play – looking at the sheet music it was as dense in black notation as a spruce wood plantation in Scotland or new growth forest in Newfoundland, and incomprehensible to me'. Ian also marvelled at Martyn's sense of pitch and rhythm and that he could also commit the tunes in his head to paper with great ease. 'On one trip to the Cairngorms to ski, we were discussing tunes and without any hesitation he swiped out a pen and pad, drew some staves, and proceeded to notate a tune for me – such gifts I wish I had'.

Kingussie

On moving to Scotland in 1976, Margaret and Martyn spent a short while in Mull where Margaret performed tourist concerts in a local hotel before securing a job as a teacher. This took them to Dumfries which at the time had one of the most active folk clubs in Scotland, and they quickly became part of the 'folk family' with the likes of Billy Henderson, Phyllis and Billy Martin and Lionel McClelland all adding to Martyn's passive repertoire. After two years a supply-teaching job took them to Glasgow, where Margaret re-married. The folk scene there was a big part of their lives, as her husband, Joe McAtamney, loved to sing and other 'folkies' often gathered at their house. In 1979, the three of them settled in the town of Kingussie in Badenoch, some 40 miles south of Inverness. 'The small town with a big heart', it brands itself nowadays, and for a wiry young lad with an acute sense of adventure and a liking for the hills, it provided a fine playground indeed. These were key formative years for Martyn: it was here he underwent a good part of his schooling and here that he learned to play the bagpipes, making his first public performances as a musician. It was from here that he ventured out with his mother to folk festivals across Scotland where he peered into the deep well of tradition, and here, too, that he began to develop a sense that he was just a little bit 'different'. Martyn later reflected that he felt something of a 'social misfit' at school there, his small stature now very noticeable next to the hulking shinty-playing locals who seemed to dominate his new school environment:

> I hear people say that they felt like they were a bit of the odd ball at school you know. In Kingussie High School I was the smallest in the whole school and kind of lived in amongst strong, strapping farmer lads! I had to get tough and I found when I later went to the city I was the toughest and I was the most motivated.[16]

His memory of this discrepancy in size is corroborated by accounts from adults who encountered this unusual wee boy for the first time. David Taylor, his main piping teacher, recalled him being 'very tiny', while storyteller Dolly Wallace remembering

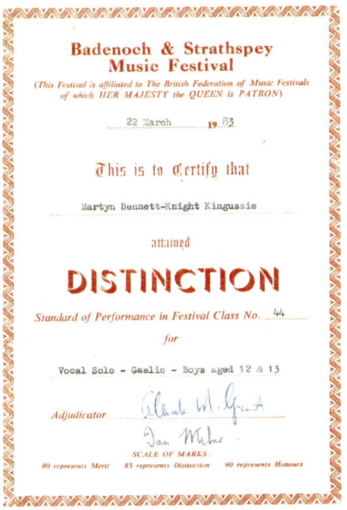 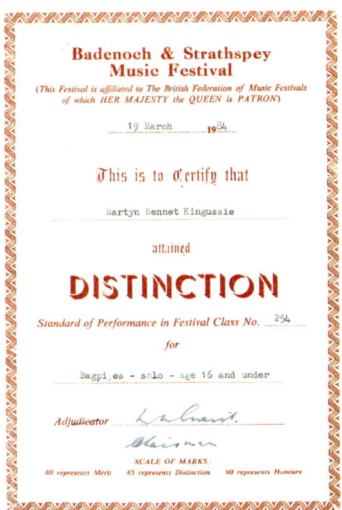

Highland Nights in the Grampian Hotel in Dalwhinnie where Martyn would pipe for a six-year-old dancer, remarked: 'And they must have been the most photographed pair in Britain at the time, because they were so small, so neat, and so sweet and pleasant. It was just flashing lights round them! Oh the tourists loved it!'[17] In Martyn's own later recollection, in learning to play the pipes, he went from feeling diminutive and unremarkable to having a special talent that got him a great deal of attention:

> By the age of 12 I was winning prizes in many of the junior piping competitions around Scotland, however I was really more interested in playing the folk scene. Being a young prodigy meant that I got a lot of attention at the folk festivals, as there were very few young musicians around at that time. It was also a total gas being snuck into the pubs under someone's coat and getting the pipes out before anyone had noticed the under-age drinker. By the time I'd got through the first tune and the place was jumping they were hardly going to chuck me out, were they?[18]

Piping was in the family, and the first set of bagpipes Martyn ever heard was played by his grandfather, Margaret's father, George Bennett. It was 'Papi' who gave his grandson his first practice chanter, and the two of them would discuss the merits of certain tunes, playing styles, and the etiquette of kilt wearing (no red shoes!). Margaret would later donate her father's pipes to be used by the students of the Royal Conservatoire of Scotland, Martyn's alma mater, a gesture to the influence George had on the path his grandson was to take in music. That said, that relationship wasn't always totally harmonious, as Margaret recalled with amusement:

> My mother and father spent a lot of time with us when Martyn was growing up, and my father – who gave Martyn his first chanter – could be bit a Victorian about manners. We were sitting down to dinner one day; I'd called Martyn, who was about 14, and he came bounding into the room and plonked himself down in a chair – just exuberant, like he was. But my father was not impressed at all, and said to him, 'Young man, would you mind leaving this room, then returning and sitting down like a gentleman.' So Martyn just seemed to take it, went away and came back and sat down quietly; there was a bit of a silence as we all just carried on eating, and then Martyn piped up: 'Papi, do you know what I've just been thinking?' 'No, Martyn, what's that?' 'Sometimes I think you're a bit of an old bastard.' I nearly died: dropped my fork, almost choked on my food, but then I could tell my father was stifling laughter, even as he tried to be stern: was I going to allow my son to talk to him like that? So I spluttered something about how I'd certainly never encourage such behaviour and then found myself saying, 'But I have thought the same thing myself, sometimes!' Ever after that, whenever Dad phoned, once he and I had

spoken he'd say, 'Where's my grandson? Tell him it's the old bastard on the phone.' Even I'd been a bit scared of him before, but Martyn saw beyond the strictness – and completely disarmed it.[19]

While it was George who first stimulated Martyn's interest in piping, it was one of his teachers at school in Kingussie who nurtured it and set him on his path to greatness. In an interview given to publicise *Grit* in late 2003, Martyn confided to Ann Donald of *Scotland on Sunday*: 'I was really below average academically for a lot of my life and it wasn't really till I knew this amazing teacher, David Taylor, who taught me piping, that I felt here was something I could do really well.'[20] David Taylor became the single most important influence in the discovery and development of this young man. A history teacher in Kingussie High School, he has a strong piping pedigree himself having been taught by Bert Barron in St Andrews, a hugely influential and slightly eccentric character who could count among his piping pupils several future gold medallists and major pipe band leaders. Bert was also a dab hand at procuring, refurbishing and selling on high-quality sets of old bagpipes, and it was from him that David secured Martyn's first ever set. They were full ivory-mounted Henderson's, often considered the 'Stradivarius' equivalent of their kind. They cost the equivalent of a month's teaching salary, recalled Margaret, who paid for them by taking in Bed and Breakfast guests. Martyn was later to inherit an even older set from his grandfather Bennett, but according to David, he took to that first set as if they were just made for him. That said, he had to grow into them: for the first couple of years he couldn't reach the tuning slide on the bass drone over his shoulder, so he came up with a unique method of turning the pipes upside down to tune them! As his mother remembered, 'he used to wonder why some folk laughed even before he started to play!'

The respect that Martyn held for his main piping teacher was certainly mutual. In his contribution to Margaret's collection, *It's Not the Time You Have*, David's admiration and pride in his star pupil was obvious:

> I first remember Martyn as a very tiny, excited, desperately enthusiastic wee boy with wide shining eyes. I've never seen anyone learn the chanter so fast. In his first lesson (1980) he mastered everything I gave him first time round – I probably gave him a month's worth of lessons in our first meeting. He was the most natural learner I've ever encountered – even making a practice chanter musical and playing grace note scales with perfect rhythm. It was only a few weeks before he was playing his first competition tunes on chanter. He had such light musical fingers when he played and even the hardest tunes flowed in such a natural, musical way. His impish sense of humour combined with his amazing talent meant he was always tremendous fun to teach. I looked forward to our lessons as much as he did.[21]

Martyn also took some piping lessons from John MacDougall, one of the leading competing pipers of his generation who lived locally, and who was employed as a piping teacher in the Badenoch and Strathspey schools. In the 1970s his fellow competitors began to call John 'The Highland Hoover', as he dominated the Highland games circuit, sucking up all the prizes! He reputedly used to practise in a nearby disused quarry, in all weathers, to prepare himself for the unpredictable conditions of the outdoor competition circuit. Perhaps some of that meticulous attention to detail rubbed off on his young pupil who was certainly in expert hands there, but Martyn did make the point on several occasions that he considered David Taylor to be his key musical influence: he was unequivocal on that. And others who benefitted from

BEGINNINGS

David's teaching in the school – whether history or music – also concur with Martyn's view. Pianist and composer Mhairi Hall, one of today's leading Scottish traditional musicians, attended the school some years after Martyn:

> Retired history teacher David Taylor was one of my most inspirational teachers at Kingussie High School. He really brought the subject to life and got very animated in class, especially regarding Scottish and Highland history. He used to run two-week long school trips up to Orkney over the Easter holidays so that every child spent time on the islands there, living the history and feeling connected to both our past and present. He taught many pupils piping, including Martyn. Rather than a pipe band, he ran the school folk group and that was where I started playing traditional music. He taught us the best traditional Scottish repertoire, that has stayed with me throughout my musical life. He regularly spoke about Martyn pushing the boundaries of our music and once suggested I go to a concert he was playing up at the Daylodge of Cairngorm Mountain. That was my first live concert seeing and hearing 'Cuillin Music', having listened to his first album and *Bothy Culture* until they were worn out. He gave me a letter to give to Martyn. I don't know what was in the letter but Martyn spoke to me as if we had been in school together, learning at the same time. We had a connection and shared experience being taught by this incredible teacher. (I was a bit of a starstruck teenager!) On reflection, David gave us an understanding and connection to our history, our present and how these veins run through our music. This of course is so abundant in Martyn's music, and I'm sure some of David's teaching must have rubbed off – it certainly has with me.[22]

David himself can recall in detail one of these field trips to Orkney that Martyn attended in his first year at the high school.²³ 'For all his sense of fun and mischief he was actually a very serious young lad in many ways, and he was determined to get everything he could out of the trip'. He remembered Martyn lying on the wall of one of the houses at the Neolithic settlement of Skara Brae, 'sketching it in incredible detail and wouldn't leave until it was right'. Martyn was indeed a talented visual artist, and at that stage it was art rather than music that excited him most, and it did seem likely for a while that this would be the path he would follow. 'It was a brilliant sketch for a boy of just 12', David concluded. When the art teacher saw it he dismissed it as having been copied or traced from a book. 'But no', remarked David, 'I watched him drawing it with hands numb from the bitter Atlantic breeze that sweeps over Skara Brae'.

As with so many recollections concerning Martyn, humour is never far away, and David continued with a classic of his own:

> Another story from there that illustrates the impish sense of humour. I was commenting to the kids how much I'd like to get down into the one of the houses to get the real feel of it. So Martyn 'accidentally' dropped his clipboard into the house, and said with a twinkle, 'Mr Taylor, I've dropped my worksheets – could you possibly go in and get them for me?' I was just about to seize my opportunity when the old Custodian said, 'Don't you worry boy, I'll just go in and get it for you'. Martyn just laughed so much at how his ruse had failed! Years later I got a postcard from Orkney from Martyn, who was playing at the folk festival there. I still have it. He not only remembered, but took the time to write. That was Martyn.

> ᛈᛁᛈᛁᚾᚷ·ᚷᚱᛁᚾᛏᛋ
>
> Dear Ailsa & David,
> I thought I would drop a line from the inspiration behind that lovely music you taught me so many years ago. We have a gig with the trio in Kirkwall tonight (14th) and tomorrow in Thurso. Things have been busier than we thought they would be since August with no break till Dec. I am writing a new classical ensemble piece encorporating the piobaireachd "Lament for Mary MacLeod" and I would love to run it past you. I loved the type you sent me, by the way, of Hullachan Mor. See you soon.
> What incredible talent you have nurtured.
> Much love
> Martyn
>
> Ailsa & David Taylor
> Kingussie
> Inverness-shire
> PH21

    Alongside his art, Martyn soon became obsessed with piping; according to his grandmother Peigi, a frequent visitor to Kingussie, 'he used to read the *Kilberry Book of Pibroch* in bed, he'd write music in bed.'[24] He began to compete in mods and other competitions, with a good deal of success, although he was very clear to his teacher that the rigid formalities of that kind of playing was of little interest to him. 'He found it restrictive and felt unable to express himself the way he wanted to. He wanted to play folk style – the rhythms of Aly Bain and Cathal McConnell rather than the more stilted reels of competition style'. He may not have enjoyed the established competition repertoire, but he could certainly play it, and play it very well. Margaret has a recording of her son playing a strathspey and reel on his pipes aged 12, and having heard it I can say with confidence that he was indeed exceptional. The tunes were of the complex, heavy form – 'The Shepherd's Crook' and 'Pretty Marion' if I remember correctly – and he played them with both technical precision and great musical lift. It was a remarkable performance for a boy of that age. There is also a recording of him singing a Gaelic duet with a young local girl, Lucy Anderson. Lucy carries the melody, while Martyn provides the harmony. To extemporise a harmony was something Martyn found easy, and I twice experienced this directly when he was in his teens and he played his pipes along with me, going for harmony all the way. I didn't know what tune I was going to play next, so there's no way he did either!

As well as formal instruction on the bagpipe, Martyn was able to soak up the styles and nuances of traditional music more generally on his visits to folk festivals and gatherings with his mother, a regular feature of his time in Kingussie. In the early years of the folk revival in the 1950s and '60s, a handful of singers had gained recognition as 'the real thing'. These were people for whom the singing of traditional songs and ballads had always been part of their lives, but the flowering of wider interest in folk culture had brought them newly found recognition and they were now being placed – quite literally – centre stage. They became labelled as 'tradition bearers' and 'source singers', and Martyn got to know them all. Many were of the travelling community – Duncan Williamson, Belle Stewart and her daughter, Sheila, Willie MacPhee, Betsy Whyte, Jane Turriff, Elizabeth Stewart and Lizzie Higgins were all singers and storytellers whose faces and voices were familiar to Martyn, while he got to know non-travellers such as Jock Duncan and Flora MacNeil also. Margaret remembers when her son first came across Jane Turriff, a traveller singer from Fetterangus in Aberdeenshire:

> We were at Auchtermuchty festival and he'd gone off by himself while I was recording a competition. He came running along the street to find me. 'Come and listen to this', he said, 'you've never heard the likes of this old lady yodelling and everything!'

Martyn drank in everything these artists sang, and *they* noticed *him* too: as Sheila Stewart remarked, 'they were glad a young person was interested'. That interest would never leave him, and he was later to draw on it directly in his final album, *Grit*. Reflecting on that following its release late in his life, he explained

in an interview with the broadcaster, Mary Ann Kennedy, just how important those early experiences had been to him:

> These are voices I knew as a child – these are people that I knew when I was starting to play music. At TMSA festivals I would hear them, and they were the celebrities if you like. No Posh and Becks for me then! It was the likes of Lizzie Higgins who were my kind of heroes. I got to hear them at the likes of Kirriemuir, Keith and Auchtermuchty. I haven't been to these festivals for so many years... I didn't know what a privilege it was for someone of my age – but then no one my age was interested. And I wasn't forced into it – it wasn't like

> Margaret Bennett said, 'Right boy, you're going to become some sort of folklorist and pass on this tradition!' I was just brought up around it.[25]

The important formative years in Kingussie drew to a close when Martyn reached his mid-teens and life took a new turn when Margaret accepted a lecturing job at the School of Scottish Studies at the University of Edinburgh. It was time for the young lad to get his first real taste of city living, and although he could not have known it then, it was a move that set him on a journey that was also to define the rest of his life.

2

The Music Apprentice

Broughton

AT THE AGE of 14, Martyn Bennett travelled to Broughton High School in Edinburgh, pipe box in hand, to audition for the specialist music school there. Founded in 1899 as the main 'higher grade' school in the north of the city, Broughton had its share of notable alumni. One who made a major contribution to Scotland's creative culture was a certain Christopher Murray Grieve, who attended for a few years in his teens before later emerging as one of the nation's greatest modernist poets under his assumed name of Hugh MacDiarmid. (That said, his stay at Broughton had been relatively brief, having been expelled for stealing books!)

The specialist music unit was a much later addition, having been set up in 1980, aimed primarily at 'classical' players and so when this young piper and whistle player walked through the door with hopes of securing a place, it was new territory for the staff. Margaret had taken advice on Edinburgh schools from some of her new colleagues at the university, and had gathered a variety of school prospectuses.

Martyn had been very taken with the idea of going to Broughton when he read about the set-up there that was specifically for 'musically gifted children'. This came as something of a surprise to his mother, as up to that point he had shown little interest in playing music beyond his piping, and an earlier attempt to take up the violin had been short-lived. At the age of seven he had taken lessons but one day refused to go back to school after the summer break if he had to carry on with them. It was many years later that his mother discovered why – the teacher was something of an eccentric old maid who had been so taken with his early progress that she scooped him up and planted him with a kiss in front of the whole class. The fact, as he later divulged, that 'she had whiskers' had cemented his decision! And while Martyn was also no total stranger to the piano, his formal lessons before his Broughton days were very limited. From a very young age he would play away on his own, happily exploring the sound and mechanics of the keyboard, an approach that his mother was advised to encourage until beginning a brief run of lessons in Glasgow at the age of ten. Their move north to Kingussie put a stop to those, however, and no more piano lessons followed until his arrival at Broughton.

Mary McGookin was a principal teacher there at the time Martyn arrived, and remembered eavesdropping on his first audition:

> I wasn't on the audition panel at the time but I was in the school and I heard piping and it was unusual to hear piping because at that point I think we had a range of instruments but no traditional instruments. And I could hear it coming from one of our classrooms so I went to have a look and then I realised it was a kind of pre-audition. We normally have two stages of auditioning so this was the more informal one but I could hear this piping and I could hear that it was really, really good. And I was lurking outside the door and listening and hoping that we could take that leap and admit someone who was not on the kind of normal classical route.[1]

Margaret was also waiting on her son outside the door and recalled 'a gale of laughter' spilling out of the classroom. 'It was embarrassing,' she laughed:

> They had asked him if he could play anything else, besides the pipes. 'Yes, the tin whistle.' 'What can you play?'
> He told them he would play 'The Arrival of the Queen of Sheba in Galway,' and promptly played a flashy tune he heard on the hit-parade. It was from James Galway's *The Man with the Golden Flute* record. The playing was note-perfect, but the title made them all laugh!

Despite getting the names of the artist and the piece mixed up, Martyn clearly impressed them, and following another more formal audition in front of expert piper, Major Gavin Stoddart, he was accepted. I was in daily contact with Margaret at this time, as she was one of my lecturers in the School of Scottish Studies, and I well remember her telling me the news that Martyn was about to start at Broughton. The offer of a place, though, seemed to come as a bit of a shock to Martyn himself:

> I auditioned for a music school in Broughton in Edinburgh which was like the music unit there and to my surprise I got in on the bagpipes (laughs) and the flute. But I didn't play any classical music – didn't know anything about it. Couldn't read or write music, I couldn't really. It was much more an aural thing, an aural tradition to me, so it was quite brave of them to allow me to have my shot at learning formal music – classical training and I stayed there for three years and learned violin, piano, composition and to read and write music. And that was the most amazing three years and that was the point at which I realised this is where my talent lies.[2]

To this day, I find this one of the most incredible aspects of Martyn Bennett's story. He arrived, aged 14, having had only the briefest of spells on violin seven years earlier, with only a very basic self-taught command of the piano keyboard, and with limited musical literacy. Yet by the time he left he was ready to walk into a classical musical performance programme at one of the world's leading conservatoires.[3]

How did he do it? Sheer hard work was at the heart of it. Yet as a piper, Martyn would not have arrived quite as green and unprepared as we might assume, or indeed, as he later remembered or claimed. He may not have been musically literate in the sense of having a familiarity with key signatures, the mysteries of the bass clef, relative minor scales, chord theory, interrupted cadences and the like, for the limited nine note scale of the Highland bagpipe taught as a solo instrument requires little formal understanding of such matters. However, what he certainly possessed by then was an ingrained and thorough appreciation of the importance of clean and fluent physical technique, as well as a commitment to a practice regime requiring frequent and sustained repetition of complex finger movements and note patterns. Early mastering of these qualities is a prerequisite for success in piping, and as I well recall, by the time he came to Edinburgh Martyn was an exceptionally skilled piper. He certainly had the core values in place that were to stand him in good stead for the demanding challenges that lay ahead.

Once at Broughton, Martyn settled in quickly. Mary McGookin again:

> My recollections of Martyn are of someone who was curious, but it felt as though he'd landed somewhere where he could get what he needed and he had a real appetite for it. He was also a good communicator with people – natural – and I think other pupils and teachers responded to that. He was charming in a nice way, a

really natural kind of personality and I think once he started getting the technical basis for playing, when he started getting all that grounding, he really responded to it. He absorbed it quickly and there is no doubt he had an innate musicality but then that's what we would be looking for in people who were admitted you know?

The fact that he did not share the classical music background of the rest of the pupils did single him out for close attention from some of his peers who didn't quite know what to make of this piper from the north. He was also small for his age, making him a target for some of the older lads who liked to throw their weight around. 'He didn't particularly like being given the nickname of "drone", accompanied by *nyaaaaaaa* sounds and laughter', remembered Margaret:

> He tried to tolerate the taunting and teasing but one day he was so provoked by the school bully, who challenged him to a fight. I was sent for after the episode. The other boy was admitted to hospital with a broken arm and another injury. Martyn was suddenly ashamed and frightened of the power of anger. Apparently the doctor asked the boy, 'Who did this'? 'A wee guy in the music department. Plays the violin'. The bully was told, 'You must remember that violinists develop very strong muscles in their hands and especially in their fingers!

Despite such teething troubles, Martyn threw himself fully into the Broughton school community, not only working very hard on his own instruments, but making himself available for various ensembles and orchestras, and responding positively when Mary McGookin 'ambushed him in the corridor' when a particularly Scottish or traditional flavour of music was needed for some reason or another. The revamping of national school level qualifications was happening at this time, with the introduction of Standard Grades to replace O Grades in 1986, and Mary and some of her colleagues were keen to develop the Scottish content in their teaching on these and in the Highers:

> The best way I felt to let pupils who were starting know, was to actually hear it, to see it and so I would ask Martyn if he would just pop in and play and he always did. Sometimes the smallpipes or sometimes the Highland bagpipes, sometimes whistle so he'd look at the different instruments and look at the different dance tunes or the march or whatever and I loved it.

Having a piper on tap for Burns suppers, welcoming visitors and for trips abroad was a boon for the school, and by all accounts Martyn was happy to oblige. Yet there was no sense in which the bagpipe was to become just a plaything, laid aside while he got on with the serious business of becoming a classical musician. The bagpipe remained a serious instrument to him, and a serious instrument needed a serious teacher.

Captain John MacLellan (1921–1991) was an army man through and through. His father, William MacLellan, hailed from the Achnasheen area in Ross-shire and was a piper in the Highland Light Infantry, seeing action in the Great War, including the fierce fighting on the Somme. (Not only did *he* survive the experience, but so too did his shot glass that he carried with him at all times, and which is still in the possession of his grandson, Colin MacLellan, himself one of the world's leading pipers of his own generation.) Young John attended the Fort Augustus Abbey school with his brothers, before joining the Queen's Own Cameron Highlanders as a boy piper at the age of 15. By just 19 he had been appointed Pipe Major of the Seaforth Highlanders, but the war put paid to any thoughts of competing, and so as with most of his generation, he was well into his 20s before taking to the competition platform seriously. Success came very quickly, however, winning the coveted gold medals for piobaireachd at both the Argyllshire Gathering in Oban and the Northern Meeting in Inverness in close succession. He was also a formidable light music player, earning a total of nine 'silver star' medals, the elite bracket of contest for march, strathspey and reel playing at these same competitions. There followed a string of other major successes, and by the time he was in his 30s, he was recognised by his peers as one of the finest players of them all. The army appreciated the importance of providing high-quality tuition for its pipers, and John had received short but concentrated bursts of instruction early in his career from two of the most renowned players and teachers of all time: Pipe Major Willie Ross and Pipe Major John MacDonald of Inverness. Ross was to become a major influence on his playing after the war too, when John attended the army pipe majors' residential course at Edinburgh Castle under his instruction. In turn, John himself was to take up that prestigious post soon after his mentor's retiral, remaining Director of the Army School at the castle from 1957 through to 1976.

To become a private pupil of Captain John MacLellan, then, a decade after he had retired, was something of a coup for Martyn. It was not based on chance, however, but rather on the strong impression he had made back home in Badenoch on another respected figure in the world of piping, Dr Kenneth MacKay of Newtonmore. The man who would later inspire one of Martyn's best-known compositions, *Mackay's Memoirs*, was very active in piping circles in the north, and knew Martyn's playing, giving him a few lessons as a young boy. David Taylor, Martyn's main piping teacher in Kingussie, recalled the first time he introduced his young pupil to the venerable doctor:

> I took him along to meet the formidable old Dr MacKay of Laggan who at that time was living near me in

Newtonmore. Dr MacKay asked him what he would like to play, and Martyn replied, 'Inveran'. Doc looked at me with horror and said brusquely, 'What are you thinking of giving a wee boy a tune like that!' I replied, 'I didn't – I had no idea he even knew the tune'. When I asked him how he got it, he simply told us that he had heard John MacDougall play it and liked it. Well, he played it – and you've got to remember how small he was then, he looked a lot younger than 12, just a head and three drones sticking up above the back of the couch as he marched to and fro! Doc was gob-smacked. It was Dr MacKay that got him the introduction to John MacLellan at the castle when he moved to Edinburgh.

Dr Mackay was a good friend of John MacLellan, and would sing the young lad's praises when John and his wife, Bunty, dropped in on the MacKays when heading north to competitions in Inverness and beyond. On hearing that Martyn was moving to Edinburgh, he wrote to his friend imploring him to take him on as a pupil. Nobody else would do. John agreed, and the deal was done.

Looking back now, it is tempting to think that this must have been a rather incongruous relationship, and that master and apprentice must have occupied opposite poles of the piping spectrum. How could the inquisitive young upstart possibly sit comfortably in front of this military musical disciplinarian – a man, who as a commissioned British army officer was used to being saluted and addressed as 'Sir' – and play through his pieces in accordance only with the uncompromising rules of convention? To make that assumption, though, would be to misunderstand them both. Yes, the captain did once threaten to put his foot up his backside if he ever heard him try to 'bend' a note again, but as pipers we have all been there! Nonetheless, there was without doubt enough common ground between them for the relationship to work, and work well.

Central to that was a mutual respect – respect for each other, but also for the music. Both were lovers of *ceòl mòr* – the 'big' or 'classical' music of the Highland bagpipe also known as *piobaireachd* ('pibroch' in English) – and both were fastidious in their approach to its learning, its performance and its transmission. There may have been only one way to play each technical movement – *triplets, grips, taorluadhs, crunluadhs, crunluadh a machs* – but the music came from the 'space in between', the subtle lengthening of notes, the marginal slowing in the final phrases, the bold and brisk 'playing through' of key passages that seemed to demand an assertive execution. Neither John nor David Taylor belonged to any particular 'school' of playing, in which those subtle ways of bringing out the music from a piece were passed on almost religiously. Their approach was rather more liberal, and John was more than happy to share varying styles with his pupils. Over the years he had amassed an extensive personal archive of recordings of top players performing piobaireachd and light music, and kept a highly detailed reference system that allowed him to locate all the different versions he had of each tune, or indeed all the recordings he had of each player. As his son Colin observed, when teaching him, his father would ask which versions he wanted to listen to, not to encourage blind replication, but simply to illustrate how it was possible to find the music in the tunes in many different ways. That was an approach to learning that was music to the ears of Martyn Bennett.[4] John's wife, Bunty, recalled that visits to their Stockbridge family home for lessons were not only about piping:

> Martyn would come to the house on his way home from school. You know, he would be up there with John, doing his lessons, and then he'd come down and he always stood there, in the kitchen, with his back to the counter. I'd give him tea or clootie dumpling or something like

that – he loved clootie dumpling. And he would talk about anything except piping – he was so interested in everything – everything! ... And John said that Martyn was his last pupil and his best – that's right. That's exactly how it was – it gave him great pleasure, oh indeed, yes![5]

At Broughton High Music School.

With the captain taking care of Martyn's piping development, his violin training was overseen by another musician of deep substance and high reputation. Daphne Godson (1932–2022) was a recognised virtuoso who had come to prominence on the international scene early in her career. At the age of 25 she had attended the third International Henryk Wieniawski Violin Competition in Poznan, Poland, in December 1957. This brought some of the elite players of the world together in front of a panel of judges drawn from some of Europe's most revered musicians, with honorary jury status going to Yehudi

Menuhin. The prize list included international stars such as Rosa Fain from Odessa, USSR, and the American, Sidney Harth, later concertmaster, soloist and conductor of the most celebrated American orchestras including the Chicago Symphony, New York Philharmonic and Los Angeles Philharmonic. While Daphne was not in the main prize list, she received recognition with 'an award', and so had clearly established herself as being worthy of keeping such elevated company on the world stage. Settling back in Edinburgh, for the 30 years from 1959 to 1989 she was a regular soloist in the Reid concert series at the University of Edinburgh in performances usually conducted by Professor Sidney Newman (1906–71) until 1970 and thereafter by Professor Kenneth Leighton (1919–88). A fellow artist who often shared the billing with her at these events was Miles Baster, later to become Martyn's main violin teacher once he moved on to study at the Royal Scottish Academy of Music and Drama. To be taken on as a pupil by Daphne Godson was seen as a great honour, recalled Anna-Wendy Stevenson, who befriended Martyn when they met in the Edinburgh Youth Orchestra a couple of years after he had arrived at Broughton, and realised they shared the same violin teacher. Daphne had a reputation for being very strict in her teaching, but clearly got good results, and the two teenage pals were able to compare notes on their walks home to the capital's south side after weekly orchestra rehearsals. Anna-Wendy was impressed with her new friend's enthusiasm:

> He was clearly feeling excited about life and about his traditional music. He didn't have any kind of weird attitude about 'having to go through the classical stuff but I'm really into traditional music'. He was just into it all. And was really committed to it all. Took it all seriously. And loved it all. And he wanted to talk about whatever he was excited about. And that included kind of physical work – I think he was into hillwalking, and

THE MUSIC APPRENTICE

I remember that he had this tank top and you could see that he was obviously into his fitness! And he was just bouncing off the walls really. He wasn't the kind of person who was cliquey – he just dived between things, because he was all just about whatever was exciting him at the time. He loved a challenge. And he just loved it if there was something really hard to get his fingers around. And we were playing some really challenging work too – some of the repertoire. So he liked a challenge. And that was just like another rock that he had to find his way round.[6]

Taking to the hills.

While Martyn had arrived at Broughton with little, if any, practical experience in the realm of classical music, the genre was by no means new to him as a *listener*. As an infant in Newfoundland, he had enthusiastically taken to toddling around the family home imitating a French horn playing Mozart's 'Horn Concerto No.4'. That seminal disc had clearly left an impression, for the French horn was Martyn's preferred choice of instrument he wished to take up on arriving at Broughton. The request was rejected, however, and he was pointed towards the violin and viola instead. His very early years had also exposed him to strings and bows when he was taken by his mother at the age of three to hear a touring group of young Suzuki violinists perform Brahms' *Double Concerto* from memory. And after the move to Scotland, his exposure to 'high falutin'' music continued, including a trip to Glasgow, aged seven, to see the Mozart opera, *The Magic Flute*. Martyn, complaining that he couldn't see properly, managed to find himself a single empty seat in the front row from where he had a bird's eye view of the orchestra pit. He loved it. And later, frequent visits to the Edinburgh International Festival exposed him to a wide range of classical artists, including a particular favourite, Stéphane Grappelli, a jazz musician and multi-instrumentalist known as 'the grandfather of jazz violinists.' Martyn and his father, Ian, saw Grappelli perform in the St David's Hall in Cardiff in the early 1990s, and he played almost up until he died at the age of 89 in 1997.

Exposure to these great maestros across all genres was clearly important in Martyn's own musical development, embedding in him a rich seam of cultural wealth, an appetite for discovery, high ambition and stellar standards for which to strive. All he had to do, then, was practise! And practise he did. Obsessively! The drive and desire to practise incessantly is a trait that all successful musicians share, and was certainly one held in common with two other folk-oriented pipers of Martyn's generation whose names are often uttered in the same breath. Gordon Duncan, a piping genius from Pitlochry, played every minute available to him, while Fred Morrison does likewise. I have shared several long-haul flights to Seattle with Fred in recent years, and can personally vouch for the fact that his earphones are in within seconds, attached to his electronic chanter, that he plays without stopping for the full nine hours! By all accounts, Martyn was the same. And that, in all probability, more than any other factor, explains why he began at Broughton from a standing start and left five years later as a potential violin virtuoso, ready to take the step up to the next level of his training at the Royal Scottish Academy of Music and Drama.

Broughton was to remain a significant part of Martyn's life long after his time there. A decade later he was commissioned to write a piece of music as part of the celebrations of the school's centenary. A new director, Tudor Morris, had arrived from the Brit School in London in the mid-1990s, and soon came to hear of Martyn's work and the fact that he was a former pupil:

> When I joined the music school in 1995, I was made aware of Martyn, and so I went and listened to him and was obviously very impressed and loved the way he was taking his music, the way he was mixing genres, whilst still remaining very true to the tradition. He would always have that integrity for the big music, for the tradition, although he was doing quite daring things with it. So I invited him in – so this was before *Mackay's Memoirs* – he came in to talk to the students really about his pathway through music. I was fascinated with the fact that he had been a traditional musician, then became a classical musician, then went to the conservatoire, then started making music in his own way.[7]

Tudor invited Martyn into the school on several occasions as a mentor for the current generation of students, asking him to share some of his experiences and to generally help inspire them and encourage them to be ambitious in their approach. As Tudor recalled, 'he just came in and talked to the students and they loved him'.

The school had raised some funding to help celebrate the centenary and had decided that a commission for the pupils of the music school to perform would be a most fitting project. Headmaster, Gordon Ford, was very keen on the idea, and said he wanted 'something special, and something that's going to last'. Martyn was the obvious choice to come up with the goods, and he readily agreed. The remit was to try to be as inclusive as possible, creating space for a wide range of the instruments represented there at the time, and for all levels.

> Often people comment on the strange orchestration of 'Mackay's Memoirs', but *every* pupil in the musical school at the time had a part. Had a part that stretched them. And there are no easy parts there – but they had a part that was possible, but they'd have to work at. He'd come in on Fridays and the ink was still wet – because he was still writing it on the way in! He listened to the players and changed parts, if he thought they could do other things.

For his inspiration, Martyn had cast his mind back to his formative years in Kingussie, and to his time spent with Dr Kenneth MacKay, the man whose intervention had secured him lessons with Captain John MacLellan. Kenneth was a medical man, and a man of God. He had spent long years as a church missionary medic in Peru, and had kept detailed medical and personal journals that Martyn had been allowed to peruse. A thoughtful and colourful writer, he had been fascinated with the apparent cultural parallels between the land of his birth and his adopted home in South America. Central to those links was music in general and pipe music in particular. He and Martyn had shared a love of ceòl mòr, and both were especially fond of the 'Lament for Mary MacLeod', a beautifully constructed tune from the MacCrimmon tradition of the early 18th century. It was this that Martyn chose as the central melodic and structural thread of his commissioned piece. The tune is also just one example of how pipers can find controversy in just about anything! In this case, it is about a single quaver that occurs in just one of the variations. Generations of players, teachers, editors and commentators have argued as to whether it should be a G or an A. To some minds, the G doesn't belong there, as the tune is pentatonic, being based around five notes only (A, B, C sharp, E and F sharp). The G is an imposter. Martyn loved that idea. Listen out for the G!

Following a first performance of the piece at Broughton for the centenary celebrations, an invitation had arrived for the school orchestra to perform it in Princes Street Gardens in Edinburgh as part of the celebrations for the opening of the new Scottish Parliament in 1999. 'It's difficult to describe the feeling', remembered Tudor Morris:

> The sun was shining, the red arrows were flying over, and there was just that feeling of optimism, looking to the future. It was Princes Street Gardens. They were all playing it, and the piper at the time was Hamish Munro. Martyn was there to help with the technology and everything else. He leapt onto stage and helped tune the drones – just adjusted Hamish's drones, and just picked up the pipes and started playing along. And that wasn't planned – that was a shock to everyone. He just wanted to be a part of it. And it was filmed – there's a lovely sequence on the film, when Martyn starts playing along with Hamish, and the looks between the two of them are just fantastic. The respect and encouragement. And

particularly moving for me – I'm getting goosebumps thinking about it – at the return of the pibroch part Martyn just fades away and bows out and leaves Hamish to play it. That's captured on the film and it always gets me – Martyn just fading away and letting the younger people carry on. Very moving.

A quarter of a century on, Hamish Munro recalled that day very fondly. 'It is a moment that will stick in my memory forever' he told me. 'Mackay's Memoirs' opened my eyes to what is possible with the bagpipe. The man was a genius and it was an honour to have known him and play alongside him'.[8]

The Glasgow Years

On leaving Broughton in 1989, the next stage of Martyn's musical apprenticeship took him to the Royal Scottish Academy of Music and Drama (RSAMD) in Glasgow, where he was accepted onto the Diploma in Performance, studying violin and piano. That particular programme required a higher initial level of performance ability than the standard progression route through the degree, another clear sign of the remarkable progress he had made on these instruments at Broughton. His key mentor at the Academy was the violinist, Miles Baster (1935–2004), whom Martyn had already heard playing at the Edinburgh International Festival that summer in his role as leader of the highly respected Edinburgh Quartet, that he had founded in 1960. Martyn had been hugely inspired by the performance, making his way backstage afterwards to introduce himself and to announce that he would like Miles to teach him! The master invited Martyn to play for him the following week, and was only too pleased to take him on as his pupil once he began studying in Glasgow.

Born in Croydon in 1935, of Scottish descent, but moving

to Cornwall as a young boy, Miles showed early promise as a musician, being given his first three-quarters sized violin aged nine, and attending the King's School in Canterbury on a scholarship. While still at school he became leader of the National Youth Orchestra, and regularly made the journey to London to study with the renowned soloist, Albert Sammons. From there, he took up a place at the Royal Academy of Music, where his mentor was the Canadian-born virtuoso, Frederick Grinke, a friend of Ralph Vaughan Williams. Baster won many prizes while studying there, including the Dove Prize, the Academy's highest award, and later also the Boise Scholarship that allowed him to take up a place at the Julliard School in New York. The star attraction there was the chance to study under Louis Persinger, a giant of a musician who could count amongst his other pupils some of the world's elite players, including Yehudi Menuhin and Isaac Stern. Violinists, like pipers, are apt to place a good deal of worth on their learning pedigree, and through his time working with Miles Baster, Martyn was certainly inheriting his influences from some of the world's very best.

Miles Baster's Scottish connection was forged in 1959, when still in New York, he was invited by Sidney Newman, Reid Professor of Music at the University of Edinburgh, to form the Edinburgh Quartet. Although a career as an international soloist beckoned, he accepted the invitation, taking up the position he was to hold for the next 35 years. The International Festival apart, the classical music scene in the Scottish capital in those days was at something of a low ebb, and Miles' innovative and energetic approach to his work has been recognised as having done much to change that for the good.[9] Under his leadership the Edinburgh Quartet built up a reputation, still held to this day, as one of the foremost chamber ensembles in Britain, performing on tours throughout the world, making regular radio broadcasts and recording an extensive discography. Given its international reputation for excellence, the fact that Miles was later to invite Martyn to 'sit in' as cover for one of the players when the occasion required, is clear evidence of the high regard in which he came to hold him as a classical violinist. Miles' students and colleagues recall him with fondness as a thoroughly supportive teacher of great dedication to his art and to theirs. He would often stand at a classroom window chain-smoking as his pupils negotiated their way through their scales, or host them for lessons at his modest high-rise flat in Edinburgh's Gilmerton, dispensing his wisdom through the reek of his roll-ups, his television blaring and cat prowling.

Under Miles' guidance, on taking up his place at the RSAMD, Martyn continued where he had left off at Broughton in terms of the attitude with which he approached his studies. Many who knew him there remark on the zeal of his work ethic and his unflinching commitment to practice. He found the expectations of the course hard going, and was well aware that neither he nor anyone else could simply sail through without full commitment. The more industrious among them were in the building by 8.30am each morning to make sure they could secure a practice room, and would play for at least six hours each day. Martyn was certainly in that camp. Many of his peers had been playing their instruments almost since infancy, while he of course had come to both the violin and piano very late in relative terms, and so he did feel he had a lot of catching up to do. And there was no piping for him there! In the years that followed his time at the Academy, a piping degree was indeed established as a joint venture with the National Piping Centre, but there was no hint of that back then, and in fact very few staff or fellow students were even aware of his piping prowess. He didn't stop playing – in fact he was pragmatic enough to know that he could earn an attractive income from piping at weddings, ceilidhs and functions in the evenings and at weekends, and he had been quite comfortable busking with his pipes since his early Edinburgh

THE MUSIC APPRENTICE

days – but he seemed to prefer to maintain a clear separation between that and his daytime studies, and saw little point in sharing his dark secret! His busking brought him a healthy extra income, although things didn't always go well. He liked to take a large speaker with him powered by a battery pack in order to play 'backing' tracks he had pre-recorded, and would blast them out in Sauchiehall Street as he fired out the pipe tunes on top of them. On one occasion though, the battery pack leaked in his backpack, leaving a soggy, acidic mess on his back! It was a painful lesson!

Although now fully immersed in his classical music studies, his father recalled how Martyn was still eagerly exploring the sounds of the folk scenes of both Scotland and Ireland. In 1991 Ian took a holiday in Scotland and they travelled together to Durness in Sutherland, a place that intrigued Ian as it shares the same rock formations that he studied in western Newfoundland. On the way north they took a small, metalled track across the top of the granitic Highland moors from Inverness where they had stayed overnight. *The Storm* by Irish 'supergroup', Moving Hearts, was on the car stereo when Martyn 'whipped out his low whistle and with feet on the dashboard played along through the whole album'. Indeed, for those of us who had grown up playing the Highland pipes and who were trying to add the low concert whistle to our musical arsenal, that particular album was certainly a favourite 'play along' – it was a seminal release for many of us of Martyn's generation. In Ian's view, the 'musical adventurism' displayed by Donald Lunny and the rest of Moving Hearts was a very significant influence on his son, as indeed was *The Wellpark Suite* composed by Billy Jackson. Both 'let him see that you could break out of the constraints of traditional presentation of traditional music' and Martyn sent his father letters with copies of the albums, 'enthusiastic about both', as soon as they were released in 1985. Martyn was also posting him the music of Alasdair Fraser, Altan, and Shooglenifty, all of which provided new tunes for Ian to learn as well as 'a great mix of fast and slow tunes to train for the summer triathlons on a stationary bike during long winter months'. In return Ian sent Martyn albums like *Out of Africa* by the Kronos String Quartet and the Swedish group, JPP, and many classical albums of interest. Ian also owned a collection of traditional albums from Cape Breton as well as classical albums that Martyn would tape to take home after his summer trips. The musical influences between father and son flowed in both directions, clearly.

Yet it was *The Storm* and *The Wellpark Suite* that remain most firmly in Ian's memory as having excited Martyn most keenly. These are two very different sounding albums, and they wear their Irishness and Scottishness respectively on their sleeves very overtly. *The Wellpark* was commissioned to mark the centenary of the founding of the Glasgow Tennent's Lager brewery of that name, and captures the industrial urbanity of its theme with very subtle layering of strings and wind, performed by several of the leading traditional musicians of the time (and still, in most cases) such as Ron Shaw, Wendy Wetherby, Jim Sutherland, Tony Cuffe, John Martin and Iain MacDonald, as well as Billy Jackson himself along with his brother, George. Several of them played together in the band Ossian, one of the

Martyn and his father, Ian.

early adopters of the Highland bagpipe into a folk group setting along with the likes of Alba, The Tannahill Weavers and The Battlefield Band. For a young lad brought up in the strict musical discipline of Highland piping, the blending of the instrument's iconic voice and tone with fiddles, guitars and clarsach was a sonic joy, and there were many of us pipers who shared in this musical epiphany around this time.

And if *The Wellpark* was classy, *The Storm* was just plain cool. Moving Hearts had been formed in 1981 by two giants of the Irish traditional music scene, Donal Lunny and Christy Moore, who teamed up with guitarist Declan Sinnott along with Eoghan O'Neill on bass and Brian Calnan on drum kit. But it was the soaring reeds of Davy Spillane's uilleann pipes and Keith Donald's alto sax that gave the band that radical edge of danger and evoked a sense of life in the fast lane. Their eponymous first album of 1981 was followed quickly by a second, *The Dark End of the Street*, the following year, but after Christy Moore's departure in 1982 the band went through a few personnel changes before dropping the songs and focusing purely on instrumentals. By the time *The Storm* was released in 1985, a second uilleann piper had been added in the form of Declan Masterton to give the band a three-pronged melodic attack that was quite stunning in its power and range. Add in Greg Boland's melodic electric guitar licks, pitched in the same high octave as the twin pipes and the sax, and the result was a weaving interplay of instrumental voices that was like nothing most of us had ever heard before. There was an almost paradoxical combination of precision and wildness in there that was also to become a prominent ingredient in Martyn's own work. However we might define the idea of musical fusion, there was plenty of it in Moving Hearts. A deep, driving bass end brought the kind of depth that appealed to those of us in our teens at the time (Martyn was 14 when *The Storm* was released) while Noel Eccles' conga-driven percussion lines brought a touch of African exotica for a mid-'80s audience. The uilleann pipes sang 'tradition', the alto sax spoke 'jazz', and with Davy Spillane's championing of the low D concert whistle too, it seemed to many of us that this was it – this is what we had been waiting for. Martyn's excited response, witnessed by his father, suggests that he agreed, and it is not hard to detect the trace elements of that Moving Hearts sound in the work that Martyn was to produce a decade later.

It was while studying at the RSAMD that Martyn met his future wife. Kirsten Thomson was a year above Martyn and remembers him initially as a rather quirky lad who would always appear with his violin strapped vertically to his back (which nobody else did in those days), its case complete with a conspicuous Canadian flag. He went everywhere by bike, and never one to do things by halves, wore the full Lycra gear and proper cycling shoes. It was an unconventional look, and sometimes attracted unwanted attention in the form of stones lobbed at him by the Gorbals' youth as he made his way into college from the home of his stepfather, Joe. He couldn't understand why they would pick on him; Kirsten and his other friends could! Kirsten also noticed that Martyn was something of a social butterfly, flitting in and out of different groups of students, and refusing to adhere to the conventional behaviour adopted by most, of sticking with their own kind. He began to hang out with the drama students (apparently a very rare habit for those on his course) and within his first year, in March 1990, ended up securing a role in one of the opera school's productions, playing the part of Mozart's 'young fiddler' in the opera, *Mozart and Salieri*. 'In the show he had to do a wee dance and play his fiddle! Other people used to say to me "My God! I would *never* do that! How did he get taken in by them?! And dancing on stage!"'

As well as developing his performance skills on violin and piano, Martyn studied music history, aural skills, harmony and counterpoint. His listening skills, in particular, astounded Kirsten, who was much more of a visual player, comfortable when sight-reading but less confident when working 'blind':

> We used to go to these aural sessions, and I used to dread them every week. I was so rubbish at it! 'What's the chord progression?' And I would just go blank! Panic! Or 'sing the fifth note of this chord.' But he found it just so easy, so natural. I just always went into a massive panic, there were other people who just sat and worked it out and then people like Martyn, which was hardly anybody, who couldn't understand why nobody else could hear it! I asked him how he studied that stuff, but he didn't study it. He didn't have to. He would sit at the piano and just play a lot of chord progressions, listening to the different

effects. But then he said he was rubbish at the piano! He said that his piano teacher always kept saying to him, 'stop digging for potatoes'!

Of course, from a very young age Martyn had been exposed to a world in which people *did* literally dig for potatoes. It was a world in which music was learned and passed on through ears rather than eyes, and no doubt his frequent trips with his mother to folk festivals in the likes of Keith, Auchtermuchty and Kinross as well as his exposure to the fieldwork recordings she was making right across Scotland and well beyond, had honed his aural skills greatly. Yet there was clearly an innate hypersensitivity to sound in evidence from Martyn's earliest years. He would, for instance, ask for the sound on the television to be turned down if there was music being played on it that was not exactly in tune! The insistence that tuning be perfect, and an almost zealous readiness to point out when it was not, was a trait than never left him. The Gaelic singer, Anne Lorne Gillies, witnessed Martyn, still in his teens, boldly announce to the conductor of the orchestra he was rehearsing with that 'the second violin is out of tune'! And indeed, it was! His mother laughed heartily when telling me this – 'he had no filter'!

It wasn't all work and no play for Martyn in Glasgow, though, and the drama students were apt to have a fairly active social life. Martyn began to go to clubs with them, his first main exposure to the forms of electronic dance music that were to provide the inspiration for his future musical direction. He had always been into technology, stripping and re-building car engines as a boy in Kingussie with his stepfather, Joe, and later doing likewise with tape machines and amplifiers. Martyn's grandfather, George Bennett, was also something of a technology buff, and on retiring from his profession as a civil engineer he enrolled at Dalhousie University in Canada, where his studies included audio technology and electronics. 'Papi'

Martyn and his mother, Margaret.

and Martyn shared long conversations about music technology, and it was George who first introduced his grandson to the work of Canadian composer, Murray Shafer, who 'was right up Martyn's street', and whose writings pointed the way to a range of other composers who used 'noise' in their compositions.[10] There were various guiding hands behind Martyn's ventures into the world of electronic sound, then, and he certainly made the most of the inspiration. I well remember meeting him at a gig in Dalry in Edinburgh, probably in the early 1990s, as I was lugging a large, heavy PA speaker into the venue from the back of my car. Martyn was disdainful, pointing out that this was unnecessarily hard work, and that I should do what he had done, having made himself a nice light pair of speakers. And they could still make a big noise, he assured me. Quite how somebody could even begin to make their own speakers was a total mystery to me. (So I told him not to be such a smart arse and give me a hand with the other one. And to be fair, he did!)

Discovering a room within the RSAMD that was being set up as a studio, Martyn was intrigued to find a sampler and began to spend long hours experimenting with the electronic manipulation of sound. The basic idea is a fairly simple one: the machine captures a 'sample' from another source of recorded sound, such as from tape, vinyl or CD, that is then stored digitally to form what is essentially an archive of basic units of sound. Most samplers allow these to then be manipulated in various ways, such as altering pitch or time-stretching to elongate them, and they can be 'triggered' (i.e. played) from some form of software programme or hardware such as a sequencer or keyboard. In this way, complex passages of music can be created by layering the samples together to form a track that can then be used as one element of a recorded piece, or played live in concert. Martyn's initial use for his sampled creations was to serve as a backing track for his street busking exploits to help fund his way through college. There is something pleasingly cyclical about that, given that he was using the institution's equipment to compose it in the first place! But more significantly, perhaps, it was the beginning of the next stage of his apprenticeship, developing the understanding and techniques upon which his main creative outputs, and indeed his future career, were to be built.

Those who are serious about using samplers and their related hardware, Martyn among them, consider them to be more than mere tools. Rather, they are instruments in their own right, and so require the same level of commitment and practice as pipes, violin or piano. And as with them, mastering the technique is only the beginning, for there is a degree of artistry required to compose in a way that communicates ideas and emotions just as effectively as these more conventional musical objects can. Martyn seems to have understood this from the off, as Kirsten explains:

> People call it a backing track, but that track was more important to Martyn than anything else that went on. He had put everything into that – he had created or put down every single sound. He didn't copy and paste things from elsewhere. He was an archivist in some ways – he would sit and listen to stuff on vinyl or CD and he wrote down something that he liked – it could be a loop, or a sound or one note – and he'd write down the track, who it was, and then he'd sample it, and store it. He had huge amounts of files of samples, some of them just seconds long, some of them longer. And he stored all of that and then he would layer many sounds together. The complexity of his work – that is something that a lot of people didn't realise. The entries on the screen were huge. He would write out the bits of tune which he would physically play and use that as the score. He was incredibly organised with his filing of all of his samples and notes – there was nothing chaotic. He was ordered. In everything.

That scale of electronic production still lay in the future for Martyn, though, and while studying he remained committed to mastering his main instruments throughout his four years at the Academy. His violin playing blossomed under Miles Baster, and there is no doubt that there developed a deep mutual respect between them. Martyn played in orchestras, deputised within the Edinburgh Quartet and entered composing contests during his time there. He won the Royal Academy Prize for composing at the end of his first year in 1989 and the Hilda Bailey Prize for Excellence in the Violin in 1992. That same year he came to wider prominence by appearing as a finalist in the BBC Radio 2 Young Tradition Awards that were broadcast nationally from London. In his final Academy recital, Martyn's programme included a Beethoven sonata as well as Prokofiev's Second Violin Sonata and Miles clearly considered him to have the potential to follow a career as a concert soloist. Margaret has a recording of that recital that I saw her sharing with final year students studying at the Royal Conservatoire of Scotland in early summer, 2023. They too were about to perform their recitals the following week, and as an outsider, I felt like I was witnessing a quite beautiful moment of recognition and sharing amongst exceptional musicians who sadly never met. His mother apart, it must have been the only time any of us in that room had ever heard Martyn perform classical music, and I for one, was totally spellbound. I knew of course that he was lauded as an outstanding talent on violin, and yet I somehow wasn't prepared for the almost overwhelming emotion of that experience, nor indeed for the virtuosity of the performance. It was a moment of epiphany for me.

All of this created an air of expectation surrounding his future career that Martyn found hard to deal with, and he was not at all convinced that he had what it would take to succeed in the realm of professional classical music. Nor was he sure that he even wanted it. In truth, he could never see himself spending his life sitting in an orchestra, nor even standing in front of one as a soloist. Reflecting on that issue some three years after graduating, he was very clear that his future did not lie in the classical field:

> I love playing classical music, but it isn't in my blood, it's not in me – which was a big disappointment to my teachers. I'm not wanting to sound arrogant, but the fact was that at college they had me down as the next Menuhin, kept telling me I really had something special on the violin, and it really freaked me out, because I just couldn't feel it. It cut me up, cut me to pieces – I would love to have felt it, I would love to be able to say I am a true master on the violin, or the pipes, or whatever, but it is not in me.[11]

This is a truly revealing admission by Martyn: he recognised that he possessed the technical ability to achieve great things as a solo classical violinist, and that his teachers knew this and fully believed in him, yet he did not believe in himself. It was not enough to be brilliant. True mastery was the only goal worth having, and this was unattainable for him, he felt. And note that this did not only apply to classical music, but to his piping too. Was it really not in him? That level of self-criticism, that total lack of satisfaction with one's own ability, may well be a hallmark of many great artists as they strive for something approaching perfection, but the fact is that Martyn acted upon those doubts, and was later to leave both classical music and piping behind in pursuit of new paths.

Martyn's worries about his abilities in the realm of classical violin had certainly been picked up by his father on one of his visits from Canada:

> I visited him in Glasgow where I crashed each night on a mattress on his flat floor when he was at the RSAMD. There, we visited the electronics studio, he introduced

me to his like-minded mates and I shared a pint with Miles Baster discussing Martyn's progress on the violin because Martyn at the time lacked confidence that he was attaining the proficiency expected to be a successful musician. It's hard to believe but he was conflicted about ever getting good enough while at the same time he dropped hints that he was already bitten by the musical horizons that technology could open to him.

At times, this attitude brought a certain tension to Martyn's relationship with Miles, recalled Kirsten, although such

intensity is by no means rare between teacher and apprentice at that level of artistic excellence. And it was a relationship that remained intact for some time after Martyn's graduation, the two continuing to work together now and again, culminating in the pupil composing a complex piece of music specifically for the Edinburgh Quartet, led by the master. For reasons that remain unclear, its first performance also marked the end of the relationship, and indeed coincided with the end of Miles Baster's association with Scotland.

The *Piece for String Quartet, Percussion and Scottish Smallpipes in C* was composed in 1995. It is difficult to play. *Very* difficult to play! Snatches of traditional pipe tunes are interspersed with ever-shifting rhythms and time signatures, with a jazz-infused bass line underpinning some wild and discordant soaring string passages that take us eastwards, through the Levant, and down into Mesopotamia perhaps. It is a forerunner, it seems to me, of a passage that was later to appear, albeit in more simplified form, in *Mackay's Memoirs*. The percussionist entrusted with the job of joining Martyn and the Edinburgh Quartet to perform the piece was Tom Bancroft. The first time Martyn had seen him play some months before, Tom had been using a rather unconventional drum kit comprising a set of pots and pans, a sound and idea that very much appealed to Martyn's sense of musical adventure, and so he invited Tom on board.

In Tom's account of this period we get glimpses of the way in which Martyn was to operate professionally, with gigs in the Highlands and Islands, each trip a memorable adventure for Tom, and with Martyn already demonstrating some of his key traits – being musically and professionally demanding, yet also supportive and fun:

> He wrote this piece and it was really fucking hard! I don't know whether he knew it was hard and wanted

it to be hard or whether he was just throwing ideas out there. It was an example of these different musical worlds colliding. Martyn was so plugged into all these different kind of ethnic grooves from Iran or wherever. So he was asking a lot of these different musicians and I don't know if he knew how much he was asking of them. It was a technically very difficult piece. I was nowhere near good enough to play that part. There was no chance I could play that looking back. It was partly because I wasn't good enough but also maybe it was actually impossible to play for one person. We did some rehearsals and it was all a bit like, 'Oh Jesus!' Martyn was totally on top of his part, and he was great. Very supportive. So we had this gig which was the premier of it, on Skye, at the Skye Music Society. Me and him drove up together in this big blue Volvo estate I had, and we had this brilliant drive up there. But Miles disappeared. That day. He just didn't show up. That was the day that he disappeared. He actually disappeared for several months as far as I remember, and he eventually showed up living in another city. And you can't help but think that it was something to do with the piece. That he just couldn't face playing this piece. But when we got there the other three guys from the Edinburgh Quartet were there, but we thought, 'what are we going to do? We can't do the piece'. And everyone was really worried about Miles, and we were just freaked out by the whole thing. So they played a trio piece that they had, and me and Martyn just did a duo thing, a kind of Coltrane bagpipe jam, and we didn't play the piece.[12]

Whether that was indeed the catalyst that led to Miles Baster's decision to up sticks and leave Scotland for good is of course hard to determine now. But the incident did mark the end of the master and apprentice relationship, Miles moving south to Cornwall where he had family connections and where he continued to perform both solo recitals and concertos with local orchestras. His final performance was in January 2004 when he played Beethoven's Violin Concerto with the Sinfonia of St Mary's in Penzance. By that time he was suffering from cancer, and died, aged 69, in October 2004, just three months before Martyn's own death.

Ever hungry for new creative inspiration, Martyn also used his time at the RSAMD to explore many other musical traditions. He became fascinated with jazz violin styles of playing, for example, particularly that of Joe Venuti, whose work he chose to study as part of his diploma. Giuseppe 'Joe' Venuti (1903–1978) pioneered the use of string instruments in the development of North American urban jazz in the 1930s, recording many violin 'breaks' on jazz dance releases. His style of playing was described as 'hot' and listening to clips of him, especially in duet with his childhood pal, guitarist, Eddie Lang, that is a pretty accurate description.[13] And I suspect his light-hearted and jokey attitude to life was a further attraction for Martyn: stories of his comic exploits abound, including his filling of a tuba player's instrument with flour, or calling every bass player in the New York phone book asking them to meet him on a street corner. Fifty of them turned up, with their instruments, blocking the street. But there was no sign of Joe! Martyn also loved the blues harmonica playing of Silas Hubbard Jr, the eclectic guitar style of Bennett Hammond (who he got to know well on trips to New England), the American folk duo Sparky and Rhonda Rucker, French Canadian fiddle virtuoso, Jean Carrignan from Quebec and the potent pairing of Dougie MacPhee and Buddy McMaster from Cape Breton.

Martyn's taste for the Arabesque that flowered in his piece for the Edinburgh Quartet and seasoned some of his later work was also developing strongly while in Glasgow. High on his list of favourites was Omar Faruk Tekbilek, a Turkish multi-instrumentalist and composer who practised Sufism, a form of Islamic Mysticism, and who therefore took a very deep and holistic approach to his music-making. His playing on a range of traditional string and wind instruments was highly technical and fluent, and so all the qualities that Martyn most admired came together in this one virtuosic artist. Kirsten herself spent an extended period in Turkey, and could understand her partner's obsession with Tekbilek, recalling that Martyn was '*completely* besotted with his instrumental playing. When you hear him you can feel where he's coming from, where his roots are, where his passion is. It's really powerful. He was influenced by him massively'. Inspiration also came from 'Northern Lights' music in Scandinavia, Martyn finding a great deal of substance in the playing of some Swedish and Finnish musicians, the nyckelharpa player Johan Hedin, in particular. And a favourite discovery was the considerable output of Silex Records, a French label founded in the late 1980s by the producers André Ricros and Philippe Krumm, specialising in what by then was becoming known as world music. Much of this was esoteric to say the least: Kirsten found it 'hard to listen to' concluding that most people would simply 'file it away'! The chanting of Tibetan monks inspired him greatly, while back on more culturally familiar territory, the music of the Lithuanian-born but American-based musician, Jascha Heifetz (1901–1987), remained top of Martyn's list of heroes for the rest of his life. That is perhaps not altogether surprising, given that for many, Heifetz was the greatest violinist of all time.[14]

And yet Martyn was also being drawn increasingly towards electronic dance music. Julie Thomson, Martyn's future sister-in-law, clearly remembers the night when he announced to her the direction he wanted his music to take. It was 1992, she was studying at the Glasgow School of Art, and was in a bar 'dancing away upstairs with my pals, when Martyn showed up. He started dancing around like a total Dervish saying "this

is the music! This is what I want to do. This is the very thing I want to do. I want to combine my music with this!"' Thereafter regular nights in the Glasgow clubs with the drama students and his own sampling experiments in the RSAMD studio led Martyn to investigate the early output of electronic artists who were destined to become household names. Leftfield, formed in 1989 by Neil Barnes and Paul Daley, led the way in Britain's embracing of this new form of popular culture, combining elements of existing sub-genres such as Dub, House and Reggae to form a hybrid that came to be labelled Progressive House. Martyn loved it, and from there discovered the early work of the Chemical Brothers and the creative mixing and sampling of Fat Boy Slim. In the USA, Moby had emerged out of the underground punk scene to begin experimenting with electronic dance music, and his early 1990s releases on the labels Instinct Records and later, Elektra Records, were greatly admired by Martyn.

These are just some highlights of Martyn's eclectic sources of musical inspiration discovered during his apprenticeship, and it would take hundreds of pages to do justice to the list in full. But these were mainly artists he could only admire from afar. To progress, he had to be exposed to different approaches to the electronic music-making process itself, and the chance to do that came when he met a Sheffield-born multi-instrumentalist, composer, producer and violin-maker by the name of Martin Swan. From Martyn's many collaborations with him beginning with the band, Mouth Music, through to Swan's production of the *Mackay's Memoirs* recording on the day Martyn died, the two forged a musical partnership that had its frictions but remained a constant throughout Martyn's life.

3

Making a Name

AS WITH MANY young musicians, Martyn was by no means content to wait until he had finished his formal training before taking to the public stage, and by the time he graduated from the RSAMD in 1993 he had already built up a substantial CV and had an impressive track record of both live and recorded performances under his belt. While still at school in 1987 and again in 1988, he took part in tours of Denmark with the Lothian Schools Orchestra, while also appearing as a guest of the Scottish Chamber Orchestra on a tour of the Highlands and Islands playing smallpipes on Edward McGuire's piece, *Hebridean Suite*, in 1988. Later that summer he took on the role of arranger and performer for a series of concerts in Edinburgh entitled 'With Heart and Voice' featuring his mother and Scots folksinger Alison McMorland. On one occasion Margaret was running a little late, and arrived just on time for the beginning of the show. That was not something her son appreciated, being rather keen on punctuality. He said nothing in the moment, but when it was time to accompany her on the song, 'Jock o Hazeldean' – one that demands a big vocal range – he pitched it two tones higher than they had practised. Margaret gave it her best shot, but it was a strain, and after the concert, mentioned to him that he had played that one in the wrong key. 'Yes', he announced. 'Next time, be early'!

Two television appearances on Channel 4's breakfast show

followed, when they featured 'The Best from Edinburgh Festival'. The next year saw him tour the American east coast performing in Portland, Boston, New York, West Virginia and Tennessee, while on his return to Scotland that August, he joined 'The Young Champions' tour under the guidance of fiddler, Aly Bain. He was no stranger to the recording studio by this time either, contributing Highland pipes at the age of 15 to the 1986 album *Scotland Sings: 100 Great Scottish Songs* along with established folk musicians Andy M Stewart, Cilla Fisher, Davy Steele and Phil Cunningham, and appearing on *Borderlands* by Northumbrian musician Kathryn Tickell the following year. A collaboration with his mother that same year saw the release of the album, *The Thistle and the Pitcher Plant*, featuring songs and tunes from Scotland and Newfoundland, while American flute player, Sarah Bauhan, invited him to play a variety of instruments on two of her albums, *Chasing the Moon* and *The Untamed Grass*.

Martyn also travelled to perform in the USA on many occasions, initially accompanying his mother there to play in clubs and festivals. One of the first trips was in 1989, where they were booked to play at the Pinewoods Camp folk music week in Massachusetts. Musician and organiser, Lorraine Hammond:

> I wanted Margaret there for the transatlantic ballad connection and I wanted Martyn because he was a musical joy and delight – eloquent on his instruments and full of the kind of mad energy that enlivened a setting that can get a bit studious. Martyn loved the rustic setting – the 'no cars', the basic cabins in the woods, the lake to swim in, the mix of all ages, the freedom – and the endless opportunities to play music. He even seemed to like his daily kitchen chores, wearing an apron and washing dishes! A sort of 'Will o' the Wisp', he'd always do his own thing, find his own

space, his own musicians. And Martyn jammed with
us all – bluesmen Silas Hubbard and Sparky Rucker,
songwriters Gordon Bok and Bob Franke – he shook
up our perceptions and pushed musical boundaries, and
just when he seemed dangerously close to the edge he
pulled back with an exquisitely played set of Scottish
traditional tunes on the pipes. It was a brilliant week.
Mind you, my favourite Martyn musical memory that
summer was coming upon a music lesson that Vermeer
would have loved to paint! A rainy afternoon in a musty
cottage by lamplight and guitarists Bob Franke and
Bennett Hammond were patiently coaching Martyn
who was struggling to erase note after note from his
fiddle riffs until he could find and feel the deep guts of
the blues. Martyn always reached for the deep guts of
music. He found it and he communicated it. Playing with
Martyn was exciting. The experience was never trivial or
shallow. Whatever our musical gifts were to Martyn, that
was his great gift to us.[1]

Another of the extra-curricular projects with which Martyn had become involved while still at Broughton was the traditional music and dance ensemble, Drumalban. It was to prove to be a crucial step in his career, particularly because of the personal links it led him to forge. Jamie MacDonald Reid, a friend of Margaret, had spent some time in Boston, where he got to know Talitha Claypoole Nelson (later MacKenzie), the two playing together in a dance band there for three years or so. Talitha had grown up in New York, learning classical piano from a young age and teaching herself Gaelic in her teens. On graduating with degrees in Russian and later in ethnomusicology and music history, she followed through on her developing interest in the music and dance of a range of cultures, while harbouring a desire to move to Scotland that had first taken root at the age of seven. While working together in Boston, Jamie MacDonald Reid discussed with her his idea of forming a group that was committed to what they saw as bringing more authentic approaches to traditional dance than had become codified in both the Highland and Country dance worlds, with appropriate musical accompaniment and costume. Jamie returned to Edinburgh to see to the initial set-up, recruiting Martyn as their main instrumental musician, describing him to Talitha as 'a highly precocious 15-year-old', who played Highland pipes, smallpipes and violin. Jamie had announced to Talitha in Boston that she should come to Scotland 'once your marriage breaks down', which indeed did come to pass, and so she arrived in Edinburgh in July 1987, taking on the role of lead vocalist as well as a dancer. Getting to know both Martyn and his mother socially and professionally, they would come to spend a fair amount of time together in the years that followed. Her railcard allowed Martyn to travel to gigs with her cheaply, in impersonation of Owen, her son of similar age, and Martyn was later to pipe at her wedding to Ian MacKenzie, photographer in the School of Scottish Studies. Talitha took to her young bandmate immediately, although shared the frustrations that some of his other collaborators were later to experience when it came to trying to work with him:

> He was a real laugh to be on tour with. He was playful. A bit mischievous. It was like herding cats – he was always fiddling and twiddling. He couldn't really focus. If you said, 'Ok, Martyn, stand here for ten minutes while we tune up or go through something', he'd be off on another tangent doing something that was distracting. I came across quite a few people who said, 'Oh I just can't work with Martyn Bennett, he's just impossible to control. He's just away'. He was just sparking electrical energy all the time. And his ear was so attuned to what

he felt was an appropriate pitch, and he could tune for 15 minutes and not be satisfied, and he would! Everything just had to be perfect.

Because he was learning classical violin by this time, and had never really played in a traditional 'fiddle' style, Martyn was concerned that his approach might sound incongruous and might not fit the concept that lay behind Drumalban:

> I remember on a number of occasions him saying 'Is it folksy enough? Is it too classical sounding?' He was concerned that he was playing too well, or at least that he was playing with equal temperament and that it should have been a bit more rustic. He wanted to make sure it sounded more like a folk instrument, despite his classical training.

This tension between folk and classical styles of playing was a theme that was to remain towards the forefront of Martyn's concerns throughout his apprentice years and well beyond.

That summer, 1987, the members of Drumalban were invited to perform at a festival in South Uist. Martin Swan had also travelled to the island to make a documentary entitled *Dancing to My Shadow* with his collaborator, David Ray, and recorded one of the Drumalban performances in the village hall in Bornish. Martin Swan was very taken with Talitha's singing of a Gaelic song:

> I was really stunned by her performance and it turned out to be all much more anthropologically interesting than I knew at the time. I knew that they weren't local but at the same time it was really beautiful and I remember kind of watching the audience and they were loving it and then Martyn played with a local piper. They played

Martyn in Drumalban.

smallpipes for somebody for a couple of Highland dances and I was struck by the fact that they both played with this real kind of Western Isles swing. I don't think I had really heard music from that part of that world properly and you know, ok Drumalban had their own sort of odd take on the thing and you know they were sort of pretty cross-cultural but for me it was a really great experience of hearing all the material that they played.

Swan was not meant to be creating the soundtrack for the film, but while listening to the music that Drumalban was performing it occurred to him that it would be fascinating to blend that repertoire with 'something much more contemporary'. This was the early days of the world music phenomenon, and while there was no shortage of such crossovers emerging from West African artists such as Salif Keita and Mory Kanté, attempts to do likewise with European musical traditions were few and far between. He decided that this was a golden opportunity to experiment to that end, and so contacted the members of Drumalban afterwards and arranged to have them record some of their repertoire in a studio, using it as the basis for the soundtrack to the documentary. Talitha recalled that Martin Swan had initially asked only herself and Jamie to the studio, but she insisted that they should bring in Martyn Bennett as well. He duly obliged, playing on some of the tracks, which was when Martin Swan first began to realise what a special ability this teenager had, later describing his talent as 'electric' and 'bursting out all over'. The soundtrack raised a good deal of interest, leading Swan and Talitha to discuss collaborating on a full album. And so Mouth Music was born, a project that was to have a significant influence on Martyn's developing approach to his music-making. Martyn himself contributed to the album, playing smallpipes on 'Martin Martin' and whistle on *Mile Marbh'aisg Air A'Ghaol* and 'a few other bits and bobs here and there'. 'He was really good at recording actually' remembered Martin Swan. 'I suppose it's quite an odd thing for me to meet somebody who had no fear of recording you know. He was great, he was just really natural'.

Mouth Music's eponymous first album, released in 1990, was met with critical acclaim and commercial success both within the UK and North America, where it reached number one in the *Billboard* Top World Music Albums and the *Music Week* chart. *Folk Roots*, *Q Magazine* and *The Guardian* each considered it among the best releases of the year, reviews generally lauding it as a ground breaker in the marriage of tradition and modernity, and in demonstrating that world music did not have to be confined to 'African or Brazilian exotica'.[2] And there can be no doubt that it served as a catalyst for Martyn Bennett's own musical pathway. Chatting with Martin Swan in 2003, he re-stated his enthusiasm for it, and reflected on its importance:

MAKING A NAME

I'll tell you what, when you did that first album, *Mouth Music*, what a revolutionary album it is. I don't care what you think about it okay, I'm not wanting you to say what you think about it really, but you can listen to that album now and hear what was so revolutionary about it. It was the first one in the whole of the world that was the starting block for all these people coming to, trying to take something new that was actually something old and why you would want to do that you know? It was the first stage in this deconstruction of the dark thing of dance music.

That said, there are almost always antecedents for what appear to be new approaches to music, and in this case, by Martin Swan's own admission, it was a collaboration between Brian Eno and David Byrne that had been the key inspiration for his approach to *Mouth Music*. Their record, *My Life in the Bush of Ghosts*, released nine years earlier in 1981, was, in Swan's view, 'the first album to randomise, to re-order the universe' in the way that he felt Martyn had later done 'as a matter of course'. Although by no means the first album to include sampling techniques, it was certainly one of

the earliest major releases to do so on a large scale, where sampled voices drawn from other artists' previous commercial recordings as well as snatches of conversations on radio stations formed the dominant verbal presence – the 'lead vocal' as it were. It was also one of the first albums to be delayed due to the complexity of gaining clearance for use of the samples, a constant headache for all those who followed in their wake, Martyn included. For Swan, what Eno and Byrne achieved on that album was to 'take these fragments and create new beauty out of seemingly unrelated elements', while introducing 'this glue of heavy rhythm' as the binding agent that made it all work.

The highly positive reception of *Mouth Music* created a demand for live performances of it and although, as Swan explains, 'it was really a concept, a project, a studio album', he put together a band and invited Martyn to be in it because he was 'the best musician I'd met'. The first live performance was in the Queen's Hall as part of the Edinburgh Folk Festival, and it wasn't without its mishaps. Expectations were high, and they were supported by The Cauld Blast Orchestra, itself a highly innovative blending of folk and jazz, and comprising a significant number of Scotland's most respected musicians in those fields. Mouth Music took to the stage for the second half, as Swan recalled:

> We were about half way through it and I suppose it was going okay but it was pretty lumpy you know. It was a really strange thing to try and do a live performance of, but Martyn was a fantastic asset because he played pipes and played flute and played fiddle and everybody accepted him utterly. It was all this kind of keyboard stuff and lots of samples and it was all quite burdensome technologically and suddenly there was this massively loud kind of farting PA sound which was deafening! I mean people were covering their ears and it took about

five minutes to sort that out, obviously they turned the PA down so we were just kind of standing on stage looking like complete pricks. This was the first gig and had been built up you know? This bunch of idiots standing on the stage not knowing what to do and you know Martyn just picked up the pipes and played a bunch of tunes and he was the only one that could redeem that situation. And that was an eye opener for me because I had come at this not wishing to be in a band particularly, it had just evolved out of a piece of TV production and I just recognised the incredible power of somebody who can play quite a loud instrument with confidence in front of a big crowd. What a thing that really is.

Martyn Bennett's direct involvement with the live version of Mouth Music was limited to a couple of initial gigs, as he was still in the early stages of his degree and so touring was not a practical option for him. Perhaps it was just as well, because as Martin Swan has since explained, it was not at all clear that they would be able to work together successfully in such an intensive way as a tour demanded. There was no falling out, but both of them possessed strong characters and even stronger convictions regarding their approach to the making of music. And Martyn's youthful exuberance and Tigger-like enthusiasm was hard for his older namesake to cope with:

> In rehearsal Martyn was impossible, just impossible. Firstly, he would never shut up and anytime you were talking with somebody about how we should do this bit, how should we do that bit, Martyn would be diddling on a flute, he could not stop playing. Every time you wanted to stop mid-song and think about what was going on he would carry on playing for a minute and although I

always really liked him that just drove me mad! He was suddenly finding his voice, and he was bursting with energy and there just wasn't room for him. And that was pretty much what we talked about because we had a very friendly and civilised breakup. And I said, 'Look, you need to be doing your own stuff. This is you, there isn't room for you in this band you know? You make too many notes, too much noise!' which is a kind of theme of his life and our relationship.

It was a relationship that developed in other ways, however, and the two continued to collaborate on a range of projects throughout Martyn's life, (and indeed, beyond, in terms of the posthumous recording and promotion of his music). Around a year after the recording of *Mouth Music*, Swan was still heavily involved in creating soundtracks for various forms of television programming, including commercials. The Leith Agency, one of the leading marketing and promotions companies in Scotland at the time, had secured the contract to produce an advert for the whisky-based liqueur, Drambuie, and had liked the general approach Swan had been taking, including on the *Mouth Music* album. The advert itself became something of a cult classic, featuring Robert Hardy, who, hosting guests in some far-flung exotic sun-kissed location, discovered he had run out of Drambuie. One phone call set in motion an action-packed chain of supply, beginning at the Vaults in Leith, via the Forth Bridges, a private jet, a parachute drop of the precious replacement bottle, an abseiling adventure girl, and a Bond-esque speedboat escapade, culminating in its safe delivery to Hardy's butler. Who dropped and smashed it.

Just as memorable as the action, though, was the soundtrack, featuring a rhythmic conga-driven musical bed created by Martin Swan, with a highly fluent and driving eight-bar snatch of a reel played on smallpipes by Martyn Bennett. I well recall that it caused quite a stir within the piping community at the time, with people intrigued to know who was playing this great music. The bellows pipe revival was still in its infancy, and the sound had yet to filter back into popular consciousness, even amongst Highland pipers. In fact, I can think of several players who were inspired to take up the instrument having first heard it on that advert. And it is something of a paradox, perhaps, that this piece of piping probably reached a bigger audience than most of his future projects, yet very few people knew who the player was. And behind the scenes, the track continued to be the source of regular discussion for many years, but for other reasons. While not quite on a Lennon and McCartney scale, Martyn and Martin did engage in prolonged banter (but perhaps with a fairly sharp edge of annoyance) as to which of them actually composed the piece. In an interview in the *Evening News* a year or two after its release, Martyn bemoaned the paltry nature of the fee he was given for the soundtrack. 'I was just playing an instrument', he noted, 'but there was a loophole in the contract that said right, a one-off payment, £250 – bang, that's it, bye-bye'.[3]

Martin Swan, reflecting on that issue too, viewed those kinds of arguments as a product of the ambiguity involved in defining 'authorship' when creating sampled electronic music of that form:

> This was a period of recording or music-making when the producer was the artist and you were used to using loads of samples or found footage and things like that and I think the reality is that I probably regarded Martyn as a bit of found footage. He may have played a fragment of the melody and I went, 'Well we can use that.' I probably developed it, he probably added a bit more, I probably added a bit more. And I'll have seen that as him kind of working for me and he will have seen that as an important artistic statement.

The issue didn't prevent them from continuing to collaborate, however, and the partnership stretched into a Tennent's Lager commercial, several adverts for Baxters soup, and 'a whole load of stuff for the Scottish Tourist Board that was all his playing. So basically I got him in to doing loads of stuff where I would write the music and he would be the star turn'.

Mouth Music, whether as band or album, was by no means universally accepted in positive terms despite its success, and as is often the way of things, its most hostile reception came from within the tradition from which it borrowed. We are back to the question of 'authenticity' here, and what that really means in essence. Does it matter who is actually making the music, where they are from, and what their relationship is to the traditions with which they are engaging? Can a musician's 'outsider' status debar them from acceptance and legitimacy? Can a voice from across an ocean carry the weight of another language and the cultural depths it supports? Where might the line be drawn between celebration and tribute on one hand, and cultural appropriation on the other? Such questions are encountered all the time by those who cross musical boundaries, who draw on multiple traditions, and who are in the business of 're-ordering the universe'. They were questions that were certainly pondered by Martyn at various points of his life, bringing different responses in different contexts. But for Swan, his young collaborator was fully behind the Mouth Music concept, and was very supportive of it:

> He was always really encouraging to me because obviously Mouth Music was quite controversial and not everybody liked it. He was massively indignant on my behalf – the fact that I wasn't really 100 per cent Scottish and all this kind of thing and he was like, 'Fuck em!' you know? 'What do they know, idiots, losers!' It was nice to have him say that because he felt like somebody who

was from the tradition. He really liked things that got up people's noses so he was really, really positive about that, the more kind of irritating it was to people the more he liked it! I don't think he just wanted to irritate, I think he wanted to make people angry.

Talitha MacKenzie agrees that Martyn had a liking for the ruffling of cultural feathers, and feels that this was one reason why the Mouth Music project appealed to him:

> The fact that this was so controversial – I think that he got a taste for that. That he could do something with traditional music that would cause a storm, really. That he would be involved in that.

Yet on a personal level, Talitha certainly saw a sensitive side to her younger colleague, and recognised a level of emotional maturity in him which belied his youth:

> There was a certain wisdom that Martyn had. And I remember when I was going through the tough times with the Mouth Music debacle he was very good about saying exactly the right thing. He was very comforting, and he could be very conscious of when people were needing a hug or needing some support. He was very good about tuning into that. I remember being impressed with the maturity beyond his years, really. I still think of him as being very young. Because he's frozen in my imagination as that age.

The debacle she refers to relates to the fact that she and Martin Swan suffered a serious breakdown in their relationship early in the Mouth Music project in June 1991, resulting in a parting of the ways followed by legal proceedings. The end result was that Talitha left to follow a solo career, Martin Swan taking the band on tour to North America with emerging South Uist singer, Mairi MacInnes, being brought in to provide the lead vocal. A follow-up recording was released as an EP in 1992 entitled *Blue Door, Green Sea*, attributed to Mouth Music and Mairi MacInnes, with Martyn Bennett returning to contribute a version of the 'Drambuie Reel' as one of the three tracks. The Mouth Music project carried on thereafter under Martin Swan's direction with a series of vocalists including Jackie Joyce, Ishbel MacAskill and Michaela Rowan, with a further six albums appearing between 1993 and 2005.[4] Martyn's active involvement with the Mouth Music project was relatively brief, therefore, but the experience must certainly go down as a key influence in his emerging approach to music-making, and as an important step towards becoming the innovative artist he was.

Dreadlocked

At the inaugural Celtic Connections festival in Glasgow in 1994, Martyn appeared at the Royal Concert Hall on the same bill as Mouth Music. Referring to him as 'a young multi-instrumentalist breaking down the walls of the musical ghetto' Kenny Kemp's review succinctly captured some of the key traits that were to become recognised as defining ingredients in Martyn's work: 'from the beginning, when he bended the evocative notes on his Overton flute through to Nigel Kennedy-esque jazz fiddling, he controlled his sound environment with supreme dexterity'. Kemp also admired Martyn's piping, which was 'ethereal against a thumping techno-base backdrop' while his 'quirky stage presence was a source of mirth'. His prophetic conclusion was that 'this guy is going to be mega'.[5]

That may well have been the first comparison of Martyn with Nigel Kennedy to appear in print, an oft-repeated one, that Martyn grew to despise! He was no fan. It carried on in rather more overt fashion the following year, particularly in an *Evening News* feature by Colin Somerville in November 1995. A full colour, double-paged spread featuring two dominant photos of Martyn, dreadlocked, tartan-trousered and leather-jacketed, carried the huge headline 'Piping Hot Martyn Reels 'Em In' and with a byline 'With his debut album out soon, Edinburgh's own rock n' reeler Martyn Bennett is Scotland's answer to Nigel Kennedy'. It's not hard to see why the comparison was being made: virtuosic violinists with a penchant for spectacular hairdos were not exactly common currency, and their shared determination to nudge forward the boundaries of their respective musical traditions must have made the perceived connection between them just too tempting to avoid.

The punk piper had arrived.

In these early years of his professional career, Martyn was not only catching the ear of critics and audiences alike, then, but catching their eyes too. His childhood obsession with sketching and drawing was still in him, clearly, and he grew to realise that creating a style and image – 'a look' – could play an important part in being noticed. And people *did* notice. The fashion designer, John Rocha, came north to the Festival Theatre in Edinburgh to show his autumn/winter collection in August 1994. Rocha had recently won the British Fashion Designer of the Year award, and so his arrival in the capital was met with a great deal of interest. Martyn had been booked to provide some of the music for the show – supposedly playing a minor role only – but it was he who grabbed the headlines the following day. 'Piping Hot' proclaimed the *Daily Record's* coverage, for instance. 'Martyn Bennett ripped off his shirt and played the rousing finale bare-chested' the paper reported gleefully, alongside a sizeable photo of him standing amidst two of the models.[6] To be fair, he was only really joining in on what was a general flesh-fest, for the women only had enough clothes on them 'to take the kettle off the fire' as my granny might have said!

Martyn's manager, Kenny MacDonald, certainly recognised the potential advantages of a talented young musician developing a strong 'look'.

> And when he was doing the semi-naked, dreadlocked thing you could see there was a marketability there. As artists tend to do, a year later he wanted to change that look! He's sexy, he ticked all the little boxes but he had no self-awareness of that. He was a beautiful man.

Women certainly seemed to agree. Kenny again:

> I recall him playing in Cannes when he still had his dreadlocks. Walking from one end of the pier to the other on a promenade – about a mile and a half to do a sound-check for a showcase. As we walked along I became aware that every ten or 20 seconds the ladies of Cannes were coming past us. Very elegant, from their teens to their 70s. I became aware that every single woman was drooling over Martyn. He was blissfully unaware. It became a caricature comedy. You could just see it – virtually every woman was transfixed. They were just drooling over Martyn's beauty. They were loving Martyn, and he didn't have a clue. Blissfully unaware![7]

Securing Kenny MacDonald as his official manager was something of a coup for Martyn. Kenny had been managing the Proclaimers since the mid-1980s and had played a central role in their rise to fame, having landed them an appearance on *The Tube* on Channel 4 that led within months to a record deal with Chrysalis, a hit single with 'Letter From America' and a debut album that achieved gold status. The international fame that followed kept Kenny very busy, of course, but he was instantly drawn to Martyn and his music when he first discovered it in the mid-1990s:

> I'd started to hear about the dreadlock piper, but I didn't know much about him. But I got to know his music and he needed a little bit of help with deals and promotion and things, so I formed a relationship with him over that time. We just got friendly and I started to listen to him and you couldn't fail to be blown away with how good he was. I wasn't a bagpipe fan, I wasn't a folk fan, but as a music fan, I certainly developed a great love for his music. It was just so good.

Once he agreed to work with Martyn, Kenny encouraged Lisa Whytock of Active Events to come on board as Martyn's agent:

> Kenny phoned me up and said, 'Look I've got this great new artist – would you be up for working with him?' He sent me a tape, I met up with Martyn, we got on really well, and that was it. That was the beginning, and we worked with him from that point until he died.[8]

When Lisa first started representing him, 'it was just Martyn, his bare chest and his DAT machine'. He disliked 'having to' go topless, she remembered, and would have much preferred focusing only on the music without need for 'the brand'. 'I wish I'd never taken my top off', he also confided to Kirsten, and dismissed it as having been a spur of the moment decision where he was just going with the flow and vibe of the occasion. That may have been so, but he does seem to have developed a taste for it and repeated the partial striptease several times! Although his father, Ian, wasn't able to see Martyn perform all that often he did catch a few of his live performances at various stages

 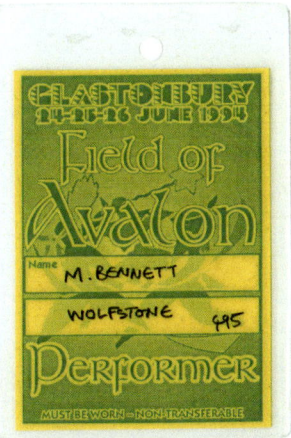

On tour with Wolfstone.

of his career. Witnessing him play with the band, Wolfstone, in Colorado, he was amused at his son's semi-naked and 'rock and roll' stage antics:

> But there was a hint of what it would have been like based on seeing him play in Telluride and his raucous vest-stripping performances in Glasgow and Edinburgh clubs. The air in the Telluride theatre was thick with pot smoke and he happily stamped on his pipe's bag at the end of the wonderful show, bringing up the last anguished musical wails much to the glee of the audience. I suspect he knew that a little raunchy acting only helped to win his audiences and he had a good sense of an occasion when he performed. I was pretty happy being there![9]

Martyn was at it again on two consecutive nights at the New Year celebrations in Edinburgh. On the second night, at the Atrium in the Traverse Theatre, he explained his shirt removal to *The Herald*'s Sarah Villiers as having been his remedy for the heat of the lights, but given that he had done likewise the night before on the Mound rather suggests he knew exactly what he was doing! That mixture of sex and music made him, for Villiers at least, 'the man to watch in '95.'[10]

Despite the fact that he was clearly very good at it, creating and developing this kind of eye-catching stage persona did not sit comfortably with Martyn, and he often admitted that he preferred working quietly on his own away from the public gaze. Music composing was therefore something he was keen to develop, and with their guarantee of income, commissions were especially attractive. In 1992 he wrote the score for a play by Raymond Ross, *The Haunting of Billy Marshall*, for the Edinburgh International Festival, and two years later he recorded all of the music for a run of *Kidnapped* directed by Tom McGrath for the Royal Lyceum in the capital too. The following year saw him complete a commission to compose and record the music for an animation production entitled *The Scottish Urisks* for Grampian Television, working with Leslie MacKenzie of West Highland Animation. This colourful folkloric tale of tiny 'happy-go-lucky' Highland sprites or brownies appealed to Martyn's sense of humour and adventure and his score using bagpipes, synthesiser, percussion and his own voice worked together 'to produce a wonderful theme tune which gives us a feel of the strength and gentleness of the shy yet powerful Scottish Urisk'.[11] But it was his work for a new stage play that premiered in 1995 that brought him the widest recognition for his composing talents when he wrote and performed the music for the original production of David Harrower's play, *Knives in Hens*, for the Traverse in Edinburgh. Now widely regarded as a modern Scottish classic, it transferred to London, and has since been performed in 25 countries across the world. Some of Martyn's score was arranged by Robert McFall and included on the album, *Birds & Beasts*, released on Delphian in 2010.

Left: Poster for the original production of *Knives in Hens*. Right: *Knives in Hens* on tour: David Harrower, Martyn Bennett and Michael Nardone.

'*Knives in Hens* is a satisfying, serpentine dalliance of whistle, violin and percussion across a medley of five Bennett tunes', concluded *The Independent*.[12]

The Jack Plug Generation

Having made the move back to Edinburgh following his graduation from the RSAMD in 1993, Martyn found himself in a city whose music had moved on during the years he had been away. A new generation of highly skilled jazz-influenced musicians had begun to coalesce around a number of sessions in pubs, clubs and private flats. Broughton High School had actually served as one catalyst for this, when several young players, still in their mid-teens, arrived there for a jazz course in the late 1980s. Brothers Tom and Phil Bancroft, Tommy Smith, John Rae and Colin Steele all attended, most of them meeting each other for the first time. All had gravitated towards jazz for different reasons, said Tom Bancroft, and they stayed in touch from that moment on, with others such as guitarist Kevin MacKenzie and pianist Brian Kellock arriving on the scene soon afterwards too. As Tom recalled, they started to gig together, but they all shared what he described as a 'condescending view of the folkies' who at that point were definitely considered 'the enemy'.[13] 'We didn't know anything about folk music and we all thought it was shit!' The relationship wasn't helped by the fact that 'they then started taking our gigs'. L'attaché, a basement bar just off the west end of Princes Street, had been one venue they had regular work in, but in the late 1980s the management decided to move more towards informal folk sessions and regular weekend staged folk band performances. My own band, Ceolbeg, had a regular gig there around 1990 and 1991, as did around half a dozen other folk bands (although I hadn't realised then that we were taking work away from the jazzers!). This economic rivalry didn't help bring harmony between the genres, then. As Tom remembered it, it was a case of just 'Who are these people? What the fuck?'!

But then a chance friendship changed attitudes. Freddy Thomson, a longstanding regular around the Edinburgh folk scene generally and in particular its 'head office', Sandy Bell's bar, became friends with John Rae, who began to play folk tunes on the fiddle. The others followed his lead and started to learn traditional tunes too, while percussionist Tom Bancroft also took up that archetypal 'folkie' drum, the bodhran. Suddenly, explained Tom, they realised that 'folk music was fucking amazing. And we realised that the young folk *musicians* were amazing – and great fun to be around too'. The two scenes began to discover each other, and very quickly formed a mutual respect. Tom felt that 'there was something unique about the

Scottish music scene – it had a fantastic energy'. This was undoubtedly fuelled, in part at least, by the symbiosis that was emerging between the jazz and folk worlds that initiated a range of new connections and musical cross-referencing, each providing the other with a rich source of melodies and rhythms to draw on. There was a wider context to this, however, for it was not a coincidence that the jazz scene globally was moving away from being predominantly black American music. 'It still is and always will be', Tom argued, 'but in addition to that, jazz was becoming an international music – people all around the world doing the improvisation thing, but drawing on different countries' traditional music or different musical identities. So for us jazz musicians it was important that we understand traditional music from Scotland'.

One early manifestation of this crossover in Edinburgh was the formation of The Giant Stepping Stanes project founded by John Rae and Dundonian musician and composer, Kevin Murray, and that featured several of the young jazz players who had met at Broughton. Key figures who had begun their careers mainly in the folk scene, such as Jim Sutherland and Simon Thoumire, were keen to meet the jazzers half way, and so bands such as Someotherland and Kevin MacKenzie's Vital Signs began to emerge, as well as a range of duos, one-off collaborations and hybrid productions of varying kinds. Tom again:

> Behind that professional level there was a lot of partying and hanging out and playing at sessions – and just having fun – having a good craic and enjoying the vibe. It was one of the things that made Edinburgh feel like a great place to be. It was tangibly different to London where I was also living some of that time. Where even just the jazz scene was cliquey and not particularly welcoming and you didn't get the feeling that the jazz scene had any connection with any different scene. But it was easy in Edinburgh.

Another key contributor to the Edinburgh music scene was percussionist James Mackintosh who Martyn had got to know when they both played with Mouth Music. Martyn would often visit James in his Marchmont flat, and the two would explore the joys of music production software such as Cubase, share and discuss samples, and generally hang out together. They would later perform together many times in live shows, on television and on various recordings, but in those years of the early 1990s they were both just beginning to make their way into the music scene. James also played with the band Shooglenifty, and he remembers that he and other members were invited to jam in La Belle Angèle in Edinburgh's Old Town:

> It was just a concrete box with a café at one end. It was incredibly sparse. We were invited to play a tune on a Wednesday night, and they paid us a few quid. We sat round a two-bar electric fire in the middle and within five weeks it was so busy we moved onto the stage and plugged in. That's how La Belle kicked off. Martyn was dotting about then.

It was into this world that Martyn stepped in 1993. Having already dismissed in his mind the need for barriers to exist between the worlds of classical, folk and jazz – or any other genre for that matter – he was naturally attracted to any situation in which collaborations and experimentation might be formed, as Martyn himself recalled:

> There were a lot of great musicians around at that time, mid-'90s in Edinburgh, and we were all in the same boat. We were all on the dole with no job and what do we do with our time? We went to the pub and played music together. I remember Monday nights being fantastic. Black Bo's and then on to Legends and there were some

great sessions happening. It was inspiring. The music was inspiring and in amongst that there were jazz musicians as well who were getting into it as well. They were joining in so there was this input and I could hear this kind of hunger from all this music wanting to get onto the big scene and present it to the world in a form that was on a screen or on a CD or something.

The Black Bo's sessions had been instigated by multi-instrumentalist and producer, Jim Sutherland, who had been keen to adopt the idea of the pub folk session, but with other genres of music mixed in. 'Martyn was a big contributor to these', recalled Jim.[14] 'People were noticing him as he could play the tunes, but also contribute beyond the folk stuff which is what these sessions were all about.' Gatherings also took place in The Transporter Room and other venues that Martyn also attended. 'There was a lot of dope-smoking and taking psychedelics' admitted Jim: 'so there was more than music going on at that time – it was quite a heady scene. There was a kind of great romantic escape that we were all involved in as musicians'. There was a new-found freedom of expression at that time in the relatively early days of easy sampling techniques:

> You could do anything – you'd listen to Hip Hop and you'd hear samples of whatever – Gene Pitney or some other old '50s album – so it was kind of cool to be able to include different kinds of things. We were getting used to music getting mixed up. Edinburgh probably had a big impact on Martyn in terms of allowing him to join himself up. There was a sense that ideas were king.

Martyn developed a particularly close relationship with Tom Bancroft following a chance meeting in the heart of Edinburgh's Old Town:

The first time I met Martyn, we had done a Someotherland gig in the Teviot Union at Edinburgh University. We'd done the gig and we were heading across to South Clerk Street. We were walking across the car park and Martyn came up to me. I didn't know who he was. And he said 'I really liked your playing. I like the way you play a little bit in front of the beat'. American jazz musicians do this, talk about playing in front or behind the beat but it's quite a specialised way of playing and thinking. And so this little guy comes up to me and says this, and I'm 'OK'. And he asked if I'd like to do something and I said sure. He was very charismatic, and he knew Jim Sutherland, but that was the first time we'd actually met. We went to a party in a flat on South Clerk Street. I remember it was 3.00am in the morning and there were was a lot of drink and joints or whatever, and suddenly Martyn gets his pipes out. And up until that point my only experience of bagpipes was I used to live near Calton Hill and these guys would play outside on a Saturday morning and it was really annoying. I didn't like the sound of them because of that and hadn't ever really got them as an instrument. Martyn started playing and it was really fucking loud in a flat that had flats above, below and at the side, but it was incredible. I can still remember the precision of his trills and ornamentations and it was just 'holy shit this guy's amazing!', and this is an amazing instrument. Wow, it blew my mind. It was a brilliant way to meet him. And he did it the way he did everything with complete charisma and style. He was such a beautiful guy. Physically beautiful guy.

Thereafter Tom and Martyn started playing together, seeking out or creating gig opportunities. Tom curated part of the Glasgow Jazz Festival, and invited Martyn to join him on a 'jazz ceilidh'. Nobody came to it! But afterwards they headed to a jam session at the Marriot hotel that was 'a big deal' in that festival at the time, attracting significant numbers of musicians and aficionados. Tom describes it as having been 'quite a macho and intimidating atmosphere' but it appealed to Martyn's sense of adventure and he loved it, and wanted to be part of it:

> I don't think anyone had ever taken bagpipes out there before. We'd been doing some duos – bagpipes and drums – just fucking around with that. I was playing stuff like you'd play with John Coltrane and he was playing reels and jigs and it was quite a good combination. So we just did that and the whole place erupted. And everyone wanted to play with Martyn – all the jazzers wanted to play with Martyn. It was really interesting taking him into that world. There's something gross about it – it's very showy-offy and macho but there's a bit of me that likes it. In a way I was showing off by taking my cool mate in there. But on a musical level it was very interesting – they loved the whole energy of what we did. I think it's important to remember how he was a leader in that way for the scene. Because he did things to such a high standard that he set the bar at a very high level for everyone else to aim at. But also that the music he made was so Scottish and so personal and so original. Even though I know that he had struggles with it in lots of ways, and it wasn't straight forward for him, but it seemed so uncompromising that he was laying down this incredible music with complete confidence and assuredness.

As his professional career took shape, Martyn was therefore moving forward on several musical fronts, jamming and performing with Tom and the other jazzers, playing in straight down the line folk sessions in the likes of Sandy Bell's and the Tron Bar, and not yet having turned his back on the classical world completely as he continued to 'sit in' on occasion with the Edinburgh Quartet. Several television appearances followed too, including on the BBC's *Transatlantic Sessions* alongside such luminaries as Phil Cunningham, Aly Bain, Emmylou Harris, Mary Black and Dougie MacLean. But he was eager to pursue his ambitions in the dance scene, and to build on the electronic tracks he had been developing in Glasgow. A number of pubs and clubs in the capital's Old Town – Black Bo's and La Belle Angèle chief amongst them – latched on to the burgeoning interest in techno dance nights and Martyn began to attend them regularly. He was particularly impressed with a young DJ who manned the decks from time to time in both venues, Andy Levy, aka Dolphin Boy. Martyn did what he always did when he discovered someone he admired – he introduced himself and befriended him! He was keen to learn from Andy, who was happy to help:

> It was mainly the beats he was interested in because he could do everything else himself. Where he was lacking experience was in making beats – programming beats. I remember we had some discussion about that. I do remember him coming round to a flat I lived in in Leith and showing him how I did things on Cubase at that point.

Martyn worked hard to develop the technical skills he needed to realise the ideas that had been forming in his head, and was soon ready to secure some slots in these clubs himself. He was determined to produce a sound that was bolder and edgier than that which prevailed, as Andy Levy recognised:

> I remember he was a lot braver. His music was a lot harder on the beats and bass side of things. It was a lot more

challenging than what I was using. He seemed to be going for something a bit more aggressive – a bit more epic.

One of the first club gigs he performed was witnessed by *The Scotsman* journalist, Bob Campbell who ventured into this underground world and was intrigued by what he found:

> It is 1.30am, it is hot and lights are low in a barely furnished rectangular space that has the air of ex-industrial usage about it. Apart from the small stage, the biggest features on view are the biggest pair of huge speakers through which the beat of some dance music mix threatens to atomise your very breast bone. This is the Squid Club in La Belle Angèle, down and out the back of Edinburgh's Cowgate and on the way in you are body-searched for bayonets or Stanley knives or other implements of modern night manoeuvres. 'It's for your own safety and our reputation', smiles the brisk young man on the gate. And what's the attraction this late on in a mid-December night among a company of techno freaks and trance dancers? Come on down Martyn Bennett, billed as 'the future of ceilidh'. How was that again? In the week-by-week billing Bennett is sandwiched between Dunni, 'Afro fusion Lagos groove', and Sons of Arqa, 'legendary acid tabla dub experience'. The future of ceilidh? A short, slight figure appears on that small stage wearing a kilt as a wryly chosen fashion statement. Off on an ethno-techniq trek (his term). This is racy subterranean stuff.[15]

It may have been racy, but being 'subterranean' was not going to cut it for very long. Underground is hip, yes, but it doesn't pay the rent. As his agent, it was Lisa Whytock's job to secure Martyn gigs and she set about the task armed only with a few basic resources:

MAKING A NAME

One of the first gigs we got for him was King Tut's in Glasgow. There weren't many places then that were cool. And at that time in order to get anyone any gigs you had to send a VHS video, so we video recorded that King Tut's gig and used that. So we had that and a cassette tape that we'd send off – tapes which we called 'white labels' – basically just a cassette with a piece of white paper inside with 'Martyn Bennett' on the spine! And that's how we started getting him gigs and it really took off.

For Martyn, the new sound was coming together, and it was going down well. His reputation was spreading, clubbers and journalists were beginning to take notice, offers of gigs were coming in, and things were heading in the direction he wanted. But white labels weren't going to get him to the next level. It was time to make an album.

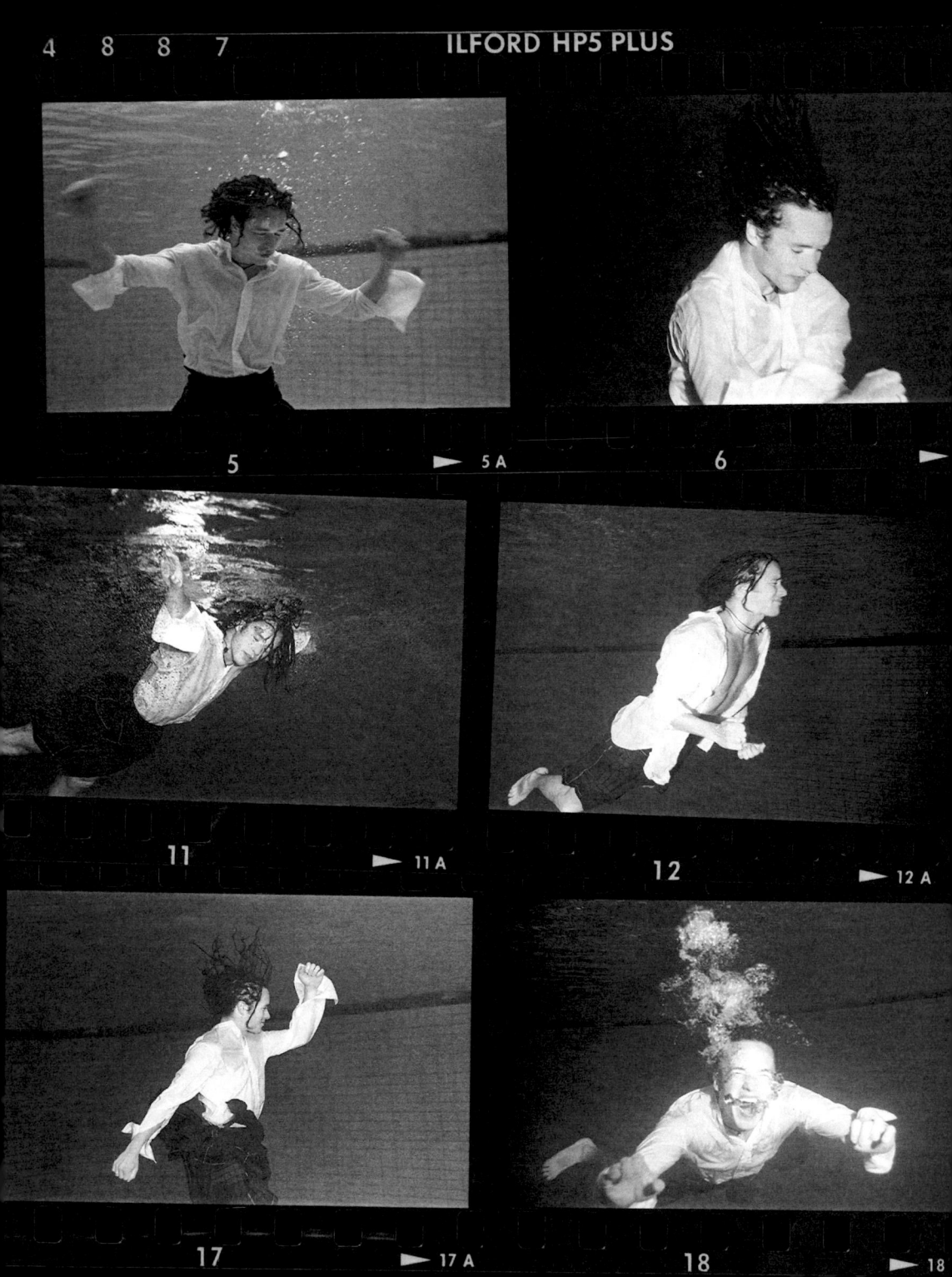

4

First Born

IN MARCH 1995, Martyn headed to Pencaitland in East Lothian to record his debut album, originally planned as *Jacobite Bebop*, but eventually (and perhaps, thankfully) named simply as *Martyn Bennett*. It is a true 'solo' album in that he arranged and performed everything on it himself, although in that regard there were multiple Martyns who came together to achieve the goal, making full use of the latest multi-tracking and programming technology. And there was much more than just music in there: as he declared on the sleeve notes, it was 'produced by mothers, fathers, friends, cousins, lemmings, lovers, lemons, bees, trees, mint, mountains, rain, sun, love, pain, birth, life, death, god, buddha, spirits, weed, energy, hope'.

Described by one exuberantly enthusiastic *Herald* reviewer as a 'pumptastic Caledonian-folk-roots-ambient-hoose cross-fertilisation', this debut album was generally well received, although not by everyone. Reacting to one rather dismissive assessment, Martyn was moved to do that thing artists have probably all done from time to time – review the reviewer!:

> The guy goes on about 'karaoke highland piping' and 'house and techno rhythms' – which he obviously doesn't have a clue about, and then he's talking about the tunes and he says, 'Unfortunately they're nearly all Irish. Why unfortunately? It's like it can't be good, it can't be

quite right, because he is playing the bagpipes and he is playing Irish tunes – it makes me want to scream. He says nothing about the fact I made all the backing tapes myself, all the 'karaoke' stuff – and that's new, original Scottish music, if you like. It is ignorance – a DJ would never say anything as stupid as that.[1]

He had a valid point. Whatever else the album was, bagpipe karaoke it was not. Granted the arrangements did not reach the layered levels of sophistication of his later work, but overall, it represented a bold statement of intent, and an emphatic announcement of his arrival on the cultural scene of Scotland. It is also the finest recorded showcase we have of his instrumental virtuosity, and the only extended studio recording in which we really get to appreciate the scale of his abilities on his four main instruments – Highland pipes, smallpipes, whistle and violin. It is, first and foremost, a 'tunes' album, melody reigning over rhythm for really the only time in his main recorded output. As Martyn himself recognised, the tunes are mainly the kind of fare he was playing in pub sessions in the likes of the Tron Bar or Sandy Bell's in Edinburgh, and as such most of it was fairly familiar territory for followers of the folk scene at the time. And the accusation that the material was 'nearly all Irish' may well have been influenced by the session trends of that mid-1990s period: for a while in the 1980s, folk sessions at the likes of the Green Tree in Edinburgh's Cowgate and the nearby Tron Bar were dominated by Irish influences, with a gradual 'reclaiming' of the Scottish tradition emerging in the early '90s. Perhaps for that reviewer this was a renegade step therefore, although the idea that Martyn Bennett was ever *behind* the times is not one we hear too often!

The album is a solid reflection of the music Martyn had been performing live since his busking days in Glasgow, and so it came together very quickly in the studio, taking no more than

Above: Probably the most iconic image of Martyn's early career. Somewhere along the line the photograph was accidentally reversed – his face looks odd and his pipes are clearly on the wrong shoulder. In early conversations with BJ Stewart, Martyn had forgotten the identity of the photographer – 'A nice Scandinavian bloke' was as close as he got. It remained a mystery until, about two years ago, his ex-manager, Kenny MacDonald, handed The Martyn Bennett Trust a box of 'paper work' which had been gathering dust for decades. Inside was a print of this image, with 'James Holm' stamped on the back. A Google search and we had contact. James couldn't have been nicer and within days The Trust had access to dozens of marvellous photos of Martyn that had never seen the light of day. All scanned the right way round too! Martin Honeysett's cartoon is clearly taken from this reversed image.

a week to complete. That is a very short time for an album of this level of sophistication, although it was certainly in keeping with the norm for traditional artists, budgets rarely stretching much beyond that, then or now. In this case, the task was made easier by the fact that he had already spent a good deal of time composing and creating his tracks that he had been using in live performance, and these had been carefully crafted and meticulously arranged over many months. The main task that remained on arriving at Castlesound Studios was therefore to capture high-quality performances on his live instruments, and to then stitch it all together into a seamless whole. The collaborator who helped to achieve this was Stuart Hamilton, at the time a young and emerging sound engineer who was to go on to earn a widespread reputation for possessing one of the best pairs of ears in the country, and with the technical knowledge and creative flair to match.

This record stops just short of being revolutionary. Rather, it can be seen as one step in the *evolution* of the traditional instrumental music that had been emerging from Scotland and Ireland over the previous three decades or so. It isn't hard to spot the influences: the Bothy Band (who he especially admired), Planxty and Moving Hearts from Ireland are all in there, while the use of Highland pipes thoughtfully integrated with the voices of other instruments was already commonplace in Scotland in the music of the likes of Alba, Ossian, the Battlefield Band, the Tannahill Weavers, Wolfstone and Ceolbeg. Martyn's style of piping on the album was in similar vein to a group of players who were a few years his senior, particularly Fred Morrison, Gordon Duncan and the brothers, Angus, Allan and Iain MacDonald, from Glenuig in Moidart. All superb technically, and steeped in the Highland piping tradition, between them they had at times cast their gaze westwards, selecting and arranging traditional Irish tunes for Highland pipes, a tricky operation given the limited single-octave range of the instrument. Each of them had also shown the way in developing a flute and whistle style that drew heavily on that of Ireland, but that had unmistakable Highland piping flavours. That clearly influenced Martyn, although his close personal connection to Irish musician, Boys of the Lough flute player, Cathal McConnell, certainly opened his ears to the unadulterated flute style of Fermanagh. If there was more than a dash of Ireland in Martyn's whistle playing, there was no mistaking it when he picked up his bow either; his hard-won conversion from classical violinist to folky fiddler that had taken up so much of his time following graduation was achieved through an obsessively deep engagement with the playing of a small group of Irishmen, Martin Hayes chief amongst them. Martyn was greatly inspired by Hayes' ability to combine technical virtuosity with a drive and flair that flowed from deep inside the traditions of County Clare, and he studied his style in exhaustive detail. It is unsurprising, then, that the flavours of Ireland were very much to the fore on this debut album.

Also in its early stages of development in Scotland by the time the album was released was what the musician and scholar, Lori Watson, has described as the 'beyond tune' approach to musical arrangement whereby conventional melodic structures of two or four parts, each comprising eight or 16 bars, were replaced with short repeated phrases or motifs, and where 'the backing' was elevated to a sophisticated dominant presence in its own right, and brought forward to centre stage in both the arrangement and the mix.[2] Shooglenifty and the Peatbog Faeries, formed in 1990 and 1991 respectively, were among the bands leading the way in that direction, and in doing so, they were also shouting loudly and boldly: this music is DANCE music! And as is underlined by the fact that the tempos are noted on the sleeve notes for each track, so was the music on *Martyn Bennett*. The 'beyond tune' approach does not feature

heavily, but it is there, certainly, as he put down a marker for what was yet to come.

While the trace elements of all of these influences can be detected on this album, it was his step into the *Mouth Music* territory of a programmed electronic underpinning that brought a fresh feel to the soundscape he created here. The actual units of sound were not unfamiliar – luxuriant keyboard chords, deep and pulsing bass and percussion loops evoking the voices of congas, bongos, shakers, claves and snares – but when performed by computer rather than by human hands, the effect is markedly altered. Musicians, however consistent they may be, naturally pull the tempos and rhythms around whether playing live in front of an audience or when recording in a studio. Even when playing along to a click track or metronome to aid in the process of multi-tracking (the layering of instruments or voices on top of each other), these pulses just become reference points, and there remains plenty room for subtle rhythmic deviation. As listeners, when suddenly we are faced with its absence and it is replaced by unwavering precision, we know we have arrived somewhere else.

One minute and twenty seconds into the opening track we suspect we may have reached that place. Until then we have been led by the hand into a sonic space that is common enough: this could be Capercaillie, or Clannad, perhaps – a lush, 'Celtic' strings pad on keyboard opening into the voices of two low whistles in harmony, shimmering with reverb. There is a melody there, underpinned with a drone, but the notes glide along gently, and only later does it register that this is the track's theme tune played at half speed. Sparse and light percussion – a clave and a shaker – are joined by a tuneful riff on conga. Or tabla perhaps? The overall sound is sumptuous, what engineers might call 'expensive'. A rich, deep percussive bass announces itself, setting up a more regular rhythm as we begin to sense that we are heading somewhere else. The drone has morphed into something more complex, higher in pitch, raspy and grating, and for a second or two we're in *Doctor Who* theme tune territory! And then here it is, the other place, as the rhythm breaks into full tempo, and we are cast into that electronic dance world, our feet tapping at 120 beats per minute as the whistle leaves behind its meanderings and plunges full speed into 'The Swallowtail Coat'. Martyn Bennett has announced his arrival and he's inviting us to dance!

After partying in Ireland, Martyn next takes us to the Isle of Skye to scale some musical heights on 'Cuillin'. Presented in two parts, it is our first chance to hear his own composing style as he offers up a handful of reels, those on Part 1 played on smallpipes before moving to the more strident sound of the Highland pipes for Part 2. They are cracking tunes, but again it's everything else that is happening all around them that catches the ear. For Martyn, the Cuillin is 'a contrasting, gentle, magnificent and terrifying' mountain range, and he pretty well manages to fold all these qualities into the many layers of keyboard chords, violin, programmed percussion, chants and other assorted sonic ingredients that probably shouldn't work together but do. That is true also of another two-parted piece later in the album, '3 Sheeps 2 the Wind', a track that includes another self-penned tune wonderfully entitled 'Sheep Running About'!

Reflecting on the album towards the end of his life, Martyn could see its immaturities, but remained justifiably proud of his first born 'child':

> Written in Edinburgh in 1995, this self-titled album
> is my first venture into the world of electronica and
> crossover. Prior to this, I had been involved with Martin
> Swan and had recorded a couple of tracks on his
> album *Mouth Music*. As well as listening to DJs in the
> Edinburgh club scene, working with Swan was probably
> the biggest initial influence for me. It gave me the insight
> I needed to explore technology and traditional music
> within the same grounds, but more importantly it was
> like a voice of consent – it gave me the courage to step
> forward with my own ideas in the knowledge that there
> was, at least, one person who understood my wish to
> graft two contrasting forms of music. Recorded and
> mixed in just seven days, I listen to this album now
> with a hidden smile. Yes, I can hear the limitations of
> my knowledge of electronics and the small amount of
> equipment I had at my disposal, but this album, for me,

is like a child. It's full of fun and abandon. It does not care about the 'correctness' of the sounds or complexity of arrangement, it only cares about energy and light. I often wish I could repeat that energy now, but it was the energy of the moment. An energy of being unknown, an energy of no expectations, and an energy of being in love.[3]

'Energy and light': yes, that seems to me a pretty good summation of *Martyn Bennett*. It is a party album, certainly, with fun and laughs aplenty, but with moments of quiet contemplation and intellectual reflection along the way. As far as the laughs go, the most blatant ones are literal, and they belong to that much maligned international superstar of his day, Sir Harry Lauder. Tracks 5 and 6 on the album are paired under the title, 'Deoch an Dorus' and feature Lauder's own voice delivering the jovial musings from his 1930s hit of that name. 'Ha ha ha, that's alright boys', he chuckles. 'But I must tell you this first of all, that where there are one or two or three or four Scots gathered together, the general rule sometimes, just before we part, you know, is that we have a wee *deoch an dorus*'. Every 'r' in the sentence is rolled far beyond reason, as he invites us to have a 'drink of the door' or 'one for the road'. Martyn didn't 'particularly like what Lauder did' but 'he was as big as Michael Jackson in his day – and he was Scottish. ... Up yours, Sir Harry!'[4]

Martyn was by no means the first noted Scottish artist to flick a finger at Lauder's clownish self-parodies of the drunken, jocular Jock. His fellow Broughtonian, Hugh MacDiarmid, had done likewise two or three generations earlier, and if Martyn's teasing was gentle enough, MacDiarmid held nothing back. Lauder, to him, was the epitome of the crass stupidity of building a culture on caricature and ridicule, and whose version of Scottishness had to be resisted – indeed swept away – at all costs. 'The reason why the Harry Lauder type of thing is so popular in England', he complained, 'is because it corresponds to the average Englishman's ignorant notion of what the Scot is.' That was not to say that it was *all* the fault of our neighbours to the south – far too many Scots embraced it too: 'The fact that this over-paid clown gets £1,500 a week is a shameful commentary on the low state of public taste'.[5]

The intensity of MacDiarmid's dismissal of Lauder's approach to entertainment was by no means unusual, for he rarely let anyone off lightly when their art displeased him. And an awful lot did. He has not had it all his own way, however, for some commentators have been much kinder to Sir Harry, recognising that the mass popular reach he had, that brought the urban workers of Scotland out to the theatres in their thousands, was proof of a hunger for amusement and light-hearted entertainment as an escape from the poverty and drudgery of the time. Lauder had given of his time freely in entertaining the troops at the front in the Great War, for instance, a war that had taken the life of his only son, and so he had his own forms of escape to seek too. And what is wrong with a touch of self-parody: isn't it a healthy thing for a nation to be able to laugh at itself? Literary scholar, David Goldie, for one, is very keen that we give Lauder his place, and that MacDiarmid's charges need to be answered critically:

> Harry Lauder is far from being a figure on whom one would want to found a national culture. But his work, like that of Billy Connolly or the *Chewin' the Fat* comedians after him, needs to be recognised not only for its technical excellence, but also for the way it speaks directly and in differing ways to a wider national culture than that normally reached by serious literature. As such, it is a complement rather than a threat to literature. If such a view is allowed, the picture of the national culture that emerges is both more generous

and humane than MacDiarmid admitted, and also more open to cross-fertilisation and revitalising change. To see *both* MacDiarmid and Lauder as important national figures is to imagine a culture open to possibility and not one bound by either a narrowing intellectualism or an inhibiting deference to tradition or precedent.[6]

So what was Martyn Bennett's motivation for introducing his listeners to this 'over-paid clown' and knight of the realm (and indeed later re-visiting him on his third album, *Hardland*)? Was he simply adding his name to the lengthy list of those artists and commentators of the MacDiarmid variety who had installed Lauder as their chief whipping boy? Was Martyn setting up a contrast of extremes, saying 'listen, *that* is what Scottish music once was, but *this* is what it can become'? Or was there in fact just a hint of admiration there, a recognition that there was a dash of clownishness in his own public persona, as he himself took to the stage as caricature, dreadlocked and bare-chested? Whatever else Lauder was, he was master of his art, and never failed to own the stage completely, and those were qualities Martyn generally admired. Perhaps Martyn Bennett, also a consummate showman, felt just a touch of empathy there?

Keep the album running onto the next track, and we are met with the work of another huge cultural figure of the 20th century, Hamish Henderson. Poet, folklorist, collector, song-smith and political campaigner, Henderson grew up in the years when Lauder's fame was at its height, and like MacDiarmid, saw the entertainer as an anti-hero and representative of all that was wrong with his nation's view of itself. On returning to Scotland after serving as a captain in the Intelligence Corps during the Second World War, Henderson set out to develop a cultural agenda for the second half of the century that was socialist, internationalist, positive, forward-looking and peaceful. Heavily influenced by the thinking of the Marxist

BRAVE NEW MUSIC: THE MARTYN BENNETT STORY

Sardinian intellectual, Antonio Gramsci, who had developed his philosophy while incarcerated as an enemy of the Mussolini regime, Henderson's vision was to follow a path in Scotland that put 'Gramsci in action'. The serious study of folk culture was to be at the heart of the movement, Henderson sharing Gramsci's view that folk song could be a force for good in the world, and one that could serve to unite rather than divide. Henderson had seen that for himself at first hand, as his interrogations of both German and Italian prisoners of war, in their own languages, had shown. The questioning invariably drifted towards chats about what songs they knew, as he honed the techniques of enquiry that would later make him one of the most prolific collectors of folksong Scotland has ever seen, and chief instigator of the Scottish folk revival.

Henderson was to become a looming presence in Martyn's life, both personally and culturally. Reflecting on this, following the release of his final album, *Grit*, Martyn saw some parallels between himself and Hamish:

> It would be hard to describe Hamish Henderson in a nutshell I have to say because he was a kind of unique fella. He was kind of similar to me in some ways, although he was brought up in Perthshire, and he knew the traditions even better than I do. He still came from an outsider looking in sort of thing and he had a unique perspective on what was really special about the whole Scottish scene. Hamish was a folklorist principally and a collector. He travelled around Scotland collecting music and songs from people he met at a time when no one else was doing that in the early '50s and he is responsible for kind of starting off an archive of this wonderful music and song before it really became in danger of dying out. If it really hadn't been for Hamish I think possibly much of what Scotland is today would be lost... I think in

some ways Hamish and I have a similar thing which was basically trying to keep traditions moving and keeping them fresh and not as a museum piece. I don't think it's a good thing to have a museum full of relics if you don't know what they mean culturally and that's the problem with a lot of archives is that they can end up as big pickling jars unless they are used every day, and that doesn't just mean taking them out of a tape box and playing them. I'm talking about actually going out and singing them and Hamish was certainly someone who did that. He was an academic but he also was someone who was very humble in many ways.

Martyn had met Hamish in the late 1970s at a festival he was attending with his mother, but began to spend more time with him after moving to school in Edinburgh, during his frequent visits to the School of Scottish Studies in George Square where both Margaret and Hamish taught. As Margaret recalled, poetry readings were a regular part of the cultural scene in Edinburgh through the 1980s, and so Martyn was being exposed to live renditions of their work by a host of the big literary names of the time: William Montgomerie, Norman McCaig, Sorley MacLean, Iain Crichton Smith, Edwin Morgan, Duncan Glen and Liz Lochhead among them.[7] Yet it was one of Hamish Henderson's own poems that piqued Martyn's interest in the spoken word. Margaret remembered that her son first heard Hamish recite 'Floret Silva Undique' at a poetry reading when he was around 14, and later discovered it in printed form:

> I have a vivid recollection of the sound of youthful, wild enthusiasm, bursting through the kitchen door: 'I've found it! Listen! Listen to this! This is fantastic!'... Book in hand he began, 'Floret silva undique...' and reading on in measured pace, with intonation echoing Hamish's voice.[8]

The poem is a sensuous salute to Edinburgh in springtime, set in the open greenery of the Meadows, the expanse of parkland between Henderson's home in Marchmont and his university office in George Square. Loosely translated by Martyn as 'all around the flora is in bloom', the title is borrowed from a line in the medieval collection of poems and vagabond songs known as *Carmina Burana*, a motley compendium of the kind of bawdy and irreverent verses that appealed to Hamish Henderson's anti-establishment tastes. Yet there is little that is overtly satirical here in the poem it inspired, as Auld Reekie goes about its business one Sunday in May. There is an earthy undercurrent, certainly, for the month is 'lusty' and as 'The sun goes doon under yon hill, Jenny and Jake are at it still'. However, read by Martyn as being 'basically about springtime in Edinburgh, with everything coming alive in the Meadows', it is innocent enough, and provides a textual seed from which new music might grow. Not content to simply draw on a selection of verses lifted directly from the poem, Martyn and Hamish discussed the choice of lines for inclusion on the track at some length, agreeing on three verses, each composites of lines drawn from different stages of the original.

Track 7 on the album begins with the voice of the poet himself:

> Floret Silva Undique
> The lily, the rose, the rose I lay.
> Floret silva undique
> Sweet on the air till dark of day.
> The bonniest pair ye iver seen
> Play chasie on the Meedies green.
> Floret silva undique
> The Lily, the rose, the rose I lay.

Immediately we return to that ethereal space we entered at the start of the opening track on the album, an improvised low whistle melding with light keyboard strings, punctuated with assorted tinkles, chimes, bells and cymbals, before the percussion slips into a regular rhythm and off we go. We are aware of another human voice now, or voices, chanting in Islamic flavours, reminiscent of the call to prayer. But as Martyn later explains, it is a nod to Henderson's time spent with the 51st Highland Division in the North African campaign during the war. Martyn's own voice joins in, repeating the opening verse in hushed tones, before picking up his fiddle and transporting us to Ireland. It is a self-composed reel, but unmistakably and liltingly Irish, and if anyone had ever doubted that a classically trained violinist can convincingly recast himself as a loose-armed fiddler, then here is the proof that they were wrong. The phrasing is supple and flowing, seemingly aloof from the automated regularity of the breakbeat underscoring, yet invisibly anchored to it. And then

Martyn's voice returns, a new verse telling of the goings-on of the Edinburgh folk out for their 'sabbath stroll', but delivered at a full shout. His screaming is a foretelling of another mood change, as a full corps of pipe band snare drummers, albeit in programmed sample form, strike up a drum fanfare, while the Arabesque chanting re-emerges underneath. Magnificent incongruence? Or the 51st Highland Division marching into Cairo, perhaps? That idea is given weight when we hear the pipes set off with another of Martyn's own compositions that he describes as a march. But it is played on smallpipes, gentle in tone and subtle in feel, and much more evocative of a sprightly hornpipe than a military advance. Nothing is ever quite what it seems. A final verse of the poem brings us back to the Meadows, as the smallpipes round off our odyssey in jaunty mood and Hamish, most likely, shuffles off for a dram in Sandy Bell's bar.

As a track, it is a fine piece of musical storytelling, but in embarking on this collaboration with such a towering cultural presence as Hamish Henderson, we must surely read rather more into it than simply that. Placed immediately after the Lauder tracks (and mastered with virtually no time gap between them), in combining 'Deoch and Dorus' and 'Floret Silva Undique' we are presented with a dozen minutes of music that serve to embed Martyn generally, and this album specifically, into a creative continuum that spans almost the whole 20th century. Martyn was well aware of the trajectory Scottish music had been taking down through the decades, for bad and for good, and with the release of this album, he was helping to shape the direction it was to take next. And on the following track, 'Jacobite Beebop', it was certainly heading somewhere new!

This is the track that folkies found most challenging, and if most of the rest of the album was a re-worked version of the kind of material he was playing in sessions, this probably would have had them running for the door in Sandy Bell's! As Martyn himself recognised, the track was 'somewhat aggressive' and acid folk   Highland heart-throb

Gaelic house music. techno dance folk   Peat Smoking electronicelt

the celtic equivalent of Beck

Tradition for trainspotter

Jacobite hip-hop   organic hard-hoose-roots-fun dub-hop grooviness

a techno-Hebridean Jean-Luc Pont

hip-hop bagpiper Martyn is the ne

wave of rave folkies   tartan techn

dread-locked, Scottish,   play that funky bagpipe, white b

hip-hop bagpipe-playing

sex symbol cut-up tartan dub beat

The Pied Piper of Dred

Deep Forest-meets-Braveheart techn

a Celtic-pipin'-danceclub-boy ethn

Martyn Bennett is Scotland

Highland heart-throb   The cutes

sound in dreadlock

boldly goes where no folkie has gone befo

imi Hendrix of bagpipes

Celtic techno

Playboy of the Western Isles

elic-ethnic-electronica?

Acid croft meets Highland house.

Celtic karaoke

the devil's own music; Oatcake Exotica for the nineties

The future of Celtdom

skirl'n'bass

hiphop piper

hard-house ceilidh beats

remendous in a kilt and knows what o do with his pipes.

Martyn Bennett, the world's only dreadlocked piper

techno-teuchter

fiddling

Cuillin e gang

piper sex-god Bennett.

Martyn

electro-trad

hoose music

THE RAVE PIPER

nswer to Nigel Kennedy

In your face/croft kitchen ceilidh/grooves on Afro-Islamic/dread ge dub jungle jazz trip hop

Bennett's whirling blond dread locks and cherubic fizzog

e's more hip-hop than heedrum-hodrum

a foretaste of the style he would later adopt on *Hardland*. He does sound like an angry young man here – angry perhaps, at the political and cultural fall-out that the Jacobite defeat brought about, and the heavy price the Highlands paid as a result. As he lamented in his retrospective notes to this track:

> The following genocide and breakdown of the clan system marked the end of a long history of Kingship and the beginning of an era of oppression for the Scots. The next hundred years saw the mass emigration of the Gaels as the Highlands became emptied of people and replaced instead with sheep. A very sad end to a noble cause, and one from which Scotland has never recovered fully.

Unsurprising, then, that there is not much sign of a cheery bebop jazz standard going on in this music which begins with a hint of dark mystery, with an eery ambience that might be a storm crashing on the window with an ominous warning of thunder drawing near, or else a horror movie underscore that foretells of the terror yet to come. 'The Marquis of Huntly's Strathspey' is in there somewhere, but what emerges is a dance track that's about as far removed from our concept of a strathspey as it's possible to be, and one that might be most at home as the soundtrack to Tam O'Shanter's stupor in Kirk Alloway as his unbelieving eyes witnessed the dance of the devil. It is uncomfortable musical territory. And while we're talking of being uncomfortable, the final track on *Martyn Bennett* doesn't exactly round things off with a brief and safe musical statement to bring things to a pleasing closure. 'Stream' contains some gorgeous string sounds, yes, but it mainly features 21 minutes of Martyn pissing in a pond! No radio broadcasts for that one, then!

The album was released on the Eclectic Records label based in Edinburgh run by Gordon Stevenson, a master violin-maker and member of a well-known family of musicians and actors led by his father, the late Ronald Stevenson, a highly regarded composer and pianist. Gordon's daughter, Anna-Wendy Stevenson, was a close friend of Martyn, playing together in youth orchestras in their teens and remaining close friends until Martyn died. Eclectic was a small label but a good fit for this project, having previously released two albums by the innovative jazz/folk collective, the Cauld Blast Orchestra, and two by Gordon's sister, Savourna Stevenson, a harp player and composer who draws on an eclectic blend of folk, jazz, classical and world music in her compositions. Another band that was represented on the label was The Easy Club, a folk group that brought strong elements of jazz and swing to their arrangements, while Dundonian singer-songwriter, Michael Marra, who would later make a cameo appearance on Martyn's final CD, *Grit*, released four albums on the label in the early 1990s. The common thread was clear to see, for each of these artists explored the blurred edges of different genres, but all had 'trad' music somewhere in their core. It was a natural home for *Martyn Bennett*.

The 'bagpipe karaoke' dismissal apart, the album's reception was highly positive across the board. For *The Scotsman*, it was 'a bold and brilliant statement of intent', while *The Guardian*'s reviewer admired its 'exhilarating confidence'. 'A breath of fresh air in the folk scene' was the *Folk Roots* conclusion, and *The List* commended Martyn's technical prowess and creativity, noting that he 'demonstrates a musical intelligence and an imaginative flair that's rare in contemporary music'. *Songlines* went higher still in its praise, proclaiming the release a game-changer, that 'reinvented traditional music for a new generation'. Even the self-critical demanding perfectionist within Martyn had to admit it was an excellent start to his recording career. *Martyn Bennett* placed Martyn Bennett firmly in the spotlight. Critics and public alike were taking notice, and were eager to know where he was heading next. The pressure was on, and Martyn was loving it.

5

Bellows Boy

MUSIC IS ABOUT many things, and prime among them are *connections*. These connections run in several directions, linking notes to rhythms, sounds to ears, composers to performers, players to audience, ideas to emotions. The connections of past to present are also key, especially when an artist perceives himself to be part of an ongoing tradition. Of course, all artists do belong to a tradition, for they are nearly always sensitive to what has gone before in their particular genre, what their own place is within that journey, and where they wish to take it next. Martyn Bennett, for one, was acutely aware of each of these things, but for him, tradition was central. Sometimes its power disturbed him, sometimes he wanted to break free. But he always remained fascinated by the threads that connect *people* and *time*. Let's take a moment to explore one such thread – a very long thread actually – that connects Martyn with another piper. It stretches for some 270 miles and about the same number of years. It starts in Northumberland, winds its way via Peebles, Edinburgh and Dunkeld to arrive on the Isle of Mull. The tale takes us back to the early 18th century.

Martyn and William

Let us imagine William Dixon is sitting at his table, his quill pen poised over a small notebook he had gone into town to buy that morning, the oil lamp giving off just enough yellow light for his task ahead. He has been planning this for some time – weeks, or actually months now – and he is itching to begin. The tunes are all bouncing around in his head, and it's high time he let them out. They are not *his* tunes exactly, although he feels he has made them his own. He'd known most of them for years, heard them played so many times in the taverns of Fenwick and Morpeth, the annual fairs of the parish of Stamfordham, and at a good dozen or so weddings, and his fingers could drum them out at will. He was amused to find that they were doing just that right now, there on the pitted oak of the tabletop. There was something about a piper's fingers that seemed to inhabit a world of their own.

The thing he loved most about the tunes was that they were constantly changing. They were old, *very* old as far as he knew, but they never stayed still for long. He himself had added a few twists and turns of his own, and plenty others had done likewise too. They were tunes that refused outright to be boxed into a predictable sameness, and stubbornly avoided succumbing to mere replication. No, they had discovered the joy of *variation*, always seeking their own diversions through the melodic line, and the best pipers knew better than to ever try to play them exactly the same way twice. In truth, that was why he had been putting this task off. If he was going to write them down, commit them to the page, would he be caging them in? Was he tethering them down, falsifying them, condemning them to a soulless life within the prison of the stave? The thought had caused him quite a few broken sleeps and it was a nagging fear that would never quite leave him be. He had worked long and hard to unravel the mysteries of lines and black dots carved into paper – nobody else he knew had ever even tried – and he had to admit the scribblings he had been practising had their own form of beauty. But it was a false beauty, a poor reflection of the real thing. These tunes had to feast the ears, not the eyes!

Yet what might become of them if he did nothing? The young ones now were not interested in them. Even his own boys, Parcival and John, teased him for his old ways, for living in the past. 'This is the 18th century, for goodness sake. Move with the times, father!' So yes, imprisoned is better than dead, and if that is the case for people, it's just as true for music. And so off he went. 'William Dixon His Book. May ye 10th, 1733.'

Well, I like to think that is how it may have happened! What we do know is that sometime after 1738 William had finished his book, and 40 tunes in all had made their way from his head to the paper. More than two and a half centuries later, Martyn Bennett took some of William's tunes and made them *his* own. What happened to them for most of the long years in between we have no idea. As far as we can tell, William Dixon was the first person ever to commit a substantial collection of bagpipe music to paper anywhere on these islands, his manuscript pre-dating the earliest surviving Highland bagpipe equivalent by a generation. He must surely have been proud of his work, and certainly deserved to be, but what he did with it next we can only guess. It re-appeared in Inver, near Dunkeld, Perthshire, in 1909 when it was given by a local man, Charles MacIntosh, to Lady Dorothea Stewart-Murray, daughter of the Duke of Atholl. The story goes that he was so offended when she offered to pay him for it, he threw it in the fire! She duly rescued it before any harm was done. On her death, it was bequeathed as part of her extensive collection of music to the library in Perth where it lay largely unnoticed until being re-discovered, rescued and published by piper and researcher, Matt Seattle, in 1995.[1] How it had come into the possession of Charles MacIntosh, later described as a 'post runner, naturalist and musician', we do not know.

Martyn was invited by the Lowland and Borders Pipers' Society to perform a selection of William's tunes at a celebratory gathering in Peebles in 1997 and later recorded a few on

Hardland, while adding extended versions to his live set when performing with Cuillin. I have a live recording of them playing right now, here at my desk, and I have the published version of William's book in front of me. And so before my very eyes and ears, there is a fascinating musical conversation going on between these two pipers, separated in time by almost three centuries, both departed from this world, yet alive, immediate and visceral and truly connected in art.

In spite of this unequivocal musical connection, and perhaps making it all the more remarkable, is that the intervening 270 years saw the decline, virtual extinction, then eventual revival of the instruments that William's tunes would most likely have been played on. The bagpipe is an international family, the members of which come in all manner of shapes, sizes and sounds, and even here in Scotland there has been considerable variation down through the centuries. The Great Highland Bagpipe, Martyn's first main instrument, is of course the best known, having achieved iconic status as our 'national' instrument, but William's music did not belong on these 'big pipes'. Almost certainly, his was the music of some form of smaller, less strident bagpipe, and by his time in the 18th century, almost certainly powered by bellows rather than human lungs. As musician, researcher and 'discoverer' of the Dixon manuscript Matt Seattle has proposed, there are two likely candidates, which in today's terminology would be called 'Border pipes' and 'smallpipes' (although he argues strongly that this was probably the music of the former). To the untrained eye these two instruments look rather similar, both driven by bellows, with three drones attaching to the bag via a common stock, plus a chanter. 'You play the melody on the chanter!' (to borrow a phrase that Martyn was later to sample in a refrain on his final album, *Grit*). However, the two instruments sound quite different, as the smallpipe chanter (favoured by Martyn) has a straight bore, while that of the border pipe, like its

Highland cousin, is tapered into a conical bore, producing a louder and 'wilder' sound, pitched one octave higher than its smaller sibling. (By way of comparison, it may help to consider the difference in sound between the clarinet, which has a straight bore, and the saxophone, which is conical.) Both bagpipe forms have long and fascinating histories, the more involved details of which need not detain us here, but if we are to understand Martyn's place within that story, we must at least lay out the key facts as far as we understand them.[2]

In general terms, the Border bagpipe (also termed the 'Lowland' pipe, the 'Reelpipe' and the 'Cauld Wind' pipe) was played across much of Scotland, and while most often associated with the southern half of the country and the North East, it was by no means unknown in the Highlands, especially for playing dance music. Known in Gaelic as the *piob shionnaich*, these smaller and quieter instruments were certainly not dismissed by the top Highland players of the day through the 19th century, with the likes of Sandy Bruce in Skye and Glenelg and Calum *Piobair* MacPherson in Badenoch often giving their lungs a rest by pulling out the bellows pipes of an evening. That said, Calum *Piobair*'s lungs probably didn't get much of a rest: one of the attractions of bellows power for him was that it left his mouth free to smoke a pipe!

In the Lowlands, Borders and the North East, the conical Border pipe was the instrument of choice of the town pipers employed by many burghs to parade through the streets morning and evening, and to play at various civic events. For this they tended to be given a home, a uniform and a small retaining wage, making up the rest of their income by playing at weddings, dances and fairs, and perhaps entertaining the better off members of local society in their own homes. Their wanderings often took them well beyond their home towns, and they were seen by some as the last of the old minstrels, gathering and dispensing news and gossip as they plied their musical trade through the countryside. In many cases, the town piper became a hereditary role, as with many other trades, and so certain families became associated with certain towns, such as the Hasties of Jedburgh, the Andersons of Kelso and the Allans of Kirk Yetholm. The ostentatious nature of some of their uniforms made for striking figures: Geordie Syme of Dalkeith, for instance, wore 'a yellow coat, white plush breeches, white stockings and buckled shoes'. When Martyn Bennett took to the stage with a similar instrument to perform some of William Dixon's tunes two centuries later, bare-chested and dreadlocked, the detail may have been different, but in essence this latter-day minstrel was adhering to a longstanding tradition of pure visual spectacle!

For various reasons, although not all of them entirely clear, the bellows pipe tradition began to go into a steep decline through the second half of the 19th century. The increasing popularity of the Highland pipe, especially after its formal adoption by the British military in 1854, was certainly one contributing factor while the patronage of the towns and burghs began to dry up as demands for modern urban infrastructure such as clean, running water and improved sanitation began to shift financial priorities. When times are hard, the arts suffer – it was always thus! And perhaps the town pipers, with their ostentatious yet outdated garb, simply began to be seen as an archaic survival of times gone by. Whatever the reason, by the dawn of the 20th century very few bellows pipers remained.

For a good part of the 20th century, the bellows pipes were largely forgotten, with only a handful of people playing them in the 1960s and '70s. Then on the final day of the Edinburgh Folk Festival in 1981, a small group of players held a meeting with a view to promoting the bellows bagpipes in a more focused and concentrated way. A note of the meeting was published just a few weeks later in the magazine, *The International Piper*, along with an invitation for anyone who was interested to get in touch with the organisers, namely academic and specialist museum curator, Hugh Cheape, Gordon Mooney and Mike Rowan. Regular meetings followed on for the next couple of years, until in April 1983, the Lowland and Borders Pipers' Society was formally constituted. To encourage the revival, it organised annual competitions and conferences (or collogues) and instigated a journal called *The Common Stock*, giving a platform for researchers to publish their findings into the history and decline of the instrument and its associated traditions.

Another of the key figures in the bellows pipe revival has been Hamish Moore. Hamish, a Highland piper from a young age, was pursuing a career as a vet before discovering the bellows pipes in the early 1980s. Just around the time of those very early re-awakenings of the tradition, Hamish was living with his wife Maggie and their family on the same street as the Bennetts in Kingussie:

> Margaret and Joe were just two or three doors along the street – it was Middle Terrace in Kingussie – I suppose we got to know Margaret through the music, and she would have sessions in the house, and we would go along. And we got to know Martyn in his own right because he would come for Highland dancing lessons with Maggie on a weekly basis. This was the early '80s . Martyn would be ten or 11 – that sort of age. And we were good friends with Davy Taylor who was teaching history at Kingussie High School, and he also taught piping on a voluntary basis and I remember him saying to me that Martyn was incredible. Like a child prodigy. So he taught him right through I think until Martyn left Kingussie and came to Edinburgh.[3]

As Hamish recalled, there was a healthy music scene in Kingussie in these days of the early 1980s, with several amateur musicians meeting up regularly for an informal session together:

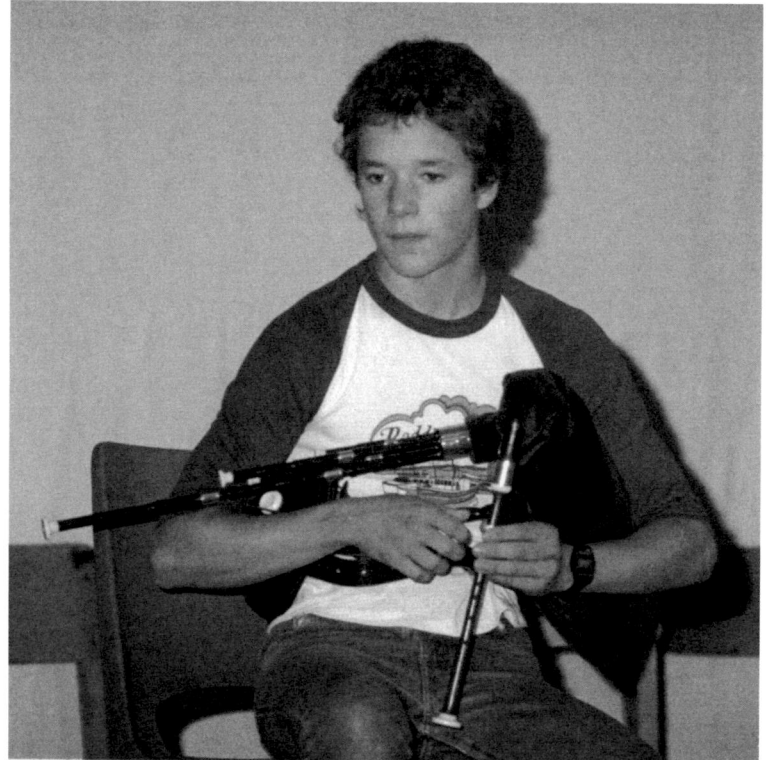

Young Martyn with the smallpipes.

The local doctor, Greg Sutherland played mandolin, and Keith Campbell sang, and Rory Morrison was a decent flute player, and then I got the smallpipes, and then Davy Taylor got the smallpipes. Cameron MacNeish was involved in it too. And Margaret was part of that, and of course Martyn as a child was part of that whole thing.

Reflecting back now, we might say that Middle Terrace, Kingussie, played a vital role in what was to become the bellows pipes revival and their eventual return back into the carrying stream of tradition. It was there that Hamish saw his first set of original smallpipes that belonged to John MacRae, a cousin of Margaret Bennett, and who was the Moores' immediate next-door neighbour. A piper himself, John ran the family milk business in the town, as his father had done before him, and they delivered milk all over that part of Strathspey and down to Laggan. His father had also been a piper and had collected what turned out to be an early 19th century set of Scottish smallpipes. Hamish had just returned from a spell in Ireland where he had been greatly inspired by the Irish uilleann pipe scene, and was intrigued to see this set of straight-bored pipes, complete with bellows, that were lying in a wooden box, unplayed, right on his own doorstep. Martyn too, was very taken with them, and was later inspired to sketch them from memory in fine detail.[4]

Hamish was aware that a Northumbrian pipe maker, Colin Ross, had already been exploring the technical constructions of other sets of old Scottish smallpipes. He had refurbished at least one, experimenting with the design and manufacturing of a new chanter that would be compatible with modern approaches to fingering and hole-spacing, and which, crucially, given the importance of that potential market, felt comfortable for those brought up in the Highland pipe world. Colin Ross agreed to refurbish John's set for Hamish, supplying one of his new chanters and reeds. And so from 1982, Hamish was playing these smallpipes in the ceilidhs in Margaret's house, with Martyn's piping teacher, David Taylor, doing likewise a little later. Within four years, Hamish had taken the decision to give up his career as a vet, and commit himself to learning how to make bellows pipes. He did just that, and along with Colin Ross, Jimmy Anderson, Ray Sloane, Julian Goodacre and a handful of other makers, began to manufacture his own high-quality instruments, helping to provide the material means for the revival to take hold and then flourish.

BBC radio producer, Iain MacInnes, one of the first Highland pipers to adopt the bellows-driven Scottish smallpipe early in its revival in 1982, and to this day one of its finest exponents, recalled his own discovery:

> I was attracted to the mellowness of the instrument, the ease of playing, and the wonderful drone-to-chanter harmonics when heard at close quarters. This was very different from the Highland bagpipe, and infinitely superior to the various mouth-blown parlour and chamber pipes which occasionally surfaced at ceilidhs, rarely to good effect. The instrument was well-balanced and sufficiently loud to play comfortably with harps and fiddles. Other musicians looked on with interest: here was a new repertoire to be explored, much of it relatively unknown. Inexorably and wonderfully, the bellows bagpipe was drawn back into the body of the musical kirk.[5]

By the time Martyn arrived in Edinburgh, then, the revival had taken root, and he was keen to procure a set for himself. The chance was to come fairly quickly, as Margaret later recalled in her book, *It's Not the Time You Have*,[6] an event I well remember myself. By the second half of the 1980s, Colin Ross was making smallpipes fairly regularly, and had left a set in the School of Scottish Studies to be passed onto Willie Haines, who ran the Blackfriars Music shop in the old town. One of the advantages of smallpipes is that they can be made in a variety of pitches – A, B flat, C and D are all possible. Colin had made a set that came with two interchangeable chanters, one pitched in C and the other in D, and there was enough play on the drones to be able to tune them to either key. This made them doubly useful, and helped make the playing of pipes in sessions and in other multi-instrumental contexts much more practicable and indeed sociable. Martyn was in the department on his way home from Broughton and was waiting for his mother to finish her lecture (which as a student there, I was attending). Martyn had volunteered to 'look after' the pipes and to deliver them to Blackfriars himself, but not before he had them out of the box and under his arms. He was hooked, as I could well see and hear myself when I came out of the lecture! Willie observed that too, and offered them to Martyn to be paid up gradually as he could afford it. It was indeed a generous offer, as Willie would have been well aware that the demand for these pipes would have been high, and that he almost certainly could have sold them very quickly, cash up front. Martyn jumped at the chance, and paid them up by busking on Princes Street every Saturday with his Highland pipes. Always one to have his eye on a marketing opportunity, he reckoned he would earn more if passers-by knew that he was saving up for a specific thing.

Given that he clearly already owned a set of pipes, he didn't feel that 'saving up for another set' would cut it, so decided to busk in jeans and t-shirt with a sign that said 'Saving up for a kilt'! His takings rocketed immediately!

I bought my own set of smallpipes, made by Hamish Moore, just around about this same time, but I had decided on a set pitched in A. Martyn and I had already had the odd jam in the department, mainly using whistles as I recall (I had bought my first Low D whistle from Blackfriars Music too, but don't recall ever being offered it on tick!) It was only when Martyn and I first tried to have a tune together on our new smallpipes that I realised they were in different keys, and so were totally incompatible. Or so I thought. Martyn had other ideas: he plugged in his

With Rory Pierce, friend and fellow Cuillin member.

D chanter, asked me to play some jigs, and began to join in with no problem at all! Sometimes he went for harmonies, sometimes counter-melodies, always immediately spotting the few short passages where there were enough shared notes for us to play the main melody in unison. I was flabbergasted. I couldn't begin to understand how anyone could do that, completely off the cuff, apparently without even thinking about it, and it was the first time I realised just how good a musician he really was. He was exceptional and the fact he was just in his mid-teens made it all the more astonishing, not to say infuriating! Leading Northumbrian piper, Kathryn Tickell, had the same experience. She met Martyn when he was 15, and he immediately began to play along with her in harmony – she booked him to play on her next album there and then.

And so began Martyn's love affair with bellows pipes, and

indeed his part in the long story I have been telling here of their survival, decline, and revival. He later added a set pitched in A to his arsenal, made by Hamish Moore in the beautifully-toned wood, *Lignum Vitae* – the tree of life – and tended to use these when playing solo, sticking to his Ross set for most performances in his later band, Cuillin. It was smallpipes that were featured famously in Martyn's contribution to the soundtrack of the Drambuie advert of the early 1990s, and he played them for a few sets in a BBC Radio Scotland broadcast in 1994. They also featured in several of the theatre plays he worked on through the '90s, but it was his appearance at a high-profile concert in the old Royal High School on Calton Hill in Edinburgh in 1995 that really cemented his reputation as one of the finest exponents of Scottish smallpipes to have emerged within the revival. 'The Grand Concert of Scottish Piping' as it was billed, was arranged by the Lowland and Border Pipers Society and curated by Hamish Moore. The line-up comprised some of the best established and emerging pipers of the time, including Angus MacColl, Allan MacDonald, Iain MacInnes, Gordon Duncan and Gordon Mooney as well as Martyn himself. The event was recorded, and was released as a CD on the Greentrax label early in 1996.[7] All the artists were in excellent form, but for Hamish it is Martyn's performance that stood out. In fact his praise could not have been higher: from that night right through to the present day, he has consistently referred to it as the best recording of Scottish smallpipes he has ever heard.

Not everyone agreed, however. It is a well-recognised fact that when cultural revivals of whatever form begin to take root and re-seed, some of the participants can begin to pull in different directions in terms of their aims and aspirations. By this time in the mid-1990s the bellows revival in Scotland was taking a 'classic' form, adhering very closely to what scholars were seeing as a typical blueprint.[8] There was a group of identifiable 'core revivalists' who provided the initial idea, energy and impetus to get the ball rolling, while they, and others, were working hard to find the historical sources that would help shed light on the tradition as it had been in the past. They were reaching out to a wider community of performers and audience, while instrument makers, teaching activities, concerts and recordings were providing the backbone of the commercial framework that is always needed for a revival to succeed. But there is another ingredient, labelled by one scholar as 'ideology and discourse', and it was in this that cracks were beginning to appear.[9] At the heart of the issue was the music itself: when the bellows tradition was at its height, what tunes did they play, and how did they play them? And perhaps more to the point, how should we approach them now? I often wonder what William Dixon would have made of the fact that it was the discovery of his little book that would allow those questions to be addressed seriously for the first time more than two and a half centuries after he had finished it. As Matt Seattle himself declared, this was not so much the missing link, as the missing chain!

When Martyn stood to play through his selection of William's tunes at the launch of the book in Peebles in 1997, he was getting embroiled in an ongoing debate on some fairly fundamental issues relating to music, identity and place. Some of those at the heart of the revival were very keen that it didn't become 'hijacked' by Highland pipers who might inevitably treat it as just a variation on their own tradition, using exactly the same finger technique, phrasing and musical aesthetic. It was already the case that most players who were taking to the bellows instruments *were* coming from a Highland piping background and the rigid training which that involved. Martyn, like many of us, was of course very much in that situation. There is no doubt that he was conscious that this music was different however, and that it was by no means familiar territory for him. Introducing his set that night in Peebles he explained his thoughts on this:

BELLOWS BOY

One thing I did pick up from being at music college was this thing called tri-tones. The period that these are written in, if you'd written anything with a tri-tone, then it was Devil's Music! Well this music is full of tri-tones and diminution. It's technically very very clever, and it is quite tricky to play, I have to admit, and it's not something that's very sort of comfortable under my fingers... I feel like an alien in someone else's music. When I first got the book... it said in the back that Charles MacIntosh said 'It's no use to anyone. I'll put it in the fire'. And after a bit of trying them out, I wished he'd left it there! But actually, having played them again and again... I've found myself going into the fire and pulling them out, and now I think they're absolutely amazing things, and I don't know what to make of them. Anyway, I think they're pretty cool![10]

Pretty cool or not, his treatment of them that night was not universally acclaimed. Matt Seattle was far from impressed. In the conference that followed on the day after Martyn's performance, Matt declared that he didn't know whether to laugh or cry. 'He played it exactly as I thought he was going to play it' he noted. What he meant was that he felt Martyn played it very much in a Highland pipe style, rather than with finger technique that Matt felt would have been better suited to this smaller, more gentle instrument. Reflecting back, Matt said he has mellowed in his views, and certainly found Martyn's later dance-centred treatment of the material more to his liking. Hamish Moore, however, was highly impressed with Martyn's interpretation of the material that night:

> Oh yes, now that was another amazing performance. He played the Dixon stuff. I'm not sure he'd played it before that. I remember he made a joke – he said that whoever

it was that had pulled it out of the fire, he wished they'd left it there! But he said after he began to play it he loved it. And he went on to use it in his hip hop stuff. I remember also that night there being lots of members of the LBPS who didn't like his performance because it was too Highland. But there was nothing Highland about it. The fact that Martyn could put in gracenotes and doublings, and keep it in rhythm as well, it's amazing. Because Martyn wasn't putting any set ornamentation into the way he played, he put the ornamentation in where it was appropriate, and to enhance the tune. I thought it was wonderful. I loved his performance in Peebles. I thought it was absolutely brilliant. He was playing it as dance music, which it possibly was.

What we have here are differing interpretations of the concept of authenticity, an issue that often lies at the root of much discussion within revival movements. When deliberate and proactive attempts are made to bring back a cultural form whose chain of tradition had been broken, decisions have to be made, individually or collectively, regarding the approach to the music. Should it be played the way we think it may have been played before its disappearance? How can we even know what that might have been? Or should we accept that the context into which it is returning is a very different one to that in which it had died out, and that it has to be made relevant to today's preferences and outlooks? All manner of issues can arise from these questions, and within the bellows bagpipe revival, they have.

A handful of the Dixon tunes became a staple in Martyn's live set, and in that of his later band, Cuillin. And Martyn knew precisely how he wanted them to sound. 'I love the Dixon tunes' said Kirsten:

BRAVE NEW MUSIC: THE MARTYN BENNETT STORY

When it came to playing them with Deirdre (MacLullich, the fiddler in Cuillin) he literally wrote out for her how he wanted her to play them and he was very particular about them not being jiggy or lilty or putting in her own emphasis. He wanted them to be driven. Not with any hint of expression or rhythm. I often thought Poor Deirdre! It was like having a lesson. It wasn't like turning up to play in a band. It was a fiddle lesson or a whistle lesson. He was very *very* particular about how he wanted to hear things. He used to say 'Stop sliding. I don't want to hear any of your sliding!'

And so back we go to that musical conversation between Martyn and William, as I listen to a live recording of Martyn's band, Cuillin, in full flow. The set begins with a monstrous roar followed by a deep electronic bass setting up the dance beat in 4/4 time at a relatively laid back 120 beats per minute. But it is a sophisticated rhythm, and one that assiduously avoids simply picking out the predictable beats of each bar. A snare finds the space in between. A distorted keyboard note – like static electricity – adds to the building soundscape. Then another voice joins in – invoking a xylophone or steel drum perhaps? The combination has power though. This band clearly means business. Then a brief moment of confusion. The dance beat continues in 4/4, but now the smallpipes are here, and off they go with a melody that cuts across the bed the others have made. Nine beats to the bar, not four. It's wrong, surely? No, it fits! It fits seamlessly. And William Dixon will be nodding now in recognition I fancy. It's one of his tunes! 'Saw You Never a Bonny Lass'? Well there are plenty of *them* dancing here! Yes it is his tune. Or one he had learned and spent many an hour committing to paper at least. And here it was being played note for note as he had written it down all those years ago. Precisely note for note. All seven measures. Smallpipes and fiddle locked in together with not a glimpse of daylight between them. Sometimes one takes the lead on its own, sometimes the other. But usually they are together as one. And then back to the beginning to do it all again, but this time with the elfin piper, naked to the waist, singing out in unison with the fiddle. Non-lexical vocables the clever people call it. *Diddling* will do just as well. And a penny whistle announces its soprano presence, soaring high above the others and just doing its own thing. And on they go all the way to the final bar of the seventh measure, when the melody stutters to a halt three beats from home while the drones are made to howl like a wolf. William laughs at that. A new rhythm is set up, still paced at 120, but the cousin from over the water, the uilleann pipes, now walk to centre stage. The big Irishman makes them sing, but it's not a tune William recognises. The fiddle girl joins in, layering a harmony a third below, but the smallpipes are hot on her trail. In they come once more, weaving a thread of notes in and around the others. The

effect is to float us away somewhere else entirely: ambience, those in the know call it! But in truth it transports us beyond vocabulary and rational words to somewhere else, somewhere sublime. Then the piping pixie shouts for us to get ready to dance once more. ONE. TWO. ONE TWO THREE FOUR! And off they go again, the pace edged up closer to 130 now, as they hit the groove back in common time. And William is smiling from ear to ear. Another of his tunes! 'Over the Dyke and Til Her Laddie!' He had felt a touch embarrassed at having to write that title in his book. But to be fair he had got used to it by then. There were plenty of the other tune names in there that made him blush. Earthy. We'll settle for earthy. And from there, into another tune that William knows so well. 'The Lasses Bushes Brawly'. Enough said on that title! And again, they are note for note as he had played it with his own fingers two and a half centuries before, with just an occasional foray into what sounds like personal territory: a single phrase, repeated for a full 16 bars, then back to the straight and narrow once again. It is loud, it is powerful, it has that same essence that William himself had found and felt when he first played it. But most special of all – the whole world is dancing. Dancing to his tune.

6

Bothy Culture

Martyn was always a bit of a cave man. I remember in the bothy at the bottom of Glen Etive one morning we walked naked to the sea to wash, then rinsed in the river, then gathered driftwood to light a big fire. We rubbed Bog Myrtle all over our bodies for the midges and gathered seaweed to boil up in a pot. Then sat naked beside the fire: talking home-spun philosophy like two young fellas from a previous time. Martyn loved getting far far 'away' from modern life. As well as a tech head he was also a hunter gatherer at heart. – Rory Pierce

AN AIR OF expectation had certainly been created by the release of *Martyn Bennett* in 1996, and many knew what they had liked about it. Yes, we had heard most of the individual ingredients before, but it was the sheer quality of the constituent parts that made for such an impressive whole. It was fun, irreverent, quirky and mischievous, yet layered deep with technical virtuosity, cultural significance, salutes to the past, and glimpses of the future. It was *very* good. What should come next? Martyn himself knew the answer exactly. In fact he had already been working on his next major recording project before completing the first one. Performed and recorded entirely by himself in his flat in Tollcross, Edinburgh, *Bothy Culture* was released in October 1997, and it was to serve as the turning point of his career. It was a major progression in so many ways: musically more mature, more adventurous, more challenging, more innovative. It *was* something entirely new.

The paradox that sits at the heart of so much of Martyn's work is built into this project from its very title onwards. Incubated in little more space than a cramped cupboard in the heart of Scotland's capital, it is an album of the city, a soundscape pressed from the sweat of the crowded subterranean urban dance floor, a polar opposite from the airy ridges of the west Highland mountains he knew and loved so well. And so why 'Bothy Culture'? Why a salute to that icon of *rural* Scotland? What *is* bothy culture in any case? Derived from the Gaelic *bothan*, simply meaning a hut, there are two linked yet distinct uses of the term in Scotland, and Martyn was familiar with the roots and traditions of both. In the Lowlands, especially around Perthshire, Angus and Fife, the bothy emerged in the final decades of the 18th century as a building used to house male farm servants who cooked, ate, slept and lived out their lives together under a single roof. It was a spartan existence, the only practical comforts being an open fire for cooking and as the source of a little warmth, and an allowance of oatmeal, milk and potatoes that at least meant they never went hungry. Under the older system of housing, the lads had usually bunked down in the farmhouse kitchen or in a loft above the stable or byre, taking their meals in the farmhouse with their employer's family. The innovation of being given their own quarters, then, gave them a new-found freedom that opened up their lives to all manner of possibilities that they were quick to explore. While this caused much consternation amongst the clergy, who seemed convinced that the new ways would bring about an inevitable slide towards moral decay and a slew of illegitimate children, the farmworkers themselves took to it with delight, building a vibrant and earthy new culture that had music at its heart. A fiddle was a must in most bothies, and from the mid-19th

Bedroom Studio, Tollcross, Edinburgh.

century there were few bothy walls that failed to ring to the tones of a melodeon too. Above all, there were songs. Songs that told of the daily toil on the land, songs that complained of poor wages, of tyrannical bosses and clapped-out equipment or horses. There were songs of pigs running amok, of clandestine initiation ceremonies into the secret society of horsemen that required them to 'shak hands wi auld horny' or enter into a pact with the devil. In a highly sociable scene involving regular dances with local lassies at crossroads and bridges, there were, of course, songs that spread salacious gossip of the kind of goings-on that the local ministers so greatly feared!

This bothy system as a means of housing so many of the young men of rural Lowland Scotland began to be phased out during the first half of the 20th century, and its music and song, taken out of its original context, proved ideal fare for the folk revivalists of the 1950s and beyond. That version was represented in particular by the 'bothy ballads' that Martyn encountered regularly at clubs and festivals with his mother. Yet Martyn knew that authentic and lived bothy culture, in its heyday, was both a *youth* culture and a *sub*-culture. It was a release from the hard graft of working the land, a touch hedonistic at times, and certainly irreverent, anti-establishment and with a hint of moral danger. That was a recipe that appealed to Martyn Bennett.

While he did suggest to me directly in our occasional chats that there was an element of this thinking in his choice of title for this album, he always made clear that it was another form of bothy culture that was foremost in his mind when making it. In this sub-culture still thriving today, the emphasis was not necessarily on song, that required a shared spoken language, if not dialect, bonding an already close-knit group living and working in close quarters. This culture dealt with strangers uniting and the use of sound to communicate (and entertain) across linguistic divides. This is the culture found within the *mountain* bothies, those small stone sanctuaries that once served the hardy souls who drove their cattle from all points north and west through the hills to the trysts at Crieff or Falkirk and which nowadays provide a safe haven for hillwalkers, climbers and mountaineers caught in a storm or running out of light. Once in, you never know who is likely to limp thankfully through the door behind you, but if you're anything like Martyn Bennett and his mates, you hope that it won't be someone who simply nods the briefest of hellos and slips quietly into their sleeping bag for an early night. If it is, they are likely to be disappointed, or angry, or both. Stories, laughs, drink, dope, capers and music are the stuff of bothy culture, and if Martyn was around, that was most definitely what lay in store for you! As his great friend and mountain buddy Rory Pierce recalled fondly:

> Martyn and I visited bothies all over the Highlands in our 20s. One 'Little & Large' deal we had was that Martyn was happy to bring his bagpipes if I was happy to carry them. This deal also applied to our day trips to the tops of various mountains. One of my favourite memories of this time was a day trip up An Teallach from Sheneval bothy. That day we set off late, which meant that by the time Martyn played his pipes on the summit the sky was turning golden orange, as the sun headed towards the horizon out west over the Hebrides. There was not a breath of wind, and time stood perfectly still while Martyn played an exquisite slow pibroch. Later that night the pipes made another appearance. The bothy was full of all sorts of mountain types, some couth, some not so. After we had all eaten – around 10.30pm at night – three very serious Germans headed upstairs to bed, asking us, very seriously, 'Can you please be quiet now, it is late, and we need to sleep for tomorrow'. We respectfully bid them good night. Half an hour later Martyn took out his pipes and played tune after set after tune, while we all danced around the bothy whooping and yelping. There was much music and singing and shouting that night. Craic agus Ceol (craic and music). We drank whisky, smoked and had fierce craic into the small hours. Not a squeak from

the Germans who got up at 6.00am and scuttled off. I don't think they were familiar with Bothy Culture.[1]

For Rory, bothy culture was highly sociable and hedonistic, strangers meeting and partying in the wilderness. It had a random anarchic quality for him, one that Martyn shared and embraced. The mountain bothy culture was not only part of Martyn's identity, but a portal to other cultures, all mixing and sharing in a marvellous session in the middle of nowhere, and the bothy is a liminal space inviting coincidental collaborations between strangers, a celebration of the exotic. *Bothy Culture* the album was an iteration of what Donald Shaw, the director of the Celtic Connections festival, regarded as Martyn's love of 'being on the edge', of manifesting 'something beautiful out of differences', of 'finding colours that nobody has ever found before.' These colours were not only those of Scotland but also the vibrant, iridescent colours of cultures afar, as Martyn revealed himself in his commentary on the album:

> *Bothy Culture* is a celebration of my culture. It is also a celebration of two other cultures that have really spoken to me through their music even though I did not know much or any of their language. The music of Islam has long been a fascination for me – how could it be that the modes, vocals and instrumentalism are so similar in emotion to Gaelic styles? And how is it that the music of Scandinavia could have the same solitary sweetness and heavy-beat rowdiness of the ceilidh music I had grown up playing?

By his own admission Martyn was no great linguist himself. However, he appreciated the universality of music as a language of its own, a means of transcending and communicating across borders of whatever kind. He was fascinated by the apparent ease with which that could be achieved, and by the effortless way in which he himself could not only feel the emotion and meaning of the music of others, but also just how natural it felt for him to play it in response:

> The answer is simple for me, because we, as mankind, have always had ways of saying what we feel without the need for words. If you strive to be a musical alchemist then you can discover the true message in all peoples through the sounds they make. I had understood these 'foreign languages' as soon as I heard them. I recognised them to be some past life I had lived through perhaps, or they seemed to well up under my fingers without my awareness.

Exploring the capability of music to transcend language seems to be a primary objective of this album, that opens with Martyn inviting us to face East and embrace the 'Tongues of Kali'. Kali is a Hindu goddess, the supreme of all powers, the mother of all living things, usually represented in iconography as having four arms and hands and a long, protruding tongue. Martyn's description of this track has all the hallmarks of youthful exuberance and a hint of contrariness that demonstrate from the outset that he intends to overturn any and all expectations. His tone is irreverential, conversational, as if he is sitting in the bothy. 'There are lots of Punjabi folk songs that have loads of sex and sweary words, but this isn't one of them. This is a party tune with a pile of twaddle over the top'. This 'twaddle' comes mainly in the form of a good going reel played on both practice chanter and Highland pipes, together with a layer of Martyn's own vocals 'speaking in tongues', or more accurately, singing in a mixture of Gaelic-inflected mouth music and what Martyn himself was apt to call that 'hee dirum ho dirum' vocal style pipers tend to adopt when sharing tunes with each other. The whole thing is underpinned with a full-on drum and bass line that pauses a couple of times for breath as the melody breaks

up into a shimmering pibroch-style improvisation on Highland pipes, before diving full on back into the groove for another few minutes until it fades out once more, leaving us only with a few short bursts of Martyn's babbling, blethering tongue. It is quirky, but full of fun and mischief and when Kali stops dancing and rests, we suspect she will sit back down with at least a hint of a smile on her face.

The same mood continues into the next track with more semantic silliness. In 'Aye!', the unintelligible babbling tongues that were uppermost in the opening piece are succeeded by one monosyllabic word loaded with possible meaning. It is a colloquial word, and although not exclusively used in Scotland by any means, it is very strongly associated with the Scots language where it also denotes permanence, meaning 'always', as in 'yours aye'. Whether Martyn had this in mind as well or not, he certainly seems to have chosen to root this track in Scottish soil. It is not the only utterance he makes – he also mumbles 'Uh-huh', at one point, that in this context brings in the non-lexical, and we realise that it can have meaning without being in the dictionary! We also find ourselves filling in the blanks with the other side of the conversation, which was with Kirsten. There is more than a hint of the old comic tropes of the man just agreeing with his partner, and the verbose feminine versus the monosyllabic masculine. When the music floods in it is in jazz style, witty and improvised, gathering pace, dragging us out of contemplation and onto the dance floor. Gently strummed acoustic guitar stands aside to welcome in a violin that is pure Grappelli that in turn gives way later in the track to a frenetic electric guitar sound that wouldn't have been too far out of place had it been sneaked into a prog rock record from 1971 – think 'Hocus Pocus' by Dutch rockers Focus, perhaps!

This hugely eclectic mix of sounds and influences continues on through the album, although the tracks are all in some way rooted in Scotland, hosted in the bothies. The third track, bearing the title 'Shputnik in Glenshiel' pairs the exotic other with a famous Highland Glen, a 'you-had-to-be-there' joke in the story behind it, a reminder by example of the fact that the experiences in the bothies created their own tales to be regaled at a later point, that the bothy culture was a sub-culture, and could be somewhat self-referential. The track note on the album hints at a funny story shared by only a few. Martyn wrote that it was: 'A tune about a crofter from Glenelg who spotted the Hale-Bopp comet, but was fairly Shputniked at the time.' Rory Pierce remembered the incident well:

> We arrived after dark, parked up, and we were walking in through forest tracks and farmland to the bothy, and we stumbled across these two crofters in the dark and Martyn went up in torch light and chatted to them, and asked them where the bothy was, and so on. Then one of the crofters pointed up to the sky and said 'Do you see that? That's a Shputnik, and it won't be back for 2,000 years!' And he pronounced it 'SHputnik', as he was looking up at Hale-Bopp. And later on that night outside the bothy we were all looking up at the comet, a Church of England minister was reciting Ecclesiastes, me and Martyn were throat singing, others were playing the fiddle – we were all kind of honouring it, and paying homage to it all at once.

The juxtaposition of the celestial marvel that would have been all the more visible in the dark Highland skies and the iconic Scottish glen is not just for laughs; it sets up the exotic and the familiar, the celestial and the terrestrial, and remarks on transience. The piece itself is a whirling dance tune, the melody circles in a few bars that become hypnotic as they are repeated, flavoured by the Middle East and the Scottish west Highlands, indistinguishable from each other as they burl around the dance floor. There is a pause for a rest, then back with more energy than ever, the music finally fading out, leaving the whistle to toot out the last notes, reluctant to leave the party.

From the otherworldly and nocturnal Glenshiel, we are next transported to a new day, and to the sounds of a stream gradually emerging as we regain consciousness. However, it is a dream state, filled with apparitions and the sounds and sights of nature and the voice of Sorley MacLean, incanting his own poetry about the displaced Gael and telling us that the dead are alive and walking among us. Linear time is thrown to the winds, gentle entrancing strings like geo-thermals take us up higher, above and away, before the choppy beat returns us to the ground, images of people and nature flickering past. 'Hallaig' forms the iconic 'centrepiece of the album', as ethnologist Mairi McFadyen observed, simultaneously rooting it in place and the imagination of the exile, those departed in body but not in spirit.[2] In the context of bothy culture, there is a psychoactive or psychedelic atmosphere to Hallaig here, and one that is fused with Gaelic cosmology, beliefs in the supernatural and ancestral existing as real entities in the present. It is utterly masterful.

The inclusion of the poetry and voice of Sorley MacLean, one of Scotland's greatest 20th century poets, continues the commitment Martyn had shown in his debut album to a direct engagement with some of the key artists and culture-makers of the modern nation. In 'Hallaig', often considered his finest work, MacLean speaks of the desolation of his native island of Raasay following a wholesale clearance of its people in the mid-19th century. The island had been sold by John MacLeod of Raasay in 1846, the buyer being a gentleman from Edinburgh by the name of George Rainy. By 1854 he had evicted the entire population of twelve townships, clearing 94 families in all. Hallaig, where generations of MacLean's own people had lived out their lives, was one of them. A century may have passed by the time he composed the poem, but the sadness and anger had barely subsided, and it is a work that groans with emotion. Where once his people thrived, the landscape is now inhabited only by their ghosts. As the scholar, the late John MacInnes remarked, it is

> an utterly new statement which is emotionally subtle and powerful, unsentimental, and wholly Gaelic. Through his genius, both the Gaelic sense of landscape, idealised in terms of society, and the Romantic sense of communion with Nature, merge in a single vision, a unified sensibility.[3]

How, then, is that mood of reflection, of sorrow, of regret, of anger, to be captured in an underpinning soundtrack? A bagpipe lament? A wretched, anguished vocal outpouring? No, the feel is actually one of gentle optimism, of an almost jaunty expectation that all is not lost. Indeed it is not, for as Sorley had declared, 'the dead men have been seen alive'. That deep-seated Highland belief that we each leave our indelible mark on the landscape as we pass through this life is there in this music as it is in the poem itself. It is a potent pairing. And the poet himself is allowed the space here to read aloud the entire poem in its English version. There are no snippets, no soundbites, no mere hints, nods or flavours of the lyric as is so often the case with archived narratives pressed into action in this way. Sorley's reading of the poem is borrowed from Tim Neat's marvellous 1984 film study *Hallaig: The Poetry and Landscape of Sorley MacLean*, and Martyn was hugely grateful to Tim for granting him permission to use it.[4] Sorley therefore takes the 'lead vocal' while Martyn plays the supporting role to an extent he had never done on disc before. It was, however, a highly significant early sign of something new emerging in Martyn's creative practice, an approach that would reach its full-blown conclusion on his final album some five years later. Indeed, the track would later find a new and spellbinding iteration in a collaboration with animation artist and renowned caricaturist, Neil Kempsell, in a film production of 'Hallaig', funded by the Edinburgh College of Art. This was a project embraced warmly by Martyn, who replied to Kempsell's approach saying, 'I have always thought that "Hallaig" as a piece would be lifted by some sort of film/animation'. 'Perhaps in the future', he added, 'I may also get some funding to commission more of your work to go with a couple of tracks for my new album *Grit*.' In the event, Neil did indeed create a mesmerising animated film for another piece of his music, but sadly Martyn didn't live to see it. In 2019, Neil's visual interpretation of 'Mackay's Memoirs' was premiered at the Queen's Hall in Edinburgh at a concert to celebrate the 20th anniversary of its first performance.

'Hallaig' is arguably the most significant track on this album in terms of Martyn's artistic development, gathering as it does spoken-word, poetry, music, politics and history all into a spotlight that is shone on Sorley's voice, a voice that almost seems melodic in its Gaelic intonation and expressive manner of reading aloud. This pattern of fusion, with its mingling of intellectual and primal, rational and spiritual, real and ethereal, was not only ground-breaking at the time of *Bothy Culture*; it set the sails for new voyages of discovery and Martyn's future work in *Glen Lyon* and *Grit*. While the poetry recital of Sorley invited us to consider the lyrical and melodic possibilities of language in highly literary 'King's English', the language used by the poet is in itself a symbol of Gaelic dispossession. Sorley, like all of his generation born into the British Empire, was taught this form of English at school, and in many cases pupils were banned from speaking in Gaelic or their native Scots dialect.

In the tracks following the reflective and serious 'Hallaig', the partying is resumed, as is the fun. 'Ud the Doudouk' and '4 Notes' are an exuberant celebration of the wackiness of the mountain bothy, of the experimentation involved when cultures meet and party together. Martyn's notes on both tracks get the same treatment from him as the rest of the album; they are fun-focused, irreverent and informal, yet still give us enough information to pique the curiosity. Of the doudouk he commented: 'A doudouk is an older brother of the Scottish pipes found throughout Islamic countries; it sounds really cool and out of tune.' Elsewhere he admitted that this in fact wasn't a real version of that instrument, but a cheap imitation that sounded even more out of tune than the real thing! Of its companion tune, '4 Notes', Martyn declared, 'This tune has only four notes, but I haven't worked out what they are.' Such deadpan disingenuous humour suggests that we are not to overthink these tracks but to listen and enjoy! And they have certainly been enjoyed, for as close friend, photographer BJ Stewart recalled, they had a particularly strong impact when played live:

> The crowd always seemed to love these two tracks which were nearly always played back to back like on the album. In reality they were one long epic piece which always seemed to induce a trance-like state in the crowd. Building up, building up, teasing you down, pulling you, pushing you. During 'Ud' he would introduce you to what became affectionately known as 'the hoof', a rustic animal horn with a reed on top... And it used to get pretty raucous down the front by the way. This was no folk gig with people politely watching and applauding in between sets. Martyn would often shout out, 'Let's go men-tal' and the crowd would happily oblige. Dancing if there was room to allow it but often it was a good healthy mosh pit front and centre. And at a gig in the Liquid Rooms in Edinburgh, I was trying to make my way down to the front when a guy was barging his way out in the opposite direction, his t-shirt covered in blood and his nose all over his face loudly declaring, 'That's fuckin magic!'

The Hoof!

'Ud the Doudouk' begins with the tinkling, tinkering sounds of instruments tuning and warming up. Gradually and seamlessly a groove emerges and then a simple refrain. The steady 4/4 beat shows up, heralded by a twanging electronic baseline. The 'doudouk' sounds in all its 'out of tune' glory, making detours and variations of increasing complexity as the track progresses. We hear a male voice calling out 'Waaaaaa', over and over. It sounds distant, then moves a little nearer as the whole ensemble gathers momentum. There is a call to prayer – reminiscent of the Islamic Adhan but simplified. Then there is a trance-like, floating, electronic riff, and the return of the original refrain playing out softly on a flute. The pause between this and the start of the next track, '4 Notes', is like a rest between bouts of activity. Once the 4/4 beat emerges again,

it has more bass and boom, accompanied by the return of the call to party. The Great Highland Bagpipe strikes up, playing the same refrain that the doudouk played in the last dance. The beat is now hypnotic, carrying the crowd away. All the sounds are joined together in a cacophony, not quite in unison so that we can pick out individual instruments and effects more easily, appreciate the slight chaos, the improvisation, the imperfection. It fades, and the refrain, the nominal 'four notes' prevail before tinkling bells announce another rest.

    The next track takes us to Scandinavia and the Arctic Circle, with another kind of mouth music – this time 'joiking', a form of chanting practised by the Sámi. Space-age electronic bleeping is succeeded by two chords strummed on acoustic guitar, introducing the beat for the dance. We have visions of Northern Lights in all their psychedelic glory with the electronic effects that seem to hover above the Joik. When this ends with a sudden 'Hai!', we are propelled into the penultimate track, 'Yer Man from Athlone' – an Irish fiddle tune with a jiggy beat and then yet another form of mouth music, this time 'diddling'. The pitch of the vocal raises as the tune progresses, dipping in and out of falsetto and rendered with an echo, as if it's being overheard from the entrance to a cave in leprechaun country. The playfulness with Irish stereotypes is deliberate: in his album note, Martyn comments: 'Nobody ever takes the piss out of the Irish these days, but I love taking the piss.' This subversive humour literally plays out in the track, which ends with everything fading away leaving the comic trope of the diehard partygoer still up for more craic when everyone else has gone home, and Martyn showing his keen ear for mimicry in full Fermanagh accent: 'Let's do it again. Hello? Where's everyone gone? I was having fun!'

Martyn returns us to the sentient world of the Gael in his final track on *Bothy Culture*, 'Waltz for Hector' serving as a fitting conclusion to this musical odyssey. You would do well to discover any hint of a waltz in there though, for this begins and ends in pure pibroch, sounded first on a high whistle and ending on solo Highland pipes, with much ambient and discordant noodling on low whistle, smallpipes and a host of electronica in between. The pibroch is one of the finest: 'Lament for Red Hector of the Battles', taught to Martyn by Captain John MacLellan in Edinburgh a decade before, and a musical memorial to a Highland hero of the old school who died at the Battle of Harlaw in 1411. Exactly how long after the event the tune was composed we cannot tell, but this is *very* old music. The antiquity of this final tune vis-a-vis the welter of technology is another contrast that Martyn places in our consciousness as a parting gesture, showing off his ability as a 'musical alchemist', unifying polar opposites without compromise to the integrity of either. It was a feat of extraordinary instrumental and technological ability.

While Martyn was making *Bothy Culture*, Kenny MacDonald had been working behind the scenes to try to secure a deal with a bigger record label, and had sent off some early mixes to some of those that specialised in 'world music'. While Martyn later came to dislike that term and the pigeon-holing that went with it, it did seem the natural home for the music he was now producing. 'A former colleague was now working with Rykodisc, so there was an in there', Kenny recalled. They liked it, and offered Martyn a three-album deal, which he gladly accepted. 'It was a big jump, as they had a global machine'.

In the event, *Bothy Culture* brought neither fame nor fortune, but the international reviews were almost universally positive. The *LA Times* viewed it as 'an invigorating and captivating form of multiculturalism', and *Rolling Stone* considered it the most notable release in the drum-and-bass album genre for the year. *Billboard* branded it 'a tastily idiosyncratic world music blend that ranks with the very best of the progressives' but the *NY Press* was rather more succinct in its quip that here was 'tradition for trainspotters'. *HUB (Online)* proclaimed that its blend of techno and traditional represented 'the birth of a new genre', *The Wire* saw it as 'an exhilarating achievement' and *MOJO* thought it 'a genuinely ground-breaking album'. For the *Boston Herald*, the 'grace, depth and consistency' rendered this 'sheer musical alchemy'. That particular choice of words was intriguing, for Martyn himself viewed the process of making music as a form of alchemy too. He understood that to be an alchemist required a lot of pure graft. 'He worked bloody hard', as his wife, Kirsten, recalled. That work involved seeking out, listening, sampling and as he complained to Alistair Clark of *The Scotsman*,

> I sat in that room till two in the morning for months on end. And I'm still sitting in that room. It's mad, crazy. What am I doing this for? Yesterday I spent 14 hours trying to get

the bass sound I wanted for one wee bit of music. Can you imagine how irritating and boring that can be?

Alistair Clark's rather reasonable suggestion in reply that perhaps it would be easier to hire a bass player seems fair enough in the cold light of day, but for Martyn, that was never going to be an option. Quite apart from not being able to afford one, 'a bass player just wouldn't fit in'. What he really meant is that it might take himself 14 hours to find exactly what he wanted, but he would get there eventually. Perfectionism doesn't lend itself to delegation!

The solitary nature of this album and the detailed, careful way that it was constructed is an achievement of ultimate irony, given that it represents impromptu music-making by many people, performing for a random party! Martyn played every musical instrument himself, from 'the hoof' to violin, and with the exception of Sorley MacLean's voice, provided all vocal and electronic sounds, blended it all together himself and only then had it remixed working with Martin Swan. He had little patience for those who were prepared to take shortcuts, and was suspicious of the new musical bandwagon that seemed to attract many of them. 'World music', he complained, 'has given rise to many so-called alchemists whom I believe do not actually understand the music they borrow and unfortunately they tend to tout their works as being authentic with no upbringing in any tradition whatsoever.' Martyn knew, though, that he himself was lucky to have been brought up *in* a tradition, and to have roamed the country with a mother who collected, studied and performed tradition. Folklorists are trained to seek out features of culture that transcend time and place, and to wrestle with this complex and often elusive thing termed 'authenticity'. No wonder, then, that Martyn was highly sensitive to these concepts, and was acutely aware of their importance to his own work.

While *Bothy Culture* was welcomed with rave reviews and

Martyn's technical and musical brilliance lauded, relatively little recognition has rested on the vocal and linguistic content of this album. Every track contains a human voice whether counting the music in, intoning a call, speaking in tongues, responding on the phone, reciting poetry, joiking, singing *canntaireachd*, diddling, or parodying an accent. It is all there, using the power of the word and the wordless voice to convey 'craic agus ceol'. Martyn's brief and witty track notes belie a genius hidden in plain hearing. As well as the ground-breaking dance album for which it is perhaps most recognised, *Bothy Culture* is on every level an album about communication and commonality. He saw that the culture of the bothies of Scotland had a direct link to similar contexts across the world, but also to the dance club scene that he himself had been enthusiastically embracing:

> I would say that in some ways bothies have the same, familiar atmosphere to urban nightclubs – arriving for the sound-check when they are merely cold, empty shells is always a spooky experience. Perhaps the same spirits of so many fire/spot-lit, whisky/drug charged nights have somehow imparted a memory of the ghosts of those people you have never met and can only imagine. Although the music and songs that have been played in them are totally contrasting it is this same sense of excitement that can transform four bare walls into a chamber of sheer sensual delight.[5]

And to create these chambers of delight, it was time to lift the music of *Bothy Culture* off the CD and make it happen in the air. It was time to form a band.

7

Cuillin

Mosh Pit

The experience o the live gigs – it's a lang time he's been gone but the memories are still very fresh in keepin his spirit and the music alive. We were the NCR hillwalking and mountaineering club from Dundee. We were the Bennetteers! We used to hire a mini bus at the weekend to head off and we always had the music on *in the bus – Corries, Ossian, Runrig – we were very much into Scottish folk music. One of the guys had the first album, Martyn Bennett. We put it on and right away we're like, 'Wow, this really is just something new!' He just broke all the rules with a sound that was something that the people could connect wi and we got it! The first time we saw him play was the Old Fruitmarket at Celtic Connections. £7.50. I still hae the ticket. We went to that gig which was jam packed and no really knowin what to expect. He wis a one-man band – just getting that huge sound and always when he played the pipes live over the top of the track the place just erupted and that was us hooked. We tried to get everywhere he was playing after that. He came to Dundee Rep. There were a lot of season ticket holders so they'd come and see whatever was on. And I think he'd done the first two tunes and we're aw sitting in this theatre setting. Dougie Mitchell, he's like, 'Fuck this!' Got up oot o his seat, onto the stage, doffed his cap to the band, and started dancing – on the stage! And we all thought, we'll have*

The Bennetteers.

some o that! And a couple of people had walked out – 'this is terrible behaviour'! We end up on the stage and Martyn and the band loved it. By the end there was hardly anyone sitting – we were all on the stage. Afterwards Martyn says 'You guys are nuts!' We says 'We cannae just sit there tapping our feet!' It was like a full workout – you were just a sweating mess by the end o it! And the Barrowlands was another electric gig. We were on each others' shoulders. Wherever he was playin we were there. And King Tuts, a wee compact place. The place wis jumpin. He shouts over the mic, 'Fenians and Huns unite!' That was very brave in Glasgow! He had a dry sense o humour. And in the mosh pit – smiles on everybody's faces. It was anticipation of what you were about to get. To go see the live thing was something right off the Richter scale. When he started the pounding beats everyone was off – the gig in the Rep summed it up. You had to be up there in amongst it. You were like in a trance – he knew how to play the audience. He'd put in a slower number to give us a rest, then the pipes started and we were away again! Just brilliant. – Gary Robertson, Dundee[1]

IT WAS AT Celtic Connections in late January 1998 that a new band arrived on the scene, taking to the stage at the Old Fruitmarket in Glasgow to 'a thousand mad-for-it punters', as reviewer Sue Wilson remarked. Martyn Bennett, who as his band mate and future wife Kirsten recalled 'really was the man of the moment' on the Scottish music scene, had filled a major venue with his fans waiting keenly to experience this debut performance of Cuillin, the collective comprising herself, her friend Deirdre MacLullich, and Martyn's great pal, Rory Pierce. All were highly trained instrumentalists and Rory also a composer. While it may have seemed like an eagerly anticipated and 'natural progression' to the audience and critics for Martyn to take to the stage with a band, the pressure on these new and relatively unknown musicians accompanying him was intense that night. Many years on, they each recall a sense of the crowd being there to see Martyn and a distinct feeling of impostor syndrome, with people perhaps wondering 'Who are these people?', and 'Why have they been chosen?', as Kirsten reflected. 'I can still remember the smell of my own acrid sweat!' recalled Rory. The nerves were noticed, reviews of the evening observing that the band took a while to get into its stride over the first few sets, but soon settled in, and Cuillin was born.

The notion of forming a band seems to have crystallised in Martyn's mind over the course of making *Bothy Culture* and experiencing adversity touring alone. On the one hand, the rationale behind Cuillin was mundane, as Kirsten recollected:

> He called me from Hungary where he was out playing on his own. 'I'm having a terrible time – I have a bus pass and the British Council have left me to it with a map. I've got so many cases of all my gear.' He was all stressed out. 'This is the last time. I need a band to carry my stuff!'

Kirsten had recently returned from Turkey where she had been teaching English and visiting a friend and fellow RSAMD student, and although she and Martyn had decided to go their separate ways when she had left after graduation, they had stayed in touch, met up on her visit home, and the relationship was rekindled. Although she had been teaching while overseas, Kirsten didn't have any formal teaching qualifications and so enrolled on a Teaching English as a Foreign Language course where she happened to sit next to a young woman who clearly had a flair for languages and who was fluent in French and Italian. 'She helped me with my grammar', Kirsten laughed, 'and we got chatting and realised we shared a music background'. Her name was Deirdre MacLullich, a violinist from Edinburgh, and the two became firm friends. 'We had a funny little duet;

we used to go round hotels and do gigs and stuff. And she asked me where I was staying and I said I was moving in with my boyfriend, and Deirdre said, "Oh I know him!"' She and Martyn had played together in their teens in the Edinburgh Schools Orchestra and had been on a trip to Denmark together. And so on his return from his fraught trip to Hungary, Martyn's search for a couple of musical bag carriers brought instant results! 'He came back and decided that Deirdre and I were there – we could just get on with it!'

The third recruit to the band was another former member of the Edinburgh Schools Orchestra, Rory Pierce, a cellist and uilleann piper from Enniskillen in Northern Ireland who had moved to Edinburgh in his teens. Rory and Martyn first met aged 16 in the Lothian Youth Choir, where Rory remembers forming an instant bond with Martyn, who, though small and wiry, had a remarkable 'deep bass voice'. He and Rory were kindred spirits in the bass section, irreverent yet deeply committed to music, and 'the boys at the back' soon moved on and 'chummed up' to take to the hills together at every opportunity.

Musing on the formation of Cuillin, Rory, Kirsten and Deirdre agree that it was guided in good part by pragmatic consideration, Martyn choosing from his closest circle of friends and his partner, knowing from direct experience and advice from mentors such as Martin Swan of the Mouth Music project that a band would need to withstand the demands of living and working in close quarters for sustained periods of time on tour. However, his rationale was also musical, as Deirdre recalled: 'I think the fact that we were friends was quite important but it was about more than just "we can have a great time on the road"; he was still very particular in what he was looking for.' Kirsten remarked that 'He did want people who could put into practice what his ideas were.' Rory agreed observing 'in truth I think we were a bit malleable and would do as we were told.' All of them had also evaded musical categorisation; 'We weren't anything – not folk musicians, or jazz, or classical', claimed Kirsten, adding that Martyn could give them a piece of music and 'there wouldn't be an issue with how to play something. He never spent any length of time going over stuff.' He was also very much in command: they all remember that they were 'very much given their parts' by Martyn; 'He was the despot', remarked Rory, although with fondness in his tone, an observation greeted with affectionate amusement by the others. The tolerance and acceptance of Martyn's style of leadership is a strong clue as to why Martyn selected the band that he did: they understood and loved him and appreciated what he wanted to achieve musically. And so, the 'array of entirely fresh faces' was completed.

Initial rehearsals for Cuillin's first performance took place throughout late 1997 in a Church of Scotland building on Colinton Road in Edinburgh. It was totally and conveniently soundproofed, with a kitchen and good facilities. The people were welcoming and friendly and the building was free. The schedule was demanding; Martyn was strict about time-keeping and upset if anyone was late. He was dogmatic, knew what he wanted and was a consummate perfectionist, very conscious that these preparations were for a 'big launch gig and a lot riding on it' as the band recall. The preparation for their debut performance was accordingly intense, but it established from the outset a combination of hard work and healthy fun, with the group going cycling after rehearsals. Martyn, while very much directing the proceedings, also had a highly determined vision of their performance on stage that inspired confidence in the others, and perhaps also in himself. 'He'd shut his eyes and say: "It's OK, I've seen it."' Rory remembered. There was no question of the gig going awry. Martyn was too much of a perfectionist to allow that to happen. The standards he demanded from his bandmates were exceptionally high. 'He knew exactly what he

wanted', laughed Kirsten. 'You couldn't go into the rehearsal room without knowing what you were doing. He'd go mental!' The rehearsal process was very intense, and neither casual nor democratic. Martyn was the boss, he knew exactly what he wanted musically and 'it wasn't like a jam session where you go in, have a wee chat, you play that, I'll have a go at that. He didn't want your opinion. The band members had no input. You almost had to wait in line for your music!'

The progression of this young band is a journey almost self-contained within Martyn's life, and accounts and reminiscences of band members afford intimate insight into Martyn's character and development as a man, businessman and leader. In Rory's case, these portray a lad with very traditional masculine interests, comfortable in the wilderness, where they would walk naked to wash, forage and sit by the fire in Glen Etive, and where Martyn's incredible brute strength would smash up a large piece of wood for a fire, or stop Rory from falling to his death while freeclimbing a chimney stack on An Teallach. There was a competitive edge to the technological side of bothy culture that spilled into band life. Rory again:

> The thing that Martyn seemed most excited about when we went to America was arriving in a new city and working out where the nearest outdoor gear store was. We would hit the store and spend way too much of our meagre wages on ultra-light stoves, titanium mini pots & pans, tiny little headtorches, sporks – all sorts of obsessive gear. It was one way of guaranteeing those delicious jealous looks in the bothy on our next adventure. Bothy Culture often revolved around who had the best gear.

For Rory, Martyn was both a 'tech head' and a 'hunter gatherer at heart'. Wherever the band went, Martyn took the opportunity to climb mountains, to seek the high ground, whether in Kazakhstan or in Spain or the Lake District. It was a form of escape that was crucial for him, and crucial for his music.

Nevertheless, there was undoubtedly a marvellously anarchic side to Martyn's character that would manifest most readily in the hills. Rory remembered driving up to Sutherland on a mountain foray and encountering an army convoy. Martyn quickly and without warning pulled the car in and 'mooned the entire fucking army' as they passed. On another occasion he was asked to create a soundtrack for an upcoming Conservative party campaign. Rather than decline, he feigned great interest and enthusiasm without lifting a finger to write a single note.

They eventually had to pull out when nothing was forthcoming 'and the music that they ended up using was utter shit' said Rory gleefully. Yet there was an incredibly punctilious side to Martyn also, one which Kirsten noted surfaced, paradoxically, when he smoked marijuana: 'everybody knew it made him very pedantic' – quite the opposite to what might be expected! He was very particular about matters such as car insurance and professional punctuality. When four emergency police cars mustered to a car park where Martyn was applying his trusty Leatherman knife to the task of extricating money wrongfully swallowed by a parking meter, he was, according to a mortified Kirsten, most indignant, exclaiming: 'I am a law-abiding citizen'!

Martyn's resourcefulness embraced all technology: mechanical, electronic, digital, and domestic. Rory was given a car by Martyn so that the band could tour in two vehicles with all their gear and Martyn 'also apprenticed me in the art of going to the scrapyard for parts and fitting them for yourself. This art has saved me thousands of pounds over the years. I saw him do his own house-plumbing, electrical rewiring, immaculate carpentry – you name it.' A classic example of this in the context of the band is given again by Rory:

> We were getting tired of playing gigs where the sound levels were all wrong on stage, so Martyn invented these DI boxes which he made himself from components at Maplins. Each DI box had various input cables plus three volume controls: one for the backing track volume, one for your own instrument volume, and one for Martyn's volume. He also made these perfectly sewn canvas pouches, so that the box could be attached to your belt. This meant that at any point during the gig you could adjust any of the levels which were going into your headphones.

This inventiveness and addiction to Maplins (a store selling all manner of electrical components) also resulted in Martyn wiring up the first electric Hungarian zither. Technology and tradition were being fused in a very literal sense and he was as comfortable with a circuit board as a sewing machine. He even had a pouch of designer labels that he would sew onto second hand jumpers bought by the band. Kirsten remembered an incident in Montreal when Rory was seen passing the window in the snow wearing Deirdre's coat, with 'sleeves half way up his arm'. This comic pastiche arose apparently from a combination of lost luggage and Rory feeling cold but it was all the more outrageous because 'Martyn was always trying to get us to look so cool!' said Kirsten. Rory concurred: 'Yeah, Martyn would rather freeze and look cool!' Cuillin was Martyn's band; he was in charge but he also embraced fully the responsibility that it entailed.

That included looking after the band finances, and as Kirsten remarked, 'he thought about income and expenditure a lot. Music was a business to him.' Deirdre explained:

> He wanted us to make enough as a band to be able to have a great time, to have enough income to survive, and I think that was always a driving force for him. I'd say that was just as important to him as the music. He wanted us to just be in that band.

Martyn was all-or-nothing in his approach and took the consequences voluntarily, even protectively. If the band earned less than expected for a gig, Martyn would not take any pay himself. And this strong moral code extended to his dealings with the wider team around him too. Having cancelled a tour due to illness, he paid his agent the fee she would have earned had it gone ahead, despite not having earned anything himself. 'He was insistent', Lisa recalled. '"You've put all your work in to arrange the gigs, so you should get paid". Nobody else has ever done that, before or since'. He also assumed the responsibility of main spokesperson for the group confining himself to hotel rooms for hours doing press interviews over the phone while the others headed out to shop or explore. One consequence of this is that in press coverage relating to the tours and gigs with Cuillin, there is little mention of the band, the focus tending towards the music and Martyn himself. In an interview on the second tour to North America, given to the *Ottawa Sun*, Martyn is clearly feeling the strain of touring:

> Creatively, it's been a bit disappointing. All the collaborations and all the creative input that you hope you can get by working with other musicians isn't possible because you've got to go out and earn your bread and butter. You're just on the road the whole time.

The road was repetitive and geared to the commercial expectations of record companies, business and publicity dealings. Martyn seemed to assume almost exclusive and singular responsibility for this, and then resented the results: 'Touring is like having a knife in the back of your head. But a knife's a bit quicker though.' Certainly, Cuillin's touring schedule was gruelling as they accepted invitations from festivals and events in many parts of the world. As any musician who has toured extensively knows, there are highs and lows, good times and bad, on the road, and so it was with Cuillin. Jamie Hale, the band's sound engineer, here reflects at length on one particular trip to Kazakhstan in November 1998, providing a wonderfully detailed insight into life on tour with Martyn and the rest of the band. It is included here in full for these reasons.

> 1998 was our busiest year for touring. We managed over 100 flights in nine months, and whilst most

went without a hitch, it was only realistic that some, eventually, would go wrong. We'd been invited by The British Council to perform in Almaty, Kazakhstan's former capital city. The British Councillor there was from Penicuik, near Edinburgh, and was so homesick that he regularly brought out bands from Scotland, not only to do their own gigs, but also to perform with local musicians. Our brief for those five days was to play three gigs with the band, and for Martyn to perform a piece written by a local composer, accompanied by the Kazakh State Symphony Orchestra. The time leading up to our first trip into Central Asia was typical of our insane schedule of the time, namely, finishing off a tour a few hours before check-in time for another trip. Our last date of a Scottish tour was in The Liquid Rooms in our home town of Edinburgh, and with an early finish time of 10.00pm, this allowed us the luxury of being able to go to our own homes, unpack, wash our clothes, dry them, pack them all again, say hello to the family, say goodbye to the family, get the passport, and go to the airport. A 4.00am coffee was most definitely in order as we checked in for the first flight of the day. Travelling as a band can usually rack up the excess baggage bill to an eye-twisting degree, and this time was no exception. 'That'll be £2,500 please Mr. Bennett.' A resigned Martyn reached for his wallet. 'Hang on... Martyn Bennett?' The check-in man pondered for a while, scanning our tired faces. 'I recognise you guys from the telly!' With more pondering, and having taken a shine to Deirdre, the check-in man bucked the airline trend and let us go straight through to Almaty without having to pay any excess. What a very nice check-in man!

   A short hop to Amsterdam's Schiphol Airport later and with five hours to spare before the Almaty flight, Martyn and I decided to spend the morning sight-seeing and coffee drinking in Amsterdam. We soon got rid of the sight-seeing idea, and stuck with the coffee plan instead. With last minute timing, Kirsten and Deirdre were met at the departure gate by the smiley faces of their band mate and sound engineer, and our Central Asian abyss could at last begin. As the hours and the in-flight movies passed, our body clocks started to get confused. We'd been awake for at least 30 hours by this time, and were rapidly flying into a time zone five hours ahead of our own. Never mind, we were due to land within the hour, and bed wouldn't be far away. As we started our descent however, our jumbo-jet banked sharply to the left and sped off in the opposite direction. With query written all over the passengers' faces, the captain made the heart-sinking announcement that a severe snowstorm had hit Almaty, and it would be impossible to land there. We would have to divert to Baku in Azerbaijan, another three hours away. Our smiley faces quickly wore off as concerns for the trip grew.

Baku airport at 2.00am was the slap in the face we could've done without. A small airport, seemingly stuck in an ancient time warp, controlled by soldiers with two Kalashnikov rifles each, and a plethora of stray cats urinating randomly. The plan was to get us to a hotel until morning, although with only five taxis and a 15-seat mini bus, this would take time, given that there were over 200 passengers. The four of us sat huddled together on our biggest flight case, waiting for another three hours whilst more transport was sought. We were wilting fast.

The sun was coming up on yet another day by the time we got to the hotel. Looking at her flock of cross-eyed passengers, one of the cabin crew apologised as she asked us to be back on the bus in four hours' time. With a shower, two hours of sleep and an enormous breakfast, we started to feel almost human again. If only just. Baku was an intriguing, but not particularly enticing place. Signs of extreme poverty and extreme wealth in every eyeful, with Caspian Sea oil refineries dominating the entire horizon. We boarded our now familiar 747, and waited eagerly for news. If we left for Almaty then, we would make it just in time for the sound-check of our first gig. Fingers and toes were crossed. The captain though, had other ideas. The weather was still far too bad to land in Almaty, and the airline needed the plane back. The only option was to fly back to Amsterdam. Disaster.

This presented us with quite a quandary. It was already the middle of the week, and we had to be back in Edinburgh on Saturday night to play for the opening of the new Museum of Scotland. If the weather in Almaty didn't improve, the entire trip would have to be cancelled. Bigger disaster. Still, we couldn't control the weather, and decided to leave the re-organisation of our week to agents, promoters, airlines, and fate. There was nothing else we could do except sit back for six hours and watch the in-flight movie, again, and eat the same airline pasta, again.

We were due to land back in Amsterdam around dinnertime, and had planned a quiet night out to let our hair/dreadlocks down. The smiley faces were returning. Hallucinating with tiredness upon our arrival, we collected our 15 pieces of expensive and heavy cargo, and made our way to the airport hotel.

'There's only 14 cases,' sighs Kirsten as we loaded up the trolleys.

My suitcase was missing. My heart sank to my feet as I imagined some stray cats in Baku urinating all over my case whilst laughing at me. I suggested to Martyn, Kirsten and Deirdre that they should just go to the hotel while I sorted out this latest nightmare, but we were inseparable, and stayed together to have our night out at lost luggage instead.

Another five hours of unbelievable airline stupidity passed until I was finally re-united with my beloved suitcase. I was whole again. With knuckles dragging, we descended on our hotel with enough time for a short kip before trying to get to Kazakhstan all over again. There was a certain feeling of deja vu as we checked in at stupid o'clock in the morning for our now overly familiar flight to Almaty. 'That'll be £2,500 for excess baggage please Mr Bennett.'

We tried various methods of argument with the airline, but we simply didn't have the strength or brainpower to fight, and we didn't want to land our very nice check-in man in Edinburgh in trouble either.

The weather in Almaty had thankfully improved to guarantee our arrival. With over 50 hours of trying, it looked as if we would finally make it! Time to sit back and watch the in-flight movie, yet again, and eat the same airline pasta, yet again.

After having made our way to the airport in Edinburgh late on Saturday night, our plane eventually landed at about 5.00am on the Wednesday in the snowy wilderness of Kazakhstan. The British Councillor and his party met us with beaming smiles and a huge sense of relief that we'd made it at last. We tried to be civil and as friendly as we could but the exhaustion was hideous and we could barely remember our names. Our body clocks had long since given up, and although we should've gone to bed for a good night's sleep, the sun was rising over Central Asia, and it was time for breakfast.

A nearby restaurant had opened early for us to have our first Kazakh meal, although after one quick glance at the menu, we trusted our local guides to order for us. I was desperately hungry so asked if they could order me the dish which consisted of the largest physical amount of food. We waited ages for our breakfast. They must have had to take that time to prepare the almighty feast that was soon to be in front of me. As I've mentioned a few times, we were running on fumes, but Deirdre was looking especially ill all of a sudden. We'd had the same airline pasta for days on end, so this breakfast had become an important lifeline for the very real state of our wellbeing. At last, the kitchen doors swept open with a train of waiters carrying plate after plate of hot, big food. Everybody had received their food apart from me. Where's mine? I thought to myself with fear and desperation. I'd never seen such a huge silver platter being carried with great pomp and ceremony towards me as my smile returned. There it was. All the food I'd waited days for.
'That's a Kazakh delicacy,' our guides told me as I looked down at the smallest piece of lonely limp bread I'd ever seen.
'The vegetables, meat and potatoes are coming aren't they?'
'No, that's it.'
  Everyone started to laugh uncontrollably, as I stared for minutes angrily and with utter disbelief, sadness, and confusion at my piece of dry toast on a massive plate. It's hilarious when I look back, but at the time I was devastated. Deirdre had laughed too hard. She didn't look well at all. 'I'm just going out for some air,' she whispered. CRASH! We looked around to see Deirdre collapsed into the coat stand, buried under a mound of

hats, scarves and coats. She was out cold briefly, and although we were very worried, it was almost expected and accepted.

The touring lifestyle. It can be so glamorous...

We had very little time in the ill-fated restaurant, as Martyn had to go straight to a rehearsal with the Kazakh State Symphony Orchestra. Deirdre, Kirsten and I were driven to the hotel where at last we could get some proper sleep. We had to muster some energy for our gig at night. This was the second of our planned gigs, as of course we'd missed the first one from having arrived two days late.

As the sun was setting over Central Asia, we woke up to face the Kazakh people for the first time. Our drivers met us in the hotel lobby, their arms open wide and with warm caring faces, determined to look after us like we were their own children. Our gig that night was in an enormous Irish bar. It seems that no matter where you are in the world, there's an Irish bar! This was all becoming a little too obscure. Here we were, only a few hundred miles from the Chinese border, having travelled for so long to get here, playing in front of an audience consisting of many different Asian and Soviet nationals, and they're all drinking dark Irish beer.

The gig was a real success. For us, being so tired helps you get into the zone for playing and mixing more easily, and the multi-cultural crowd loved it. What felt like only minutes after the last note had been played, the audience, press and photographers had been ushered out of the building with a ruthless efficiency. The sudden silence was overwhelming. Then, like the start of an opera, the curtains covering the back wall of the stage dramatically opened to reveal a small door. We were escorted through into a long room with an enormous dining table in the

middle. Around that table sat the Deputy Prime Minister
of Kazakhstan, various dignitaries and business leaders,
all welcoming us like long lost relatives. Surrounding
them were countless waitresses and security personnel,
all with their eyes fixed permanently on the walls in front
of them.
'We are here to toast you,' the Deputy Prime Minister
said with a rosy smile as numerous bottles of vodka
appeared. None of us were big drinkers, and by that time
all we wanted to do was to have a cup of tea and go to
bed, but we didn't want to be rude and we also really
didn't have the choice.
'We toast the fact that you made it after such a long
journey.'
Vodka.
'We toast The British Council for bringing you here.'
More vodka.
'We toast electricity for powering your equipment.'
More vodka.
I lost count and consciousness around 15 toasts later.

The next day was a write off. We didn't have to
play that day, but we were to be guests of honour
that evening at a reception party given by the British
Councillor and his wife at their house in the hills.

Martyn and Kirsten managed to peel themselves from
their bed and were driven to Green Hill, a rural idyll
just outside the city. Martyn was always keen to get to
a natural wilderness wherever we may be. Deirdre and
I on the other hand, were only capable of staying in our
bedrooms, nursing the world's biggest hangovers. Again,
we woke up as the sun was setting, dressed up for the
occasion, and were driven to the Councillor's beautiful
house in a salubrious suburb, heaving with people
keen to meet us all. The welcome we received was as

typically genuine and gracious as we'd had whilst being in Almaty. It was becoming very easy to fall for this country and its people.

On the day after, we actually woke up when the sun was rising. That day would be our last in Almaty before our hopefully less tedious flight home. It was the day of our biggest and longest concert, with Martyn performing with the symphony orchestra in the first half, followed by our own full set in the second half. Our venue for that night was a beautifully characterful opera house, with statues and busts of prominent figures from Soviet and Kazakh history adorning the public areas. The audience flowed in like a tidal wave. The energy they brought in with them was as positive and encouraging as you could hope for. Having mixed Martyn's live sound since 1995, I was always in the fortunate position to be able to soak up that energy from the audience. Every single gig had been epic, but that night it seemed more than ever that we were making a real difference.

During the first half, Kirsten, Deirdre and I listened to Martyn's performance with the orchestra from the stage wings. It was a dramatic sounding piece, with Martyn playing his pipes with his usual finesse and assurance. The temperature, noise and excitement had built into proportions probably seldom seen in that opera house by the time the curtain came up on the start of our gig. The oversized, family-orientated crowd had filled every possible space in the auditorium, cheering to the extent that the homemade sound system could barely be heard. Between the front row and the stage, soldiers from the Kazakh army stood side by side wearing their green overcoats and hats, keeping the security in check. They had the look of total discipline on their faces, yet you could tell that they were loving this as much as anyone.

At the end of the gig, I was invited onto the stage to take part in what felt like 20 curtain calls. We were each handed a bouquet of flowers from our hosts, and took the time to soak up the overwhelming emotions of a very special occasion.

This night was the epitome of why we did what we did. Of course, the never-ending travelling, the constant changing of time zones and crazy scheduling exhausted us to excruciating levels, but the joy we could bring and receive in the live environment always made everything more than worthwhile.

Kazakhstan turned out to be one of the most inspiring, heart-warming, eye-opening and memorable experiences we'd been through, either as a band or as individuals. We were welcomed and looked after to a degree of unconditional generosity and enthusiasm that none of us had experienced before. We felt very sad to leave on that Saturday morning, but we had a gig in Edinburgh to get back to that night.

The usual airport nonsense resumed as we checked in. 'That'll be £2,500 for excess baggage please Mr Bennett.'

Jamie may have been the official sound engineer, but the band's highly technological sound was another area in which Martyn would assume responsibility and thus nearly all of the workload. In an era in which boxed music was taking over live performances, that might be little more than mime, Martyn made everything live, and wanted everyone to know that it was so. Yes, there was the underpinning pre-constructed track, but his insistence that all the melody lines that wove around that were played by humans on stage was a very hard thing to achieve, or certainly to achieve exactly the way he wanted it. Kirsten again:

I think what was hard about that band was that it was all about driven playing. It wasn't about 'put some lovely expression into playing this' – it had to be driven because it was up against the track. The instruments were within the track – they weren't on top of the track – they were driven through the middle. So although you were a human person standing playing he was very specific about how it was played and the direction in which it was going and where the accents were.

To achieve this, Martyn didn't write out musical scores, as such, but worked out his own system of charts and grids, with each musical piece being divided into sections with the bar numbers marked in. These were handed out to the band members, and woe betide anyone who got lost! As well as playing keyboards, Kirsten was in control of the track, and her performance involved a great deal of counting:

So I had, say, 32 bars then hit a patch, theme one for 18 bars, rest for four bars, and so on. He just wanted something incredibly exact, incredibly in time. When I was on stage I only heard the track. I didn't hear anyone else. I had my own gig going on just myself! As long as I remembered arrangements and changing patches – the physical playing was easy. He wanted to have a dance music sound as live as possible which was a very strange concept at the time cos nobody else was doing that.

This method and depth of expectation placed enormous pressures on the band members individually but even more on Martyn technologically. 'He never found the easiest way to do things', Deirdre recalled, while Rory remembered that 'he did actually find performing pretty stressful.' Setting up the sound for gigs and dealing with glitches and repairs might mean

Martyn working for hours alone beforehand, sending the others out to get something to eat or to go shopping, saying, 'You can't help me.' For Deirdre, 'It was so based on technology people were expecting a show and if it didn't work we were really stumped.' This caused Martyn to have a love-hate relationship with the whole process, Kirsten concluding that 'Even though he loved the sound as an end product, he hated it'. On one occasion in Ottawa, she remembers him cutting his index finger while working on the tech set-up and fixing it with superglue! Sound quality was an area of frequent frustration for him; he was 'often not that happy after a show' because he had 'heard and logged every mistake.' Another irritant was the discrepancy in sound between the live arena over which Martyn had control and that on recorded performances. Needless to say, there were occasions when a power outage precipitated a crisis: during a performance at the Bongo club, the power cut out just as the band was about to play. Rory remembered that Martyn kept completely cool, shouting out to the audience a quote from an Indian mystic: 'Often, when something beautiful is about to happen, the forces of darkness try to stop it!' The power duly came back on and the show began! On another occasion the lead guitarist in Wolfstone shorted during a solo, so Martyn picked up Duncan Chisholm's electric fiddle and 'replicated the guitar solo note for note', according to reviewer, Sue Wilson. Martyn's ability on the pipes was something he fell back upon to entertain and engage in a variety of situations. After a gig in the Riverside in Hammersmith, when the crowd wanted more, he simply took out the pipes and 'enthralled them for another 20 minutes or so'. In Uist, faced with an audience in a much more intimate setting with people of all ages and including several piping afficionados, he played the pipes before the performance, preparing (if not priming) the audience to accept traditional music and instruments with which they were familiar, yet in an entirely alien soundscape.

Music was integral to experience and adventure for Martyn; a celebration of life. 'Fun' – that simple word – is mentioned a great deal as the band reminisce, and was clearly at the heart of Martyn's prospectus for Cuillin at the band's inception. Being on the road and seeing the world brought many magic moments. The intense concentration required on stage is perhaps why the events surrounding gigs seem to resonate as much if not more in the memories of band members than the gigs themselves. Rory recalled Martyn actually creating such a moment for him. Rory's bed was at the back of the tour bus and as they rolled into Detroit one morning, Martyn was awake and ahead of him, able to assess the views. He put headphones on his sleeping bandmate and faded in Brian Eno's 'Ascent', waking Rory and simply pointing out of the window. When he looked, there were 'derelict factories' and 'junkies on wastelands sitting around fires', like scenes from a movie and all to this amazing track. As Rory summed it up, 'He set that memory up for me.'

A classic and well-kent Cuillin moment was their performance of a set from *Bothy Culture* at the Buddha Bar in Paris in June of 1998, the night before the Scottish national football team was to be playing Brazil in the World Cup at the Stade de France. The audience contained a whole host of celebrity guests – in fact a veritable who's who of famous Scots, including Ally McCoist, Ewan McGregor, Alex Salmond, Kenny Dalglish, Jackie Stewart, Richard Wilson, Fred MacAulay and Sir Sean Connery, who famously leapt up onto the stage, grabbed the mic and boomed out 'Get up and dance. These guys are bloody great!' For Kirsten, this was not so welcome, as Connery (who later fell off stage right having removed his shirt and led some singing) managed to collide with and imperil her keyboard stand: 'One of the main things I remember from that performance was his sweaty back', she laughed. Spotting this situation, Ewan McGregor sat beside her to buttress the keyboards. However, Kirsten had experimented unsuccessfully with self-tanning cream just in advance of the show and could only wonder and cringe at the thought of this world-famous film star getting a close-up eyeful of her streaky legs! Deirdre, meanwhile was missing a button from her shirt and became heavily conscious of that with the celebrity presence on stage! And as Connery and McGregor later led the partying on the dance floor, Martyn was highly amused at the idea of *Trainspotting*'s Renton 'getting it on with James Bond'!

Rather than payment, the band had agreed to perform for travel expenses and a nice hotel. This turned out to be The Westminster, that was so posh that guests were never known to do their own laundry. The band had just returned from

Top: Sean Connery on stage with Cuillin, joined by Ewan McGregor (left, in lower picture).

America and all their clothes had been crumpled up in suitcases. However, the pressing of Deirdre's shirt turned out to cost a somewhat extortionate 30 euros to be ironed and was hanging from a chandelier when they reached their suites. Realising that the costs of ironing clothes for the whole band was going to be prohibitive, Martyn phoned for an iron and was initially refused. He therefore resorted to blatant exaggeration, saying 'You don't understand! These are traditional Scottish costumes. They're very delicate!' This worked, although the group hit a further snag when realising that they couldn't afford breakfast in the morning, a morning expedition for croissants took an unexpected turn when they were stopped by security on the way back, presumably for not resembling the usual clientele!

Another favourite Cuillin memory of Rory's occurred on arrival outside the Buddha Bar itself, when after going for a wander about Paris, the band found that they couldn't get through the gendarme's barricades in the crowded street outside the venue. Deirdre, fluent in French, assumed the role of chief negotiator along with celebrity impersonator Rory Bremner who seemed to find himself in the same predicament and had been booked to host the evening. Eventually, they were admitted forth to perform, to a massive cheer from the throngs outside; their own red-carpet entrance of sorts, and a source of great hilarity to the unassuming young band.

In July 1998 Martyn and the band took to the main stage at T in the Park at Balado near Kinross, one of the biggest mainstream music events in the UK at the time. Although they had played at dozens of festivals across Europe and beyond, this seemed like the big time, as they shared a platform that weekend with the likes of The Prodigy, Travis, Beastie Boys, the Stereophonics, Fat Boy Slim and Robbie Williams. It was an exciting time, of course, and yet Martyn couldn't help feeling a slight sense of frustration as he witnessed these household names perform right in front of him. His manager, Kenny MacDonald:

SATURDAY 11th JULY
Main Stage

MARTYN BENNETT
Acid croft meets Highland house.

HEADSWIM
Former rockers turned more thoughtful and better for it.

JAMES TAYLOR QUARTET
Hammond driven funk frolics.

TRAVIS
Rapidly rising good-time rock.

CATATONIA
Cerys 'Is that a canoe in your pocket?' Matthews calms the road rage.

SPACE
Wacked out, fun lovin', Scouse rock.

ROBBIE WILLIAMS
Clean, lean and mean, the non-stop pop machine wants to entertain you.

SEAHORSES
John Squires gives the frets a run for their money.

PRODIGY
Boggle-eyed techno/rock freaks slap their mics up.

I remember him wondering why he wasn't as big as Robbie Williams. And I can understand that in terms of him as a musician – he's the greatest musician I've ever known or worked with. He wasn't playing the game that Robbie

Williams was playing. But it was a valid question because, you know, 'You're better than him. But in this fake world that people buy into there's a reason why he's number one with "Angels" and you're battering your head off a wall'. And at the same time I remember his latest idea was a bagpipe version of the theme tune to Dallas! This was the new idea, and I'm, 'No, that's not going to work!' Maybe that's part of the genius – and Martyn *was* a genius – that sometimes you come up with mad ideas.

Cuillin may have been mixing now with stars of the rock world, but they didn't exactly fit the stereotype and never considered themselves to be typically hedonistic. They were all vegetarian, Martyn the strictest and for the longest period of time, from being a student at RSAMD when the BSE crisis had stimulated his curiosity about meat production and caused him to stop eating flesh on both health and animal welfare grounds. This he maintained for 13 years, Rory remembering that when Martyn picked him up in the car of a morning 'he was like Hannibal Lecter. He'd sniff and ask suspiciously, "Have you been eating *mackerel*?"' The band reminiscences reveal a robust inter-relationship that accommodated each other's foibles and in which good humour generally prevailed. Their collective eccentricities were somewhat at variance with the backstage behaviour of other bands at the time. Rory recalled their appearance at T in the Park, where 'the first things we asked for were a vegetarian restaurant and a local park' and then sharing the 'green room' portacabin backstage with Prodigy, who were 'being proper rock-n-roll.' Meantime Martyn was in the corner doing 'incredible' yoga, Deirdre was 'sipping herbal tea' and Rory himself was 'trying to meditate!'

The contrast between the huge and unglamorous challenges of meeting Martyn's musical remit and still being on a shoestring budget meant that when the band encountered big celebrities and had moments of extraordinary success, there was a large element of bewilderment. After a barnstorming session at Cambridge Folk Festival, selling over a thousand CDs on the back of one gig and breaking previous recording sales for a performance at this festival, Kirsten recalled 'We actually played after Joan Baez – it was only afterwards that I thought "What a funny gig!"' She hadn't had any time to be star struck; on the way down Martyn had changed their parts and they had several feverishly stressful hours learning them. It was hardly the epitome of stardom, and yet the contrast seems to make it all the more compellingly memorable years later.

Cuillin's performance at Cambridge in 2000 (they appeared under the name Martyn Bennett's HARDLAND) has achieved something of a legendary status. This festival is generally viewed in the folk world as 'the big one' – a chance to taste the atmosphere of a T in the Park or Glastonbury, and it regularly attracts headliners such as Paul Simon, James Taylor, Christy Moore and Joan Baez. Martyn and the team were not initially convinced that their brand of electro-acoustic music would fit in, and it seemed that their fears were to be realised when they struck up their first note in the soundcheck and a large group of dyed-in-the-wool folkies who had gathered in anticipation, fled for their lives. They actually ran away! Whether they ended up sneaking back in to join the few thousand others is not known, but it didn't take long to win the crowd over, and as the reviews, recordings and reminiscences testify, what followed was truly exceptional. In fact, Eddie Barcan, the long-standing director of the festival, voted that particular performance as the best he had ever witnessed. Paul Simon didn't have a look in!

The bothies and the hills were vital to Martyn's wellbeing. Kirsten comments that 'being in a mountainous place' was 'as important as music' to Martyn. His music and agenda were the overarching purpose of the group. While he was generous and caring, and believed profoundly in economic fairness both within the group and in the wider world, he was not essentially suited to collaboration and was also something of a loner by nature. 'I think he found friendships difficult', says Kirsten, while Deirdre observes: 'He liked the idea of community but found it more difficult than he'd have liked it to be.' Martyn and Kirsten moved to Mull in 2000, motivated in large part by Martyn's desire for a rural escape and nearness to mountains. However, Kirsten remembers that Martyn became 'disillusioned' there. The band remember a distinct 'shift' in his focus between the albums *Bothy Culture* and *Hardland*. He seemed to the rest of Cuillin to quite suddenly to reject any association with folk music, as Kirsten explains: 'After *Bothy Culture* he changed direction and almost hated the word "folk", so he wasn't, as far as he was concerned, a composer who wrote folk music. He felt misunderstood right to the end.' Martyn had also not had the gigs he had wanted, such as *Later with Jools Holland*. This combined with musical influences from listening to albums such as Leftfields's *Leftism* led Martyn onto a different tangent, of electronic sound as a 'bangin'', driving and dominant force.

This shift in emphasis tipped the balance for Rory Pierce, who was a composer himself. He decided to leave Cuillin. In his own words:

> It was getting too hard. I felt he was developing into this electronic hard world and that wasn't what I liked about his music. I liked the bothy stuff and the tunes and the folky stuff and as that disappeared I was like, I'm not really sure I can go along with this. I did leave the band early. I did love it. But it was his planet.

In Rory's recollection, the bothies and the mountains had been 'a vein of gold' for Martyn, furnishing him with creative sustenance and inspiration for many years. 'I think he fell off that. I don't think he found another vein until the songs and

Cuillin Mark 2. L–R Kirsten Bennett, Martyn Bennett, Deirdre Morrison.

storytelling' (in his final album, *Grit*). Martyn was confounded by Rory's departure, and Kirsten isn't sure Martyn ever really understood why he left. She recalled that he maintained an almost childlike, bewildered insistence 'that they were having such good fun!'

After Rory left the band, Cuillin carried on performing with just the remaining three members for a while. Martin Low was co-opted for the Millennium gig at Edinburgh Castle, when Cuillin supported Texas, and for further appearances at significant Scottish venues, at King Tuts and The Barrowlands. Subsequently, Martyn brought in a young lad from Mull, a DJ called Stewart Cattanach as a replacement for Rory. Deirdre recalled somewhat ruefully: 'Stuart was lovely but it felt like everything was changing'. The last gig Cuillin performed was a charity function in Dingwall where Wolfstone, a band Martyn had toured with previously on his own, were also playing. It was 'very poorly attended', as Kirsten recollected. Everything was soon to change forever as their lives would be thrown into turmoil by Martyn's illness. The Cuillin years would have a carefree innocence in retrospect that would seem both poignant and all the more memorable for its challenges, close camaraderie and the fun of shared adventures. Whatever the difficulties presented by Martyn's perfectionism and accompanying need for control, Cuillin was for a good time a cohesive and thriving band, and its story testament to the power of immense talent, and true friendship. Together they broke ground for a new generation of musicians, although the achievement of Cuillin musically remains uniquely visionary and inimitable, of a kind and time of its own.

8

Home

Mull. I chose Mull. I didn't really choose Mull. It seems like Mull chose me. Martyn Bennett

THE ISLAND OF Mull had been one of the starting points for Martyn's life in Scotland, a small boy newly arrived from Newfoundland with his mother, following her separation from his father, Ian. They didn't stay long, moving on after a short while, and eventually settling in Kingussie, but long enough to establish a connection. Mull was a footing stone in Martyn's life, and it was to there he gravitated when he left Edinburgh as a young man, looking to build the next phase of his life with Kirsten. As he later explained:

> We moved here when I was a small boy about five years of age and lived in a farm just up the road and it's funny to find myself back here because I couldn't think of any place else that is home to me really. I mean Newfoundland is where I was born, Newfoundland feels a bit like home too perhaps.

It certainly wasn't the case that Martyn and Kirsten were desperate to leave Edinburgh, for there was a plenty going on there both culturally and socially. Life was good, as their friend and fellow Edinburgh denizen, BJ Stewart, recalled:

HOME

We used to all hang around Tollcross in Edinburgh. It really was quite the vibrant community back then. Martyn and Kirsten had their little 'hobbit hole' flat there. It really was tiny so Martyn had built platforms in the bedroom and above his minuscule recording studio where they would skuttle about in spaces too small for your average man. So life seemed to revolve around the flat, Ndebele Café owned by Martyn and Kirsten's dear friend Jeni Ayris whose unique southern African cooking and ambient café attracted people from near and far. Then there was the Cameo Cinema and Burlington Berties pub where an incredibly diverse array of punters would gather night on night for years on end. The Ndebele crowd (featuring a very young Sam Heughan from *Outlander*), all of the Berties staff who never seemed to go home after their shift ended, the Cameo crowd, Filmhouse staff, actors and stage crew from the next-door King's Theatre, loads of musicians and Art School students, all the local chefs from the surrounding eateries – you name it. Everyone knew each other. Everyone liked each other. A huge Tollcross family. They were really happy days. If you were to go to Ndebele for breakfast or lunch or just a coffee, rest assured someone would be there to while away the day with. Any passing friends would be dragged in to join the party. I'm still amazed that Martyn got any work done at all but he clearly did. He was never a drinker so the pub wasn't his favourite place but he was no stranger to it. Sometimes he would visit just to pull me from my stupor, for a midnight sit in the Meadows, a wee 'toot of grass' on the Links or often demanding company to watch the sunrise from the top of Arthur's Seat. And then breakfast back at Jeni's Ndebele!

It would be too much of a stretch to conclude that Martyn had always harboured thoughts of returning to the island that had given him an early taste of life in Scotland, then, for he and Kirsten had no particular ambitions to settle there. Rather, it was a combination of various circumstances and connections that led to them leaving Edinburgh and moving to the island that would serve as home for the rest of his days. Kirsten's parents had moved there from Glasgow in 1993 when Kirsten and her sister, Julie, had both flown the nest in Bearsden. And on Martyn's side, his mother, Margaret, had become friendly with Mary Norton Scherbatskoy, founder of An Tobar, the arts centre in Tobermory. Margaret began to offer workshops there from time to time, along with the likes of James MacDonald Reid, and Martyn had joined them on occasion, 'blowing everyone away with his amazing playing' as An Tobar's director, Gordon MacLean, later recalled. This led to an invitation from Gordon for Martyn to take on a role as a musician in residence for a few months, and he offered him and Kirsten accommodation in Breadalbane Street in the town, where they stayed for a short while before moving across the Sound to the village of Kilchoan on the Ardnamurchan peninsula. Martyn took on the daily ferry commute with a certain relish, though often bunking down in the arts centre if he had been working on into the night, as he frequently did.[1] This residency didn't bring in much money – Gordon remembers it as being 'a few hundred pounds' – but the demands on his time were few, and he only had to do some teaching and a few workshops. The main purpose was to give him space to work, and he set his studio up in the upstairs space in An Tobar, ready to create new art. Gordon MacLean was more than happy to leave him the time and space to do so:

> As always, I think most of the time Martyn was working on his own stuff. I think what you found with Martyn was you thought he was doing something, whether it was a bit of teaching or a bit of this, but actually, he was doing

a hundred other things at the same time, that you knew nothing about. And all of a sudden you'd realise that something had happened that he'd been working hard on without you even really knowing about it until the concert happened, or the record came out, or I remember seeing him at a thing in Sabhal Mòr (the Gaelic College on Skye) where it was a very academic gathering of people and Martyn was presenting stuff to them and playing it as well, in that kind of a way that was so authentic.

Kirsten also reflected on this aspect of Martyn's character, that seemed to intensify when he was in Mull and as he became more widely known. 'He constantly developed: he never, ever had a day when he didn't do stuff.' She also described how collaborative projects and ideas involving working with others typically emerged from many of his encounters with other musicians and creatives. Indeed, Kirsten found herself fielding these increasingly as intermediary, or representative later on as his illness advanced.

He was not a manipulative person but he did say different things to different people depending on his mood, how he felt. If he felt a bit sorry for them, or if he felt he wanted to help them he would say things, and he always was genuine.

There had been a further impetus to move away from Edinburgh: 'a disastrous computer crash' had wiped out an entire new album on which Martyn had been working, as well as his materials for several theatre projects and various other commissions. Catastrophic losses of that kind were not unusual in those early days of computer-based composing and recording, and Martyn was by no means alone in suffering the consequences of unstable hardware. But to lose the best part of

a year's creative work would have been a major blow to any artist. At the end of that year, Martyn had planned to 'complete recording his third album due for release in early '99.' This album never materialised but it is nonetheless significant in his story.

Martyn had been building a collection of Robert Burns songs. Kirsten reminiscing with their friend, BJ Stewart, on the phone recalled in amusement: 'It came out of a project for Channel 4 TV; *Burns Alive and Kicking*, remember? It was a kids' TV series. So he was doing a project for the music for this kids' Burns programme and he was arranging a few Burns things for that. Remember he had Chris singing? And me playing the harpsichord, dressed up as a 12-year-old, and I was 22 or something!' BJ responded: 'It was truly hilarious. This was on Channel 4 television! Martyn was there, Chris,

Deirdre and Kirsten, all dressed up, prancing about Princes Street Garden, playing music and singing Burns stuff!' Kirsten again:

> It was funny because the context of all this stuff in the early '90s, or maybe the mid-'90s? There wasn't other people doing this funny stuff. There was something incredibly funny about it. Even we thought it was quite funny. So anyway, as with everything with Martyn, it has a knock-on effect in his mind and he thinks that he'd like to do some more Burns stuff, so he had Sylvia Rae singing as well on one of his tracks.

Sylvia Rae sang Auld Lang Syne to the alternative and lesser-known tune, while BJ Stewart also recorded in other notes that Martyn himself had sung 'Westlin Winds' and played the guitar on another track. Kirsten remembered

> he had a lot of material and he wanted to make it into an album but something happened. I remember him having months and months and months of emails and letters and phone calls to Roland. That thing crashed and he lost all of the samples, every single one. It wasn't a hard drive, it wasn't a main computer problem. He fought for a long time to get that fixed and he took it to people and ended up, it really annoyed him, he really bore a grudge about that actually, so it ended up he felt aggrieved, he felt like he'd lost a lot of work.

This was a major blow for Martyn, and one that he seems to have vented indirectly in interviews given around the same time. A TV feature in Canada but filmed partly in Edinburgh has Martyn being fairly negative about technology. Kirsten reflected on seeing this interview over 20 years later that it was 'familiar', containing

> that conflicted vibe of 'I fucking hate technology', because he did have a total hatred of it in some ways. In that interview he kind of implies that he does not like dance music, that he's using it as a kind of vehicle in order to get people to listen to the pipes. I wouldn't say that was the reality. He loved dance music, he went to clubs, he knew a lot about dance music, he knew all the latest DJs, what was going on in that scene. But he equally loved listening to pipes and playing and trad stuff, as he did for music from all over the world. He had a vast array of music that he listened to.

In Kirsten's recollection, the sampler crash and resultant loss of a whole album of material compounded increasing stress and frustration building in Martyn in relation to technology both on and off stage. She reflected:

> The unreliability of technology was really the thing. The other thing that really stressed him out was gigging. The stress of knowing that there were thousands of people coming into a room to hear you and with some click of something going wrong in this set-up it could all just go silent. When he had a band together he would get really stressed. He didn't act like that when he was performing. But it was the stress of the technology and everything needing to be looked after, tweaked, sorted. There was a LOT of technology on stage, there was hundreds of cables, and he hand-made every single one of them. He hand-made a lot of his gear.

The lost album and the intensity of touring were the flip side to the enormous amount of fun that Martyn and his

friends were having in this period. The pressures of technology arose from unpredictability, on and off stage, and the loss of the album material seems to have encapsulated this. It was not something Martyn tried to begin afresh. He moved on, creatively to other projects, and geographically to Mull, but it was a loss that rankled for a long time after nonetheless.

And so it was a combination of artistic calamity, family connections and circumstance that brought Martyn to the shores of this inner Hebridean haven as a resident in 1998. His years on Mull are important in understanding his development and his gifts as a composer and producer, artistically and technologically. At the time of moving there he had already developed a burning ambition to break into the hardcore dance club scene, something that continued to prove elusive. In consequence, his focus had shifted away from folk and traditional music and increasingly toward beats and technological sound, and so his studio set-up and equipment were at the very heart of his process. Kirsten:

> For him, production of sound was as important as what was in your head, or what you'd maybe written in your studio. It was about how to make what you'd written sound hugely amazing, so he spent a lot of money on gear and studios, and that was the most important thing – the quality of sound. So when he listened to music, it was often about how an album was put together and the sound that came out. I think by the end of Martyn's time of being involved with music he rather thought of himself as a producer, a sound engineer – a sound designer, he used to call himself – rather than a musician, or an instrumentalist. Definitely.

The seeds of this transition had been sown beforehand but seemed to harden into reality from the moment he moved to Mull and he worked long, hard hours in his studio. Gordon MacLean's recollections reveal the integral nature of the studio not just to Martyn's recording work but also to his performance and collaborations, recalling that he would revise and innovate tracks ahead of performances and after collaborative or production work:

> Probably every record that he made was made in a different way on completely different equipment, because each time he'd have maybe upgraded his computer, or he'd have new samplers. Cos he was always pushing the boundaries.

Deirdre recalled that he was forever updating or changing their parts in Cuillin between gigs, and sometimes even completely new music had to be learned en route to a performance. 'I wish people could see what his computer entries look like, because there's a lot of stuff going on', says Kirsten, describing the meticulous detail with which Martyn worked in collating, combining and crafting sound.

Outside of the studio, Martyn's maverick style suggested that he sometimes took his other duties, such as leading workshops, with less seriousness. Gordon MacLean recounted an incident when Martyn was giving a fiddle workshop at An Tobar. His approach was to take the class into a room and play his Highland pipes solidly 'at them' for the duration, the participants 'emerging shell-shocked' when it was finally over! While not everyone may have appreciated such a direct teaching style (and on a different instrument to the one which they were there to learn!), it may well have been that Martyn was drawing inspiration from one of his own early piping teachers. John MacDougall was also very fond of teaching through demonstration, and Margaret remembered how her son would love nothing more than to sit and listen to the maestro play.

Hard and Scottish

Soon after their arrival on Mull, Martyn was surprised to run into a musician who had also recently moved there, Dundonian Martin Low. Martin had been working in London as a sound designer and shared his close namesake's love of electronic dance music. 'We agreed that it was a tad weird to have turned up at the same time on an island with two recording studios and time to burn', Martyn later reflected, 'so we decided we would combine forces with the intention of forging an unusual new dance sound – one that was

The Studio, An Tobar, Mull.

intentionally Scottish, hardcore, and reflective of stuff going on in the rural and urban areas alike'.

The new collaborators' aims and ambitions may have been similar, but once they actually began working together it became clear that it might not all be plain sailing. Despite their common commitment to technological innovation in their music-making, they came from very different musical backgrounds, and this proved a somewhat thorny issue to negotiate.

'It quickly became apparent that our studio set-ups and mixing concepts were not immediately compatible' recalled Martyn. 'So he came to my studio and everything was done there. He sat with me and we did each other's heads in completely'. The starting point for their work together was a series of samples that Martyn had already been working on in Edinburgh and that had survived the computer crash, and despite their mutual frustration with working methods, Martyn did recognise that his new interlocutor could bring good things to the table:

> He's into minimal dark hardcore stuff that's really, really sparse and he did a great job of clarifying things by stripping back to perhaps one or two ideas. This was fantastically refreshing for me and I really took to his approach of clearing a space for simplicity. He oversaw a lot of the work I was doing and dismantled a lot of the arrangements. I overcomplicated things all the time and he stripped it all back to the way the punters want it to be if they want dance music cos he has no traditional music background. He'd sit there for days with me and say nothing and I'd get fed up and head off and he'd move into my seat and when I got back he'd taken virtually everything I'd done and left just one tiny element. And he'd say, 'That's the tune!'

It seems that Martyn was reciprocating, often working on his own in the studio into the small hours until sleep overtook him, and more often than not making his own alterations to their joint creations too. 'It got quite messy in the end', Martyn admitted. 'It's not really my album – but it's not his either'. And yet they did seem to settle on a division of labour that worked up to a point, and that offered new challenges to them both. 'In many ways we swapped our conventional roles', Martyn recalled. 'I ended up doing most of the urban elements as he turned his focus to the rural. It was turning into quite an interesting meeting'.

The end result of this 'interesting meeting' of minds was the album, *Hardland*. Recorded in An Tobar between March and November 1999, it was due to be released by Rykodisc, the same American label that had taken on *Bothy Culture*, and that had initially offered Martyn a three-album deal. However, the previous year the company had been taken over by Palm Pictures owned by English businessman and producer, Chris Blackwell, founder of Island Records. The new bosses calling the shots at Rykodisc 'didn't take to this new sound as readily as we had hoped', and Martyn suffered a serious setback both to confidence and finances when the label dropped him, refusing to have anything to do with *Hardland*. It was quite a blow, although Martyn did seem fairly philosophical about the whole affair when looking back on it later:

> With big labels supposedly struggling with a narrowing,
> media driven music industry, they are much less likely
> to back a maverick horse such as *Hardland*. In the end
> I had to find the money and a distributor in order to
> release it myself.

While self-releasing music is relatively common now, especially given the radical shift towards downloads and streaming, in the late '90s it was still all about CDs and actual physical distribution. It was an expensive operation to arrange sleeve and cover design, content registration, mastering, manufacturing, distribution and marketing – all of the tasks a record label normally undertakes, allowing their artists to focus on actually making music. It was that, principally, that made *Hardland* 'the difficult third album'. Nonetheless, there was no choice but to go for it, and Cuillin's continued success as a live band was earning them a solid income:

> Luckily we were fortunate to have sell-out gigs at the time. Playing King Tut's and Barrowlands in Glasgow, the Liquid Rooms at the Edinburgh Festival, a couple of big outdoor gigs in Spain and a huge turnout of 15,000 at the Cambridge Folk Festival were enormously helpful in releasing the album independently. I presumed that with things appearing to heat up we would attract some real media backing. But in fact it proved difficult to generate support from any particular musical corner and especially the dance community. It was frustrating because this was where I had hoped to take our sound.

So what *is* the sound of *Hardland?* It begins with a vocal sample of unknown origin, a Bowie-esque detached voice declaring that 'Love is Here'. The distant tones of Kurdish chants borrowed from Martyn's debut album give a subtle nod to earlier work, and the unexpected arrival of what he calls his 'naked practice chanter' points in turn back to *Bothy Culture*. The track, then, is 'basically a bridge from the previous albums', but a bridge, he hoped, to something rather more radical and hard-edged.

The fragmented tune that the chanter sounds is 'Cabar Feidh', or 'the Deer's Antlers', a piece of music that has deep resonance within the piping world in particular. It is 'traditional' in the sense that there is no known composer, generations of players therefore feeling that they were free to arrange and develop it as they pleased, and it is one of those rare tunes that sits well in many forms and time signatures, including as a march, a strathspey, a reel and a jig. 'Cabar Feidh' is the battle cry of the MacKenzies, and the tune also has a military connection and close association with the Seaforth Highlanders. It is melodically unusual too, being one of the few Highland pipe tunes in the key of 'G'. To what extent any of that mattered to Martyn or indeed to Martin Low is unclear and perhaps beside the point – it is a grand tune! It was clearly one they considered to be deserving of more than the briefest of treatments on a practice chanter, which soon gives way to the full Highland bagpipe, with a fiddle in the same pitch tracking it so closely that it is hard to tell the two instruments apart. The drum and bass undercarriage, while prominent from the start, builds to the point where it eventually overcomes the melody, which fizzles out mid-tune with a spark of static, leaving us with a finale of silence. It is deliberately severed and incomplete, and alerts the senses to a mishap, an accident, delivering the polar opposite of a conventional approach to an opening track on an album. We can read into that what we will: a sign of a broken tradition, perhaps, or a challenge to the concept of wholeness? In this dramatic beginning we are put on notice. This will not be a relaxing ride.

The tradition may have been broken, but it revives in the second track, 'Love Machine', in the form of an old reel called 'Kissing is the Best of All'. It is played on fiddle at break-neck pace, 140 beats per minute to be precise, the hundreds of hours Martyn had spent converting himself from classical violinist to folky fiddler paying off handsomely here. Underneath, on top and all around, the assorted electronic distortion, sirens, yelps and wails do their thing on a 'genuine Roland 101, 303 and 909 courtesy of Mr Low', and as always it is grounded to the dance floor with that steadily pounding bottom end. The solid ground of a pibroch forms the heart of the next track, 'The Little Spree' being another classic learned from Captain John MacLellan in Martyn's youth. It is not Martyn who performs it here, though, but rather Rory Pierce who is invited in to float his ethereal uilleann pipes over another lively and complex foundation. The tune is one of three said to have been composed by a MacGregor piper of Glen Lyon in the 18th century, all inspired by the drunken exploits of a local blacksmith, but it is about as far from a drink-fuelled dance tune as we can possibly imagine, and is generally perceived and performed very much as a lament. That contradiction would have appealed to Martyn, I'm sure, and Rory does a fine job of teasing out the pathos, 'quite beautiful – almost vocal', Martyn felt, while everything else parties on at full throttle below.

Ever one to explore varying approaches to the same piece of music, both 'Threadbare' and 'Distortion Pipe' are based on a tune called 'Out of Bed' composed for Martyn by piper and whistle player, Fred Morrison, husband of fellow Cuillin member, Deirdre. Fred was and is a player of immense talent, and like Martyn is something of a perfectionist as well as a man of great flamboyance and exuberance on stage. To Martyn, Fred is 'a true artist – perfecting his art by candle-light – one of the finest pipers the world has ever seen'. Martyn and Kirsten became close friends with the Morrisons and inevitably, when they were together the tunes would flow. One of them suggested it might be nice for the two couples to form a band together, but Martyn was quick to dismiss the idea: 'it would be too much like fucking Abba'! The work of another two prolific modern composers of pipe tunes also features on the album, 'Handshaker' by Allan MacDonald serving, according to Martyn as 'a total jibe at fuck-wit cops' while 'Good Drying', which has since become something of a modern classic by Roddy S MacDonald, forms the basis of 'Play', which Martyn considered the best track

Cuillin Mark 3. L–R Martyn Bennett, Kirsten Bennett, Deirdre Morrison and Stewart Cattanach.

on the album. As Roddy has since confirmed, he had to get in touch with Martyn following the album's release to point out politely that the tune was not in fact 'trad', but belonged to him! Martyn was apologetic and altered the registration paperwork to ensure Roddy was able to collect the royalties due. Alongside the 'fantastically mental' main melody is a 'lovely lyrical tune' on guitar and strings that was written by Martin Low for his daughter Ruby and his wife Sheena.

When Martin Low listened to Martyn's earlier work he was rather taken with the 'Deoch an Dorus' track from his first album featuring samples of Harry Lauder doing his stuff from the 1930s, and suggested that they have a go at remixing that. The eventual result was 'Harry's in Heaven', which retains the jocular Lauder quips and the melodic tones of the bagpipe reel, 'Sleepy Maggie', but which otherwise constitutes a very thorough reworking of just about everything else. It is harder and edgier than the original, Lauder's comical tartan-camp music hall delivery seeming even more outlandish in this hardcore setting. Harry is playing to the crowd, and there's more than a hint of them responding, cheering him on, lauding him as the pop star he undoubtedly was in his day. A highly catchy and moreish guitar riff breaks the mood with an apparent nod – intentional or otherwise – to 1970s television theme music, a gritty American detective series perhaps. Full of sound it certainly is: loud and mighty, bold and bawdy. On the latter theme, asked why 'Harry is in heaven' in this track, Martyn (no doubt with a sly grin) explained: 'We think that the breakdown section sounds like he's chugging on his wire so-to-speak'!

Martyn had concluded that successful dance music is 'ultimately all about finding the thing that is absolutely gorgeous and you just do it again and again and again'. That is certainly the line they took in 'Rasta Plan', his practice chanter again being pressed into service with a two-note mini phrase serving as the glue that binds the five-minute track together from top to toe. There is much barely coherent blethering from assorted random voices, a short, improvised passage on the doudouk, and a pounding drum and bass bottom end that always brings to mind, for me at least, a galloping herd of heavy horses. 'The bass in *Hardland* is unusual', Martyn warned us. 'It's very rough and I think that is kind of my trademark now'. And of course his other trademark, visual not aural, was what gave the track its title. He loved his dreadlocks and seemed especially chuffed that they made him look uncannily like the Swedish footballing superstar who played for Celtic, Henrik Larsson!

The remaining three tracks on the album all draw on material derived from the William Dixon collection Cuillin had been playing in their live sets on tour, and that Martyn had first performed as solo pieces at the Peebles gathering to launch the collection in 1997. 'How it Got There' features 'The Lasses Bushes Brawly' along with 'voices recorded randomly on a vintage Robertson wireless that was sitting in the studio'.

An anonymous voice announces: 'I know what the animal is, but I really don't know how it got there'! Next up, 'This Sky Thunders' uses a melodic phrase from 'Over the Dyke and Til Her Laddie' (as Martyn points out, a reference to 'the art of shagging'), while 'Snipe Shadow' is based on 'Saw Ye Never a Bonnie Lass'. Again, a voice joins in the track, but not a random one this time, as Martyn later explained at length:

> The poet, artist and boat-builder Ian Stephen of Lewis composed some words to it as he thought it reminded him of the old-fashioned Scottish pastime – lying with a woman in a nice field of barley-corn. The poem contains the names of various old types of grain-crops that were indigenous to Scotland that have basically died out in the last 20 years due to EU Registration policy: all grains that are now grown in Britain and Europe are subject to stringent rules that standardise their yield, shape and volume so that they can be processed by a standard mechanised system.

Martyn went on to expound theories about the potential deleterious effects of these 'new grains' on human wellbeing, and indeed on his own health in particular, a theme he returned to often a few years later once serious illness had set in.

At the time of the release of *Hardland*, the immediate imperative was to start selling the album and the best way to do that was to play it live. Some of the material, especially the sets based on the William Dixon tunes, had already featured regularly in Cuillin's live gigs, but in order to help promote the new release, the band changed its name to 'Hardland Live' – a fairly direct and unambiguous form of marketing! Rory Pierce had already left to follow his own path, and so Martyn, Kirsten and Deirdre were joined by Stewart Cattanach who operated the decks and samples, as well as Martin Low himself for a short while. This change of personnel cannot have been without upheaval, however it was a testament to the remaining members that they adapted quickly and without fuss. For audiences that had been accustomed to seeing Cuillin, the overall sound they produced on stage remained fairly consistent with what had gone before, and the musical content, in its live setting, was by no means radically altered. Martyn may have felt that the music of *Hardland* was 'hard and Scottish' but a characteristic of his work that had always been present was now front and centre, a defining force. And his later reflections that the album 'is simply about the language of rhythm and melody' came as little surprise to his fan base. Surely these elements had been at the core of his art from the start? Nor did his assertion that 'it is an album which reflects a harsh rural environment, but is also strongly connected to modern urban culture' convince us that here was something entirely new. Surely that would have served as a pretty perfect summing up of *Bothy Culture* too? Perhaps that is true, but Martyn himself was convinced that there were significant stylistic differences between the two albums, especially when it came to the contrasting moods that lay at their core:

> My previous album, *Bothy Culture*, was written for the sit-down aural experience. It is all about new melodies (non-traditional), clean mixes and exotic ideas. It is also a very positive sounding album, full of life and light. *Hardland*, on the other hand, is all about simplicity, bass, rhythm and power. I think it is also full of life, but I realise that it is quite dark in many ways.

It is hardly surprising that he was eager to reflect on its value following its release, given its rejection by the record label. Perhaps it had moved *too* far away from his previous work, he suggested, rather than being too similar, and for some, he

HOME

felt, 'it is frankly shocking'. It was without doubt a major shift to a different kind of album in his view, but they had failed to take the audience and critics with them. Maybe they were not listening to it in its right setting, he suggested:

> I would add, however, that if you listen to *Hardland* at breakfast time (i.e. quietly) then perhaps you may have missed the point. Many reviewers have said, 'Oh, I went to your live show and it was tremendous, but when I stuck the CD on at home I was a little disappointed.' I would suggest, therefore, that *Hardland* is actually a studio 'live album' and sounds best with bass and sub-bass capability at around 105 dB to the centre of the room!! (This basically means have a party, set up the PA and crank it up if you please.) *Hardland*, to some, may be 'the difficult third album' but I believe it makes an important statement about how old traditions can survive. Fundamentally *Hardland* forces a relationship between two apparently opposing worlds, but their common ground is still that of personal expression – 'the dance tune'. At one end of this spectrum are the roughest elements of a very, very old folk tradition, whilst at the other there are the hardcore elements of an ultra-modern club culture.

Kirsten agreed:

> I actually think people don't get *Hardland*, don't get what it was, what it is. They think it should somehow follow on from *Bothy Culture* and be a precursor to *Grit* and it was nothing to do with either of these, even if it used some of the same little bits of melody somewhere, it was not the same kind of album at all. It was a collaborative album in that he was looking for someone else to push out the other stuff and leave a driven, simple, dancy, punchy sound.

Another issue to deal with was where to aim for when it came to playing gigs with this new material. Cambridge Folk Festival director, Eddie Barcan, wanted Martyn and the band to play there in 2000, having loved Cuillin's performance there two years earlier:

> I'd been really keen to book him, but his management were actually quite nervous – they really didn't think he'd be right for the festival, given how hardcore his music had gone at that point. Anyway, he just exploded onto the stage, and I knew it was going well when I saw the people in the disabled viewing area bouncing up and down in their wheelchairs. It's still one of the most exciting things I've ever seen at the festival. I went to thank him when he came offstage and – being a true Scotsman under his kilt – he flashed me![2]

Live performances were still going down well, then, but the disappointing thing for Martyn was the fact that much less critical attention was paid to *Hardland* than to his previous albums. This was almost certainly a product of going it alone without the backing of a label, rather than the quality of the music itself. It was and remains a very strong album, but the reviews and press features were few and far between. Those that did appear were largely positive, Andrew Williams of *The Metro*, for instance, considering it 'the first truly Scottish sounding hardcore album', while Tim Perry of *The Independent* labelled it a 'masterwork' and lauded its 'forceful collision of urban and rural culture'. He certainly recognised that 'a new-found punkiness' lent it 'a harsher edge than his previous recordings' and had high hopes for the prospects of 'hard-won recognition from the harder edge of the dance community'. John Crosby loved it, enthusing in *Time Out* about the 'orchestra of pipe overtones, rushing forward relentlessly on a tidal wave of electronic beats'. 'Bennett and his collaborators succeed', he concluded, by 'infusing their creation with an intoxicating magic and frantic abandon'.

Perry's hopes that the album might help open doors to greater acceptance and recognition by the dance club scene were not realised, sadly. Martyn tried hard to persuade clubs such as Slam in Edinburgh to put on a *Hardland* night, but to no avail. They never 'got' the folk music aspect of it, he felt:

> It was just too hard to shake that woolly jumpers image no matter how it was played. They either think it's crap or that it's making fun of a serious dance genre. They don't hear it as serious dance music with a different edge. You'd be surprised how closed it all is.

He began to conclude that he had approached the whole crossover from the wrong end. 'The only way it could have worked would have been if I'd established myself as a dance artist first. I did it wrong. I tried to satisfy two worlds that can't be reconciled immediately'.

Although not stated on the cover, the album had actually been marketed as *Hardland Volume 1*, the intention being to follow up with a second instalment that would serve as the final release of the three-album agreement with Rykodisc. That was clearly not going to happen now, and Martyn's impending illness may well have stood in the way of that in any case. The result is that in many ways *Hardland* wasn't so much the *difficult* album, but has become the *forgotten* album. It is now virtually unobtainable, second-hand copies appearing for sale from time to time on the internet for up to £100, a price that committed collectors seem willing to pay. Martyn himself was typically both candid and philosophical about the whole process which had not been the most enjoyable of his projects to say the least. Yet he remained proud of it, and

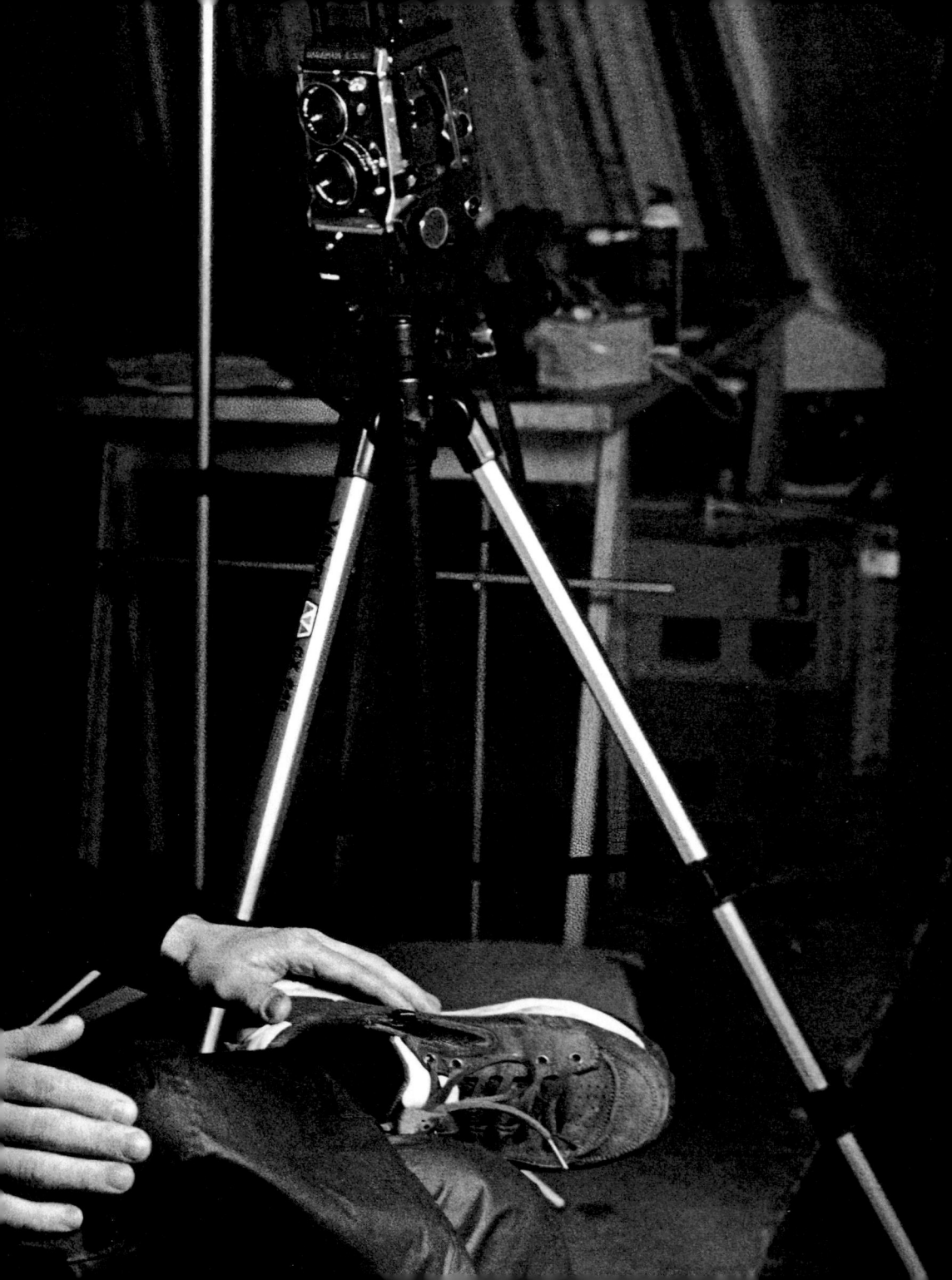

optimistic of its ultimate fate:

> Finally, I would say that the experience of making, releasing and touring *Hardland* was a bit of a mind-fuck from beginning to end. It was confusing. Perhaps it is a record that makes no sense but makes a statement none the less that old traditions can survive in a hard way.
> I hope that someday it will be viewed as an important album – perhaps one that pushed frontiers farther than they could be seen.

It *is* an important album, and is certainly one that deserves to be better known. But ever the optimist, Martyn was already looking towards his next projects, and was content to draw a line under this one and move on. 'I think that the next album, *Glen Lyon*, will soothe people's ears again, delight traditionalists and keep *Bothy Culture* lovers happy' he later announced. However, the essential mission of *Hardland*, that of 'driving traditional music into the 21st century', was anything but forgotten as far as Martyn was concerned, and was one that would resurface in his final album, *Grit*. *Hardland* hardened his commitment to reinvention and reinvigoration of traditional sound with technology. He knew where he wanted to go next, and despite the cancer that was waiting for him around the corner, he went there bravely, boldly and with his newly shaved head held high.

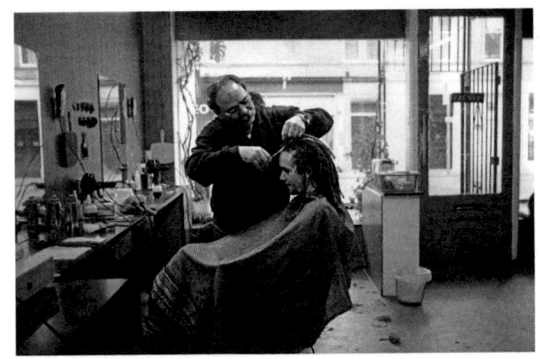

9

Glen Lyon

IN TERMS OF a preparation for the creative path that he pursued, bringing old to new and sharing authentic oral tradition with the world, Martyn Bennett was raised in an optimal environment: surrounded by the best of teachers, musicians, storytellers, instruments and opportunities. With this shared history of fieldwork, traditional song and story, it was a natural development when Martyn decided to produce an album featuring his mother's voice.

He had made recordings of Margaret singing while in Edinburgh a couple of years prior, as he later explained in an interview:

> I just actually recorded my mother singing in 1999 because I wanted to capture her voice, because she was singing very well at the time; her voice was really in good nick, and sometimes I think voices can come and go. I just thought it would be good to have them recorded, you know? And I also had a good mic at the time, which I was borrowing. And then it was about two years later, so about 2000 that I started working and I actually made *Glen Lyon* very quickly; I made it in about two weeks, just the arrangements around the songs.

For Margaret, the recording session was a highly memorable

and special experience. She was astonished by how well Martyn knew the songs and also by his authority and ability in the role of producer. She wrote in notes diarising the experience later that evening:

> Every song got a different reaction – and from his responses to them he clearly understood songs from the inside out. I had never given this a real thought until we were in the studio – this must be my first real insight into Martyn's commitment to song, for I had never really seen this close up.[1]

Margaret later remarked to her own mother: 'I learned more about singing from Martyn in two days than from anyone else in the previous two decades.'[2] He was adamant that the feel of the song had to be right, and was determined to get the truest performance of each one from his mother. In one there was a line she kept getting wrong, so she set up a music stand in front of her and sneaked a glance at the lyrics as she went for the next take. 'I can hear your eyes on the paper' he announced![3] 'Take note, all you singers', Margaret quipped to me, 'who can't get through a song without paper or a phone in front of you. It can be heard'!

Martyn was quietly revealing his profound interest and underlying depth of understanding in song and word, and starting a more serious creative journey in his exploration of tradition. Whereas he had long been highly conscious of marketing to a mainstream anglophone audience, following *Hardland*, he now had real hard-won experience of this process and the challenges involved. A new personal dimension of rootedness was emerging in his artistic observation and practice, this one running counter to mainstream and mass commercialism. It is more evident on the album that became *Glen Lyon* than perhaps any other, for this one is immersed in the

particularity of place, nature and family tradition. Martyn's own mother, grandmother and great-great-grandfather are voiced on the album and there are songs that were themselves taught to his mother and passed on to him by his grandmother, Peigi, with whom he shared a very special bond. The pipes played by Martyn on the album belonged to his grandfather.[4]

Details of nature symbolism resonate throughout this album, where the specificity of samples Martyn worked into the tracks is remarkable and deliberate, down to the buzzing of insects and the mechanical noise of a threshing machine. *Glen Lyon* as an album breathes from the inside, a living entity: it evinces real memories, events and places. While it is voiced principally by his mother, it is a personal tribute echoing key influences that had shaped Martyn's life and music: geology, history, wilderness, tradition, folklore, family.

Martyn incorporates too his longer maternal lineage, creating a fresh embodiment of traditions and memories from generations past. In this way, he evokes both continuity and change, the redemptive beauty of art and nature, and the scars of loss and war, placing the album purposefully at the intersection of artistic tradition, technology, land and livelihood.

As Martyn himself quietly emphasised, this album has been crafted with great attention to detail, each song set in its own soundscape. He described a scientific dimension to the resulting tracks in his cover notes:

> Many of the sounds that are specific to these songs may have geological implications as well as seasonal ones and I spent several weeks making field recordings of elements such as wind, water, agricultural and maritime machinery, birds, and even insects (listen for the bee!). These are the sounds that pertain to a song's ambience or inner meaning.

The album cover itself is also an expression of this fastidious attention to detail: the photographic images selected were taken at a spectacular immersive art event held to mark the millennium involving a two-hour trail in the heart of Glen Lyon, with lights and music along the way. Featured on this were the famous twin rocks in the glen, known as 'The Praying Hands of Mary' and 'Fionn's Rock', reflecting the layers of religious and cosmic beliefs of the people who named them, and the meaning this special site held for locals over the millennia. They are a symbol of ambiguity in their dual formation and have long provoked mystery about whether they are man-made or natural. 'Fionn' was the legendary outlaw hunter-warrior, Fionn Mac Cumhail, (usually termed Fin McCool in English) who is at the centre of another cycle of songs and stories, handed down over the generations in both Scotland and Ireland. The folk of Glen Lyon claim him for themselves, viewing their soils, slopes and caves as having been the main stage on which he acted out his miraculous deeds, although there are many places across Scotland that make similar claims. It is characteristic of Martyn's consciousness of paradox and ambiguity that he has a large image of the rocks on the interior of the CD, the disc itself sitting in the cleft. In what one senses is also a deliberate decision, the font on the cover notes and credits is so tiny it might itself have been written by the fairies; the effect is to pull us right in, inviting us to be inquisitive and zoom in on the minuscule in the act of reading, exploration, and engagement with the individual tracks.[5]

The physical glen itself is totemic to this album, as symbolic as the split standing stone, embodying man and nature intimately and intricately interwoven, both place and song transcending time. Such themes were clearly featuring boldly in Martyn's consciousness, artistically and philosophically, as he produced *Glen Lyon*. While he had recorded his mother singing selected Gaelic songs at the end of 1998, it was, as Margaret had emphasised, without a theme or an overarching concept, and simply prompted by opportunistic factors: he felt his mother was in good voice at the time and he had access to a recording studio in Edinburgh. Margaret recalled that he asked her to make a list of around 30 Gaelic songs, and that he would choose what he wanted! While almost all of the songs he selected relate to family, the only *obvious* thing that the songs have in common is that they are in Gaelic, as Dai Woosnam pointed out in his review in the folk music magazine *The Living Tradition*:

Martyn with his mother, Margaret.

One bit of nit-picking: the album's title bears the subsidiary title of 'A Song Cycle'. Now, this is a puzzle. To most of us, that description suggests songs that are closely linked to a theme: here, from the brief translations shown, there would seem to be no common theme apart from the fact they are all sung in Gaelic. Now 15 tracks in ENGLISH would not constitute a song cycle, would it? The album is impressive enough. To add 'a song cycle' is just a bit pretentious. A touch of 'gilding the lily', methinks. And one final thing. The album shows no running times. Why not? Is this somehow 'infra dig' with a SONG CYCLE?[6]

At first glance Woosnam seemed to make a valid point. 'Griogal Cridhe' is the only song on the album that is actually located in Glen Lyon, while Martyn's Highland family connections on his maternal line, such as his great-great-grandfather Peter Stewart (who had been the first of his ancestors to be recorded) hailed from Skye. Some thorny questions therefore surround Martyn's choices and rationale in the making of *Glen Lyon*: why did he choose the by-line 'A Song Cycle'?[7] And why did he omit running times when he surely knew that would be less advantageous for having the tracks played on radio? Above all, why did he pin it to Glen Lyon rather than any of the other iconic locations associated with the featured songs, such as Culloden or Skye?

It is through close listening to this album that we find answers to such questions. Martyn was compelling us to listen attentively and closely, for in the details, and *only* in the details, we find the themes that hold together the album as a 'song cycle': intimacy, family, separation from land, the seasonal rotations, technology, love and survival. By excluding the higher editorial categories, such as the timestamps for each song, Martyn literally blends them into one cycle but he also forces our ears and eyes to look more closely, more attentively, and then to find things we might otherwise have missed. Far from being pretentious or 'gilding the lily', he is playing with perspective, inviting us to make fresh discovery in familiar stories and landscapes, features beyond the obvious of song length and even the language in which it is sung. As a foray into sound design, it is mighty in its subtlety and nuance. The album is suffused at every turn with cyclical elements and symbolism. The songs have cyclical refrains throughout, resonating with the idea of a 'cycle' as a term for a collection of ancient stories or songs, passed down through time immemorial. This was a concept that Martyn encountered both in his time studying at RSAMD and in wider Gaelic culture, where the 'cycle' was a conventional term for song and story collections going back to the early medieval era. Using sounds of sea and shore (tidal cycles), the use of gunshot at the beginning and end of 'An Thearlaich Oig', the use of refrains, the inclusion of Peter Stewart and Martyn's grandmother demonstrating sound recording as a cyclical component in his own family – all these combine to show that songs have to be repeated to be stored, that transmission and thus tradition itself are dependent on repetition. By sampling recordings made on a wax cylinder (note the cylindrical turning object) and tape recorders (also revolving), Martyn is reflecting that mechanisation has lifted these songs out of human memory and into an archive where they can be played and replayed, mixed and remixed. 'A song cycle' seems to be a perfect summation of all this activity!

The photographs chosen for the album cover of *Glen Lyon* are entirely in keeping with this repurposing of legend, lore and nature using new sound technology, at a precise time in history when there was a hugely heightened consciousness of such things. The millennium was celebrated in Scotland with all manner of cultural events throughout the country and Glen Lyon was chosen by NVA, an arts company specialising in site-specific theatre, for a project called *The Path*. With lighting installations along a two-mile route encompassing the Praying Hands rock, it was designed to encourage public engagement with the relationship between land and people, historically and at the turning of a new millennium, looking forwards. The event ran from late May to early June in 2000, when North Perthshire nights are long and light. Himalayan traditional musicians performed en route in 'an elemental comparison with one of the world's other great Highland cultures.'[8] Margaret and Martyn had been asked by NVA for a suitable song to play at the event and they gave the recording of what would become *Glen Lyon*. It was exactly this kind of fusion, bringing old to new in an immersive experience, that appealed most to Martyn. By now he was at the forefront of a movement that embraced tradition and made it hip again, that reached out and joined hands with others globally, and that sought to raise awareness of relationship to land, nature, and place. Through individual and personal encounter with the local, something universal – not just global, but *cosmic* – was available. Though not directly involved in the project, Martyn and Kirsten walked *The Path* and it inspired Martyn to obtain a licence to use a photograph of the installation for the cover of his forthcoming album.[9]

It would be easy to overlook this highly visual element in Martyn's creative process and imagination. Art was another one of his talents, one that manifested early in his life, and in fact he thought he might follow a career in art until the time he moved to Edinburgh and music school as a teenager. His grandmother described how he would lie in bed sketching every night, and there are indeed many examples of drawings throughout his life that Margaret included in *It's Not the Time You Have*. 'He was constantly sketching', she recalled in a presentation at the Royal Conservatoire of Scotland on Martyn's life and music, adding that when sitting in an orchestra in his teens he seemed to have a fascination for the conductor's hands,

BRAVE NEW MUSIC: THE MARTYN BENNETT STORY

which he would draw as he sat waiting for his cue. When he was rehearsing the band for Cuillin performances, he would talk about 'seeing it', meaning the end result, and he would draw or sketch as part of his creative process for every album. Of the *Grit* track, 'Blackbird' he later reflected that from first inspiration 'I could see the whole thing'.[10] His close friends and family often describe him as being driven by a singular 'vision'. In light of all this, the artwork on this album cover has to be considered as significant; a pictorial guide to Martyn's overall visualisation of the album as a creative entity.

Glen Lyon, then, depicts a journey into landscape and back in time, but it also *looks* futuristic. The cover image evinces Martyn's geologist father, as well as the influences of several lifetimes of Highland lineage, of people rooted in the land. However, the coordinates superimposed on the main image pay homage to science and technology – they seem to introduce another language, this time visually, another way of orienting ourselves in space and time, another way of expressing our connection to and comprehension of place, of land. Yet they are also timeless, for these mathematical bearings would apply to the stones over many lifetimes and countless millennia. The space-age psychedelic superimposition of the code on the album cover echoes Martyn's use of technology in presenting the songs within, for audiences present and future. Coordinates, after all, are

by definition a way of making a place accessible to others, in this case so that they too can visit in person and experience being in exactly the same spot for themselves. The mapping and orientation element in *Glen Lyon* is later carried through in *Grit*, the visual emphasis on the cover there being a trig point, again suggesting that Martyn's creative train of thought was engaged in an ongoing process of reconfiguration and reorientation. And Martyn had placed song at the heart of it all.

Let us turn to the song at the centre of the *Glen Lyon* title and the final track on the album, that is known popularly as 'Griogal Cridhe', or 'Glenlyon's Lament', and which had special significance for Martyn. 'Both the song and the place have long been a source of fascination for me' he commented in his album notes. Margaret reflected on the path to this significance:

> A family favourite taught to me by my mother, it was also a favourite of Hamish Henderson's. Hamish's roots are in Perthshire, and over the years I sang it for him many times, almost always at his request – at festivals, ceilidhs, and celebrations such as his 70th, 75th and 80th birthdays, and Martyn was at a good few.[11]

The song, set in Glen Lyon, tells a story that parallels *Romeo and Juliet* in the power of its archetypal romantic plot: two young lovers from rival families in conflict with each other forming a marriage based on love rather than arrangement. This, of course, is unacceptable in a highly conventional kinship society where marriage was used to consolidate or extend political and territorial power, and where love was a mere incidental. Sung in the narrative voice of its composer, Marion or Mor Campbell, it transports us back to 1570 and the beheading of her lover, outlaw Griogair Ruadh, who was chief of the clan MacGregor, by the hands of her own father and cousin. Mor's father, Duncan Campbell, was one of the Campbell client chiefs presiding over Glen Lyon, territory that had been taken from the MacGregors, for whom Glen Lyon had been a stronghold since early medieval times.[12] Telling of the romantic love between the daughter of a Campbell noble and the young chief of the clan MacGregor, the story centres around societal restrictions and feuding between their own families, forcing the young lovers to live as fugitives in nature before Griogair is captured and beheaded in public at Balloch (now Taymouth, Kenmore) but then the main residence of Mor's cousin, the powerful Cailean Liath (Grey Colin Campbell of Glenorchy), aided and abetted by her own father. In this and the other Gaelic songs, the deeply personal speaks to universal experience. Griogair is the rightful chief of the MacGregor clan and the song composed by his grieving and traumatised widow, in the first person and addressed to their infant son. Mor was apparently forced to bear witness to the execution, and relives the vivid trauma of her experience. In the version Martyn quotes in translation in his notes this is emoted in full visceral force: 'Dearest beloved one, they spilled your blood yesterday. They put your head on an oak stob and left your body lying...' Poor Mor is utterly distraught, saying that she has torn all of her hair. Mor, as was so frequently the case for a young widow in the clan nobility, was being sent to an arranged marriage with another nobleman, this one much wealthier than the disinherited Griogair, and her agony at this prospect is heart-rending, saying that she would rather be driving cattle down the glen with Griogair than with the 'baron', wearing 'silk'. Here the public and private are intricately bound in the culmination of a dispute over land, and the distraught widow gives voice to the powerlessness of women in this situation. In its musical presentation, this track is the simplest on the whole album. Martyn plays the fiddle accompaniment with a profound sensitivity but the voice has centre stage.

The *Glen Lyon* album as a whole is rooted in female perspective and themes of loss predominate. It encompasses 15 Gaelic songs from different parts of the Highlands, a full third of these of women singing of unrequited love; four are laments, and the remainder are work songs and wildcards, in terms of genre. The first track on the album, however, features a man; a 1910 wax cylinder recording of Martyn's maternal great-great grandfather, Peter Stewart, beginning with a whistling noise transporting us back in time and place, yet paradoxically evocative of a sci-fi *Back to the Future* time machine! It arrives to an abrupt terminus at Peter, a farmer from Skye, singing in Gaelic for the briefest of moments, sounding exotic and distantly otherworldly, echoing eerily from the faraway past.

The intonation and cadence are strongly reminiscent of a Native American chant, probably, due to cinema and popular culture, a more familiar sound to many a Scottish ear than the Gaelic singing, and undoubtedly an irony in Martyn's awareness, given the 'Moccasin' song to follow later in the album. This immediately sets up the themes of the album: family, relationship to land, and the use of technology in changing Highland rural lives (the sounds of a threshing machine are included, for example), and also in recording and thus preserving the past to make it available to current and future generations. It links the local to the global in its sounds. The whole album has a subtle grainy texture, evoking a field-recorded atmosphere, lent in part by Martyn's own recordings of nature and agricultural machinery but also more generally. Martyn is 'creating new from the old' as Sheila Stewart was later to remark;[13] he honed his alchemy skills fusing family and folklore, drawing directly on what had been transmitted to him – Gaelic songs from his grandmother, ethnological recording from his mother, and songs of the landscape that had been home to generations of

his own people. Martyn in *Glen Lyon* is starting to explore how we orientate ourselves in time and place, and how we might preserve this by applying technology, recasting it with added novelty and appeal in order to carry it forwards into the as yet unknown.

The first track yields to the sound of Martyn playing the smallpipes on '*Buain a Choirce*' joined after the initial note by an echoing techno beat reminiscent of an agricultural machine. A rhythmic pulse beats out after the chorus, created from a sample of a 1920s threshing machine recorded by Margaret herself in Quebec in 1976, shortly before returning with Martyn to a new life in Scotland. Not only is Martyn moving us forward in time technologically, he is beginning with a song from an annual event, evoking the interdependent cycles of human and natural environment in confluence and harmony. Another two observations about this rhythm element bear noting: the sample was recorded by his mother; and the recording takes place overseas. The break in human patterns of existence incurred by emigration to the New World seems here to shift in his own family from actually farming land to *recording* the farming of land with new technology and now Martyn is replicating this in the music of his maternal lineage. The whistle joins the pipes as the song progresses to a simple end, the steady 4/4 rhythm evincing not just the threshing machine but the use of song to keep workers in time, here in a harvest setting.

The following track, '*Suid Mar Chuir mi 'n Geamhradh Tharram*' has the rhythmic 'tick-tock' of a clock overlaid with a gong that sounds like a Tibetan bell, footsteps on floorboards, and a peewit calling over moorland. Margaret sings acapella over the sound of the birdsong and the gently ticking clock, as if it was all taking place in the darkened room of a blackhouse. This is a song of a young woman being visited by a lover who turned out to be betrothed to another woman, establishing another theme of this cycle, of thwarted feminine love. In Gaelic song, women are able to find a freedom of expression that was frequently otherwise limited socially. Onwards now to '*Uamh an Oir*' (Cave of Gold) where strange supernatural reverberations are overlaid with Margaret's singing, echoing to the degree of threatening to catch up with the main melody, as if in the giant cave itself. The effect is eery and challenging as the ear also tracks the echo. The vocalisation in the refrain is in *canntaireachd*, a form of singing or chanting that was used to transmit pipe tunes in the oral tradition.

'*A Fhleasgaich ùir, Leanainn Thu*' has the opposite vocal quality, deadened, as if being sung in fog, or during a quiet evening outside. Margaret is eventually joined by whistles, slightly discordant and not always quite in time. '*Hò Rinn Ò*' returns to a drum sample, and soon an electric guitar and piano, playing a sequence of three chords. It is wonderfully rhythmical and exotic, the low whistle seeming to hail from another faraway land and culture. The song begins with Peigi, Martyn's grandmother, singing in an early 1953 recording made in Skye. Again the interleaving generations and technologies are invoked. 'A Thearlaich Òig' has a female choral sample shadowing Margaret's singing, recalling the feminine practice of keening in this lament. A Jacobite song composed in 1746 after Culloden, it is an account of destruction, killing and rape, again inclusive of the experience of women, who are the survivors and recorders of a history in which the men have been slaughtered. Womenfolk would go to the battlefield to retrieve the bodies of their loved ones, and according to tradition, it was not unusual for them to drink blood from the heads of their dear departed. This is no song for the faint of heart! The track begins and ends with a sample of a gunfire exchange with muffled, distant shouting, from a sample of field recordings of artillery at Karabagh.[14] By placing these samples like brackets at each end of the track, we hear the song through a cloak of new technology, and yet we are served a stark reminder of the ongoing and persistent nature of war and the eternal cycle of grief and lament that emerges afresh each time.

'*Cumha Lain Gairbh*' follows: a lament, again composed by a woman, the sister of John McLeod of Raasay, after he was lost at sea. The track launches with the Great Highland Bagpipe and the lone playing of a piobaireachd before moving to a masculine iteration of keening, or lamentation. After several bars, the vocals are introduced, an exercise in sung piobaireachd and reflecting the interweaving of genres, kinship, ceremonial musical function (here the formal mourning of the death of a chief) and personal expression (the grieving of a sister for a brother) in Highland tradition. '*Hiùraibh ò, Ghràidh an Tig Thu?*' changes pace to another song of unrequited love, a young woman wonders if her love will return from fighting in a war overseas, and relates a nightmare vision of his returning but to another. This added insecurity has a visceral expression – if she hears from him again, she will reply not in ink but in blood. Martyn seems sensitive to this Gothic theme and the emotional tumult, collating and layering a variety of instruments and sound effects in this track. A tri-tone melodramatic scream worthy of a Hitchcock horror is contrasted by the gentle rhythm of waves on the shore, evoking the disturbing dreams of rejection and suspended grief against the backdrop of a sea that is yielding only waves. Martyn crafts a track in which nature's constancy seems unsettling and unnerving.

The next track, '*Dh Eirich mi moch madainn cheitean*' ('I arose early on a May morning') is a waulking song injecting a sudden shift of tone and pace in the cycle with a catchy beat played out on bongo and introduced by rhythmic guitar.[15] Margaret comes in singing a jolly, jaunty melody and other sound effects are provided by Martyn's own recordings of rigging, barrels, and motors from boats around Mull, lending a busy workaday atmosphere to the track. A whistle features as the main instrument accompanying Margaret, whose voice has been manipulated to create a choral effect. This song ends with a return to Peter Stewart, echoing distantly down the generations. '*Air bhith dhomsa*' has a very similar set of production techniques applied to it as the previous song: a funky exotic beat, choral vocals, and a whistle as the main accompaniment.

'MacCrimmon's Lament' places Margaret's voice back on high reverb, accompanied by suggestions of fiddle that gather volume and certainty as the song progresses. 'Cumha Mhic Criomain' is an iconic lament in both Scots and Gaelic, a favourite of the folk revival movement, sung here in Gaelic, of course. Next comes 'Song of the Moccasin'. The *mogais* (plural *mogaisean*) was the Gaelic term for a type of shoe that prevailed as basic footwear throughout Scotland from the Middle Ages and presumably earlier. It consisted of hide turned fur-side inwards, and tied or sewn into a basic boot shape, similar in concept to a Native American moccasin. The Highland version was undecorated, uncured, and probably very smelly! Whether the similarity of the word *mogaisean* to moccasin is a coincidence or not is a matter of speculation on early travel and trade with precolonial North America. In this track, the only one originating outside Scotland, and one of the few composed by a man, Martyn installs a steady, plodding rhythm from the outset, reminiscent of deliberate steps and suggestive of ritual tribal dance that appears to have been used to achieve states of trance. Margaret's voice is the top layer over chanting and instrumentals derived from a recording of 'The Bad River Singers', made in Wisconsin in 1991 at a pow-wow. These choral voices have a multi-generational quality, with a mix of age and guile, they are non-lexical and in this not unlike the *puirt a beul* of Gaelic tradition. There is a downwards melodic trend on each chant, and the key is steady throughout, creating a further cyclical structure in the track. '*Fhir a' leadain thlàth*' is another song of a damsel in distress, this time left in crisis with a pregnancy, a song of sexual intimacy in the context of unrequited love. This leads to the ultimate song in the cycle of a love that was very much realised but thwarted by family in a kinship society: 'Griogal Cridhe', which, as we have already discussed, is both climax of the album and a song addressed to the next generation: a mother to her children rendered fatherless by her own kin. The female bears the child and passes on its culture in song. Tragedy and loss continue in haunting melody and lyrical narrative, memorialised and yet also a new beginning in the human cycle of existence, something with which we can contend, carry forward, and perhaps transcend, through music.

Glen Lyon is a deep and complex piece of art, layered with folkloric and historical meaning, and so much more than the simple marriage of tradition and modernity it is often considered to be. It has not had the attention or recognition it deserves, and nor has its place in Martyn's journey towards artistic maturity been fully recognised. Martyn was cutting his teeth on this project, engaging with traditional song and family through his own technology, musical trends of his time, and his own training and expertise. The album also marks a decisive move for him from instrumentalist to *producer*, fusing the personal and professional – family tradition and contemporary cool. However, the album as a whole is a salute to oral transmission, its interface with technology and its intergenerational nature. Martyn is recovering and recording songs and sounds for posterity but with a distinct and determined purpose: to reconnect a new and scattered generation with their natural and cultural heritage. *Glen Lyon* is at once an act of cultural conservation and a statement about tribal and indigenous cultures as their connection to their own land, once severed, becomes forgotten and obscured and finally lost in the stampede and hubbub of globalisation. Yet Martyn is also demonstrating a potential for a new mode of folk revival, through musical innovation and re-contextualisation in a high-tech form for a dawning digital age. This album is as much about the art (and survival) of tradition-*bearing* as tradition itself, about how each generation passes on its culture, and the practicalities of continuity in a homogenising digital world. Martyn's journey to becoming a brave new kind of producer – a sound designer – was gathering musical momentum. It continued in a recording he produced for his mother, *In the Sunny Long Ago*, but reached its zenith in his next and final album, and the one that in many ways would come to symbolise his legacy.

10

Grit

grit *noun* grit/ [uncountable]
1. small loose particles of stone or sand
2. courage and resolve; strength of character

MARTYN HAD BEEN trying to think of a title for his new album, and suddenly there it was at the side of the road, an unremarkable yellow council bin, yet highly striking in contrast to the bleak late autumn landscape of Argyll. Inscribed in black on the lid was a simple description of its contents: grit. It was a serendipitous answer to his pondering:

> Framed within the lifeless colour of the hills and a darkening easterly sky, it was probably the only thing for miles with any colour. The letters written across it in black were cracked by the elements, and made bold reference to what was once a most precious mineral, an ancient currency and a healing medicine: salt. It made such a strong and contrasting statement to its surrounding situation. Its happy colour reminded me, not of its practical use in ice and snow, but of spring, and the sign that the travelling people waited for all winter: the first yellow blossom of broom. The word Grit is strong and onomatopoeic; like an expression of a people's determination to survive and rejoice in the face

of struggle – grit which reflects the contrast found in our music and the topography of the land: colourful, dark, fine, coarse, simple, extreme – the grit and bite of a fiddle bow or the sound that a voice makes. So many analogies came to mind when I looked at it.

The humble bin itself became part of the iconic imagery associated with the album that is held by many fans and critics to be his finest work. That is true also of the photograph used for the cover, taken by BJ Stewart, and featuring Martyn, hair cropped short, standing behind a trig point on the north coast of Mull with the hills of Ardnamurchan just visible on the horizon. Martyn hadn't actually wanted to feature on the cover and preferred the idea of using something more abstract, but the record company, Real World, disagreed. BJ Stewart picked up the story:

> Martyn was also looking more unwell at the time so the photos Martyn had taken of himself at that time were judged to be unsuitable so he asked me if I had any fairly recent photographs when he looked 'fitter'. This photo that we ended up using was the 'compromise' Real World and Martyn both settled on. The photo was actually taken a good 18 or more months before *Grit* came out as part of a photoshoot of Cuillin to help promote the *Hardland* tours.

Grit has since had several iterations: as a title and tracks in the play *Grit, the Martyn Bennett Story*, as well as re-release by the record label Real World in 2014 and on vinyl in 2017, with the bonus tracks of 'Sky Blue' and 'Mackay's Memoirs'. Its orchestral re-interpretation and arrangement by Greg Lawson has brought a wave of new followers, drawing sell-out audiences in large venues and garnering rave reviews. The track 'Blackbird' was also used as the soundtrack for the film 'The Ridge', featuring internet sensation Danny MacAskill's epic death-defying cycling stunt along the Cuillin mountain range in Skye. And in October 2024 the 'Modern Scottish Classic' award was bestowed on *Grit* by the Scottish Music Industry Association at the SAY Awards at a ceremony in Stirling. Martyn joins a small elite band of winners along with Paulo Nutini, The Cocteau Twins and Frightened Rabbit. And so with each showing or performance attracting new fans and critical acclaim, *Grit* has come to encapsulate Martyn's memory in the popular imagination. The album therefore looms large in the many obituaries and tributes, and the recording process was the focus of a television documentary made by BBC Artworks. *Grit* is the release that has seen most discussion and explanation in terms of its inspiration and production, and has been the most reviewed. Indeed, in the thick wad of press cuttings and notes kept by Kirsten there is a heart-wrenchingly poignant, yellowed compliment slip from the record company that released the album, Real World, with the handwritten note: 'Dear Martyn, next batch of fantastic reviews for Grit! It's really impressive – the amount and the quality of press you've had for Grit. Do take care, Sophie'. The preserved cuttings are from the high street music store HMV, broadsheet newspapers such as *The Independent*, *The Telegraph*, music magazine *Songlines*, *Scotland on Sunday* (in which he was also highlighted as one of the top 50 young creatives in Scotland in 2004), *Billboard* in the USA, and so the list continues. Music critic Lee Blackstone observed: 'Like all Martyn Bennett albums, the production is outstanding, and even a hundred listens from now you will discover some new sound or nuance that you hadn't noticed before.' *Grit* is about the fight to survive and thrive; to pass on tradition by keeping up with the present, reworking the past into the contemporary here-and-now so that it can move forwards as the 'brave new music' that Hamish Henderson heard when Martyn played him an early version. This brings

to mind another analogy that Martyn found in the title with a magical creative catalyst; 'A piece of grit is what causes the abnormal shell to produce the beautiful pearl.' It was surely in celebration and emphasis of such a poetic spirit of innovation and vitality that he dedicated the album to Hamish Henderson.

This tribute to Henderson reflects a fundamental of the album that was largely overlooked by reviewers: the voices and songs he deployed were known to Martyn not just from his well-publicised personal associations with travelling folk and the *Gaidhealtachd*; they were known and available to him because he had also grown up in the midst of academics, poets and folklorists who, like his mother, collected sound recordings of stories and songs as fieldwork. *Grit* is an album borne of an intellectual milieu in which Martyn had been raised and nurtured from a tender age. Although born over half a century apart, he and Hamish Henderson became fast friends – so close, in fact, that Hamish soon assumed a grandfatherly role in Martyn's life. He also grew close to Sorley MacLean, eventually working on collaborations with both men, each giants of the Scottish folk revival and literary world. He developed relationships with others too as his mother Margaret recalled

> in a way that few might imagine: for example, he liked to visit William and Norah Montgomerie. When William died, and Norah was in a care home he would bring her a recording, or he would arrive with his fiddle or whistle, and play beside Norah's bedside. He visited Sorley (MacLean) and Rene in Skye, returning home with amusing anecdotes about conversations (told in a Sorley voice). In 1998, Martyn was clearly affected by the news that Iain Crichton Smith had been taken to hospital in Oban, so visited him there not long before Iain passed away... These gatherings also date Martyn's association with Sorley MacLean, Ian Crichton Smith and many of

the younger poets. It also marks the beginning of a long friendship between Flora (McNeil) and Martyn, which later inspired one of the final pieces he composed, 'Grit', with samples of Flora's voice.

As already discussed, Martyn had previously worked on projects setting music to 'Floret Silva Undique' by Hamish Henderson, and 'Hallaig' by Sorley MacLean. *Grit* was therefore personal to Martyn on every level, informed by his own immersion not just in traditional music and song, in his own Gaelic family heritage and the travelling folk, but in a whole literary and academic movement and community. *Grit* in itself is an act of tradition-bearing, reworking the wonderful legacies of archive recordings and old vinyl into a new 'crossover' of rhythmic dance beat and old song, rescuing them from relative obscurity and sending them out and forward in an explosion of new contemporary sounds. 'Bringin' the new tae the old', as Sheila Stewart, whose voice features on the first track 'Move' would observe, with delight.

It was chancing upon a recording of Sheila Stewart singing the 'Moving on Song' by Ewan McColl that crystallised the entire *Grit* project in Martyn's imagination. In many ways this was an accident of cancer therapy; in an interview with Mary Ann Kennedy, he explained that he was largely confined to life indoors for the duration (the treatment was immunosuppressive) and he felt that he had not necessarily 'got the best' songs from these tradition bearers to work with:

> I had the records that were at my disposal that were from my mum's record collection because I was in Edinburgh at the time, so I brought some of my studio down. I had some things I'd been working on before but I just stumbled upon it by accident, I just put the record on the record deck of Sheila Stewart and realised 'wow,

it's in the same key as that thing I'm doing there. And
then thought 'well, what if I try a little piece of what
she's singing in amongst this?' I think that's what a DJ
does really is find things by accident. Bits of new music
appear and they're not really your music, you know, you
write some part of it and then suddenly you start looking
for something else that goes with it.[1]

He likened the creative process of modern musical composing to a squirrel collecting and burying nuts, unearthing them at a later time. Martyn gave an account in an interview with Kenny Mathieson for the *Highlands and Islands Arts Journal* in November 2003 of exactly how this fitted in his overall creative process:

I really only used one line from each verse of the song in
my arrangement, from part of the tune which was high up
in her voice, and is the most passionate part of the verse.
She doesn't sing a big long note like that – I looped that
part of her line. (It was) the way in for me. I decided then
and there that I would use the travellers' songs and the
Gaelic songs, because they were the things I felt closest to.

In going through all the old records at his disposal, he admitted that 'not many of the songs really do work in this context. I just couldn't find a way of putting them into that musical setting without damaging them.' In this highly selective process, he ended up with song elements he could combine with a rhythm and other samples. Martyn's record collection was described by his friend Rory as 'absolutely *totemic*', and Rory would love it when Martyn was cooking dinner as he would take the chance to browse through it. No matter how obscure or exotic the tune or instrument, Martyn could join in! Martyn was an avid collector of old vinyl, 'scouring junk shops looking for old records that I can use' explaining gleefully that he had a set of 40 volumes of sound effects from America covering 'animal noises to weird sci-fi effects' that he had found in a skip.

The Edinburgh-based group, Mr McFall's Chamber, had initially been asked to record the strings parts on the album, but as their leader, Robert McFall remembered, 'the time-scale was too short and our diaries too full'.[2] In the event, Real World arranged to have another ensemble, Millennia Strings, record the parts at their studios in Wiltshire rather than Martyn 'overdubbing myself on fiddle' which he had tried initially. The recording process turned out to be a great experience that he enjoyed immensely (also taking delight in luxuriating in the same bath that Kylie Minogue had once used!). Martyn worked the musicians hard: as always he knew exactly what he wanted and was not satisfied until it had been achieved. But their efforts paid off, and the final result had a profound effect on Martyn who cried when he first heard it.

Robert McFall's role on *Grit* was not limited to the abandoned recording of the strings parts, for as early as 1998, Martyn had been chatting to him about building a project together as a collaboration. The two had first met when Cuillin and McFall's Chamber had been booked to play a double bill together as part of the Highland Festival that summer. The first concert was in Wick, but almost nobody came! They both played anyway, and so it did give them the opportunity to listen to each other's sets in an intimate (i.e. empty!) setting. The next night things were very different: 'We performed at the Cairngorm Ski Centre', recalled Robert. 'This time Martyn's fans were there, obviously knew the music inside out and jumped up and down energetically for the whole set. I also was intoxicated by Cuillin's music and from that time on Martyn and I kept in sporadic touch'. Martyn went to hear McFall's live on several occasions and accepted a commission to write a piece for them, 'though his intention was that it should be more collaboration than commission'. However, Martyn's diagnosis prevented that from happening, but they had got as far as sketching out some core concepts and shapes for it. 'Some of the ideas which we discussed ended up surfacing in his last album, *Grit*. In a way this was a studio version of the project he had originally proposed to me'.

Greg Lawson, another classically trained musician, has a depth of insight and opportunity for reflection on the composition of the album that perhaps could only be obtained from complete immersion in Martyn's creative process. Greg traced and highlighted the same elements of situational restrictions of cancer treatment, experimental spirit, and accidental discovery that Martyn had described years before:

> When he made *Grit* he was already ill and it meant his whole ability to go out as a musician on stage had changed. Music became a solitary existence for him, it became something he could do for himself. I think his whole life as a traditional musician he'd always been part of that, he'd always loved the song, the story, the history of music. And now he was actually listening to all these amazing old voices of people who had gone. And what he came up with was an extraordinary mix of completely opposing ingredients. Old unaccompanied song, song that comes from a tradition that has nothing to do with anyone else playing with you. Melody line is a free allegorical thing. It's in the air, it's not on the ground, and taking that beautiful free form and then setting it with these totally uncompromising massive dance grooves and the difference between an organic line and an electronic line. People say you can never bring those things together and I think he just thought he had the time, 'Why not? What happens if you do?'[3]

The themes of experiment and accidental good fortune are fundamental to *Grit*: trying out different tracks and sampling

With Michael Marra at An Tobar, Mull.

different sounds to see what would happen, discovering the grit bin that yielded the title, or even bumping into the Dundonian singer-songwriter Michael Marra in the Tobermory Coop, just when Martyn was looking for a male voice to read Psalm 118 on the 'Liberation' track. This was a hugely important chance meeting, as the original version of that track (entitled 'Liberation – the Bomb') was really quite different, and had featured a sample of speech from writer and broadcaster, Alistair Cooke of *Letter from America* fame. In the event, Cooke had refused to give permission for the sample to be used, and Martyn was so upset by this that he even considered abandoning the whole project. Michael Marra saved the day!

In *Grit*, authority, standardisation and stricture are constantly contrasted against the organic and dialectal. Take the sampling of Mairi Morrison's 'diddling' of the well-known pipe tune 'Lament for Mairi MacLeod' on 'Chanter', interspersed with the authoritative very English accent of a Cambridge ethnomusicologist repeating throughout: 'You play the melody on the chanter'. Yet even here variation is highlighted in the very English pronunciation of the vowel 'a' [ɑː] (as in car) in chanter, which is a sound alien to the Scottish articulation of 'a' [ə] (as in cat) and is a commonly parodied marker (in Scotland) of the English upper crust accents. The dialectal is evident throughout the album; from the stunning vocals of Lizzie Higgins in 'Blackbird' carrying the North Eastern inflections of the Doric language, with an exaggerated roll on the 'r', to the Loch Fyne Highland brogue of Davie Stewart from Arrochar in 'Storyteller'. There are, however, discernible yet subtle differences between spoken and sung dialects in the travelling people, that leans more to standard English. Lizzie Higgins, for instance, pronounces 'apron' in conversation with a strongly accented 'a' [ɑː], as in 'apple', however when the same word 'apron' appears in the line 'her apron it hung low', in the ballad 'What a Voice', it is the standard [aɪ] as in 'way' that she sings. The track 'Nae Regrets', the title of which is a Scottish version of the Edith Piaf song 'No Regrets' has the strongly Dundonian overtones of Annie Watkins, particularly the much stereotyped and parodied use of 'eh' [ˈeɪ] as in the 'e' in café for the sound 'I' [aɪ] as in the first-person pronoun or a pie! Annie belts out 'Eh'll no bide wi ma granny nae mair', which Martyn joyfully translates in the *Grit* documentary as 'I will not stay with my grandmother anymore.' The humour in accent and phonetic nuances are things Martyn enjoyed enormously, and that sense of fun is imparted here, with the emphasis falling on the first sound and a trumpety 3/4 accompaniment lending a bawdy, music hall atmosphere. Whistles, chants and non-lexical singing from Gaelic *'puirt canntaireachd'*, or 'piping song,' to Egyptian and Gregorian chants, are included at various times throughout the tracks, direct injections of traditions near and far, all sounding as if they are from exotic faraway lands and times, echoing into the present and on into the future among the contemporary techno beats and sci-fi sound samples. In 'Storyteller', the dialectal is used to create much of the rhythm, with the verbal ornamentation of 'so she says to him, she says and so he says to her, he says.' This is not without meaning, but still *excessive* to meaning, and a stylistic format often employed by traveller storyteller, Duncan Williamson, and recognisable to anyone who has heard an old man telling a long joke in Scots in a pub! Another most striking use of this is on the track 'Liberation' controversially featuring the female singing voices of Murdina and Effie MacDonald from Ballantrushal in Lewis, precenting Psalm 118 in the tradition of the Free Church of Scotland, read also by the grit-laden and serious male voice of Michael Marra. Here we have a confluence of coincidence, irony, role reversal and contrast that is nothing short of spellbinding. This tradition also has strict rules, as Martyn stresses in his notes on the track:

> Contains part of Psalm 118, in Gaelic, to the tune of 'Coleshill', sung by Murdina and Effie MacDonald and recorded by Thorkild Knudsen in 1964 (courtesy of the School of Scottish Studies Archives/Greentrax Recordings). The English translation of the psalm is recited by Michael Marra.
>   I was initially very worried about my setting of this psalm, as I was sure it would be offensive or misunderstood, so I decided to visit Murdina at her home in Ballantrushal on the Isle of Lewis. Although now in her late 80s, Murdina is a most impressive woman. She reassured me that back in 1964 she too had been very apprehensive about recording religious material for inclusion with what she termed 'the vain songs'. It had given her many sleepless nights but she was resolved by something that came to mind from the scriptures: 'I will cast your bread upon the waters…'

Psalms in the Free Church tradition are 'precented': the precentor (lead vocalist) 'lifts a tune' (selects a tune of his choice), singing each line and the congregation or family repeating, their voices following just behind his. There are well over a hundred different tunes to choose from, learned orally but also published in a collection called the *Gaelic Psalmody*. Meanwhile, the words or lyrics for the psalms came from *The Metrical Psalms of David* and were performed as part of a twice daily ritual in the vast majority of homes in the Outer Hebrides. Actor and singer Dolina MacLennan grew up in the village of Marvig, on the Isle of Lewis in a household contemporary with that of Murdina and Effie's generation.

Moving to Edinburgh as a young woman, Dolina herself became a leading light in the folk revival, and a key member of the circle of poets and musicians surrounding Hamish Henderson. As a friend of Martyn's mother Margaret, she of course knew Martyn too, often hearing him performing at gatherings and events. Dolina's memories of 'gabhal a-leabhar / taking the books', a morning and evening ritual of prayers, psalms and Bible reading, offer a fascinating insight into the religious traditions of the Free Church observed in the intimacy of the family home. She explained:

> It was always done by the man of the house. A prayer to start with. This was just what was in his head. Then a psalm. He would pick whichever tune he felt would go with the psalm. These were from *The Metrical Psalms of David*. The whole family would join in with him. Then he would read a chapter from the Bible, generally wherever it fell open. Then another prayer to finish. For this, you had to get down on your knees wherever you were sitting, clasp your hands, head down.[4]

Dolina recalled that when the men in the house were away, her mother would read a psalm and a chapter from the Bible, picking up the good book and saying 'leughaibh sinn caibeal' (we'll read a chapter); there would be no prayers or singing, no precenting. If there were no men in the house, then this would create a situation where the women would conduct the morning and evening 'gabhal a-leabhar'. Only women who were communicants in the Free Church (as Murdina and Effie would have been) were regarded as being in a position to precent, or offer up a prayer, and only then in the absence of a man. In the track on *Grit*, Martyn has not only included female precenting but in his use of Michael Marra, *reading* the psalm, he has completed the role reversal.[5]

This tendency to use male *speaking* voices and female *singing* voices extends almost without exception across the whole album. Female voices also extemporise where men tend to recite, in another twist on tradition. The Jeannie Robertson song chosen, 'Ale House' is 'an unusual song for Jeannie as it is normally a male party-piece', as Martyn points out in the notes. It has a rambunctious, defiant feel to it, telling blithely of 'the bonnie wee lassie who never says no.' In the final track 'Storyteller' Davie Stewart's rendition of 'The Maiden Without Hands' has a strong atmosphere of recitation with its emotionless, almost matter-of-fact recounting of grotesque violence, albeit allegorical. Only at the end does the human storyteller lapse into more natural speech. Whether this gender role reversal in *Grit* was conscious on Martyn's part is difficult to tell – he certainly does not seem to highlight it in the copious publicity and album notes.

During filming of the *Grit* documentary, 2003.

Another key feature of the album is the use of refrain and repetition. In 'Move', for instance, repetition is used to evoke both the constant routine of being moved along, by bringing the beat from background to foreground. Underpinning it is exotic embellishment from a sample of Turkish Ney flute played by Amir Shahzar from an album by the East–West Ensemble called 'Imaginary Ritual', that injects flurries of activity perhaps evoking an estrangement of the travelling folk as they are moved on. Sheila Stewart's voice, in imitation of authority, regularly orders her people to 'MOVE', 'SHIFT'. The haphazard nature of packing up suddenly is reflected in this frequent disruption to the flow of the song, and yet the repetition of these elements also conveys a sense of continuity, as the persecution of travelling folk persists. The time signature is a brisk 4/4 throughout, with volume and repetition of ornamentation deployed to convey changes in pace and the turmoil of their way of life. Sheila herself came from a family of travellers known as the Stewarts of Blair. She described herself as Romany, as Martyn explained; 'the oldest nomadic race in Europe. The origins of Roma are thought to be Indian.'

'The material I worked with is split between the songs of travelling people of the North East and Gaelic traditions of the West Highlands. I feel that these strands are by far the strongest links to authentic folk culture in Scotland', proclaimed Martyn. Indeed, authenticity is fundamental to *Grit*. As Martyn was to emphasise both in the interview for the *Grit* documentary and in an essay he wrote on the album for *Scotland on Sunday* in 2003, he knew, and had personal connection with, the singers he showcased in his tracks, and was raised himself with the songs and voices he deployed:

> The samples on the album are from the people and songs
> I grew up with. From the age of about ten to 15 I went
> to a lot of summer festivals around Scotland, just playing
> music. I met a lot of travelling people, heard them singing.

In sampling their songs you can bring them to a wider audience, but it's important not to exploit anyone. When Moby did the album *Play*, he used samples from the Lomax archive. Although he used it well, I have a little gripe with fact he didn't credit the Lomax (artists) as much as he should have done. On the other hand, I realise he didn't know the people he sampled personally, like I do.

In his album notes, he is able to describe these personal connections and experiences. For example, on the track 'Blackbird', he relates his first encounter with the voice of Lizzie Higgins, whose song 'What a voice!' is the main focus. 'I will never forget the first time I heard her sing this song. I was about 12 years of age and couldn't believe that a person could make such an amazing sound.' Lizzie was believed to have learned her ballads from her mother, Jeannie Robertson, however an interview given in May 1970 to researchers from the School of Scottish Studies at the University of Edinburgh describes in detail how her father also taught her to 'sing like the pipes' with vocal ornamentation and changes.

This golden thread of family and the passing on of tunes, stories and songs is woven carefully throughout the entire album. Tradition-bearing is the essence of *Grit*, indeed, like *Glen Lyon*, it is at heart an *act* of tradition-bearing in itself. Martyn sampled the voices of both mother Jeannie Robertson and daughter Lizzie Higgins as well as that of Sheila Stewart, a fellow traveller and traditional singer from a different family. Martyn would later remark: 'If I said to Sheila Stewart "Did you try to emulate the singing of Jeannie Robertson?" she would laugh and say: "What are you talking about? I just sing the way my mother sang."' In an interview with Jim Gilchrist for *The Scotsman*, Martyn revealed: 'I do see myself as a tradition-bearer, I guess, someone who can pass things on... There are maybe not so many people like myself who have been in the fortunate position to grow up in a strong tradition.'

In crafting this sonic tapestry of generations, Martyn extended the concept of combining old and new, classical and contemporary, local and global, organic and synthetic. He diverted the carrying stream of oral traditions from his own heritage into the river delta and the oceans beyond. This was a process that he had clearly begun to explore in the album *Glen Lyon*, with archive recordings of his own great-great-grandfather Peter Stewart, and Gaelic songs sung by his mother that were passed down his own family. Indeed, not only do some reviews of *Grit* identify the album as a continuation of *Glen Lyon*, Martyn himself commented that *Grit* was 'a logical progression from my earlier work.' However here Martyn understates his case: in *Grit* we see fulsome fruition, not just progress, with Martyn's design and master plan attaining glorious full bloom. Martyn's musical path was ever more concerned with the principle of 'cultural equity', an idea and term developed by the folklorist Alan Lomax, whose recordings of the likes of Flora MacNeil and Jeannie Robertson are core contributions to this album. Martyn did once meet Lomax in New York, and this notion of cultural equity is a large ambition of *Grit*. Martyn himself selected this quote from Lomax:

> All cultures need their fair share of the airtime. When country folk or tribal peoples hear or view their own traditions in the big media, projected with the authority generally reserved for the output of large urban centres, and when they hear their traditions taught to their own children, something magical occurs. They see that their expressive style is as good as that of others, and, if they have equal communicational facilities, they will continue it... Practical men often regard these expressive systems as doomed and valueless. Yet, wherever the principle of cultural equity comes into play, these creative wellsprings

begin to flow again – even in this industrial age, folk traditions can come vigorously back to life, can raise community morale, and give birth to new forms if they have time and room to grow in their own communities. The work in this field must be done with tender and loving concern for both the folk artists and their heritages. This concern must be knowledgeable, both about the fit of each genre to its local context and about its roots in one or more of the great stylistic traditions of humankind.

Martyn was applying this thesis creatively, reworking traditional song and story from Scotland into a format that would enable and encourage it to be communicated and appreciated by a mainstream audience. He was highly conscious of the purity of his material: 'All music is important but especially folk music. It's from an indigenous source, it's not affected by anything artificial, it's so completely natural.' Chris MacLullich, an anthropologist and one of Martyn's closest friends, was researching and working with indigenous people in South America in these years. Chris recalled that Martyn

> had a genuine fascination with this sort of passing generation which had things that were just being lost. And he connected with me a lot with my work on indigenous people – how many languages were lost every year. You know, there's whole coherent cultures who have their own way of doing things, their own traditions, and they're gradually just dying out. He wanted to come to South America with me.

He believes that Martyn would have done so had he lived, however 'he recognised he would only be scratching the surface' in this adventure. In Chris's view Martyn wanted to 'go deep' in terms of tradition and felt that he could do that in the culture to which he himself belonged. If we bear in mind Martyn's appreciation of the guidance of Lomax regarding sensitivity to traditional culture, most especially that 'the work in this field must be done with tender and loving concern for both the folk artists and their heritages', we can see that he understood his unique position at the intersection of the mainstream dance club movement, the classical canon of the mainstream establishment, and traditional music with a rarefied appeal that was performed mainly by an older cohort, at community level, and was fading into relative obscurity as they aged. In *Grit*, Martyn was aiming to give the traditional music of Scotland a place in that mainstream, establishing it as something of value and pride, particularly among the younger generation. He observed in the course of demonstrating his creative process in an interview for the TV documentary on *Grit*: 'That's not a dance song – and that is a dance beat. So what am I doing here?' And in an interview with *The List* magazine, the influence of Lomax on Martyn and the paradigm of cultural equity is clear:

> The tricky thing is to bring this kind of music (traditional) into the public domain in a way that doesn't compromise it. That's always a danger. A lot of the efforts in this area fail because the people writing the music don't fully understand both cultures – the traditional and the contemporary.

Cultural equity, for Martyn, was not just about publicity and mainstream popular appeal: *Grit* was also the product of a classically trained musician. Greg Lawson remarked on this on his first encounter with the album, enthused by its 'massive landscape', and later observing '*Grit* is basically a colossally structured piece of music.' As someone who arranged it for orchestra, Greg had essentially to attempt to inhabit Martyn's mind creatively, and perhaps nobody knows *Grit* as well as Greg. The contrasts within the album, he felt, are completely deliberate. The classical input he identifies, in the use of counterpoint, for instance, is as deliberate and significant as the dance beats, with both playing into the same agenda. 'There is no reason why traditional music should not be a high art. I've played with many musicians all over the world and what they do is beautiful. It is as worthy and as refined as any jewel you'll find in classical music.' Influences and elements from such traditional music elsewhere in the world are incorporated throughout the album. It is as if Martyn is taking Scottish traditional culture out onto the world stage and finding other traditional performers from other lands doing the same thing. As Chris MacLullich observed, Martyn was interested in 'putting up some kind of resistance to the loss of indigenous life... it wasn't about preserving I think.' And so, for example, on the track 'Wedding', Martyn includes samples from a Scottish classically trained pianist who took to promoting the clarsach and Gaelic musical traditions and tunes around the world. Miss Héloïse Russell-Fergusson was a spinster, a maverick who took her own path musically and creatively. Born in Glasgow in 1896 to a wealthy family, she had Gaelic nannies as an infant who almost certainly gave her language and songs from birth. She trained in piano and singing at the RAMD in London, and was teaching in Washington when she discovered a Celtic clarsach in a shop. Buying it, she adopted the instrument completely, thereafter taking Gaelic tunes around the world. The tune included by Martyn came from a recording she made in 1966: *An Treisamh* meaning 'the third', being third in 'a Unique series of fascinating Sound Spells for the Celtic harp and voice'. It also contains three tracks; 'Jabble' which she defines as 'those agitated waters of a tide-race with its contrasting eddies. A Hebridean Witch meets a Nile boatman's chant!', followed by 'Dance of the Drops', where 'the harp joins an African *m'bira* in a happy dance' and finally 'The Welkin', which is described

as bringing 'portent of nebulous Space, through which the voice wanders freely in an un-ending theme.' Although much of her life story was only researched and discovered after Martyn died, her niece Hélène and the researcher Stuart Eydmann had this to say towards the end of a paper they wrote, 'Seeking Héloïse Russell-Fergusson', detailing her life and music:

> No wonder that the late Martyn Bennett came to sample one of her pieces Dance of the Drops for inclusion in the track Wedding on his celebrated work *Grit*. In this she plays clarsach and m'bira and we like to think that at last, Héloïse had found at least one other kindred spirit who recognised her place in the history of Scotland's music.

In 'Storyteller', traditional Egyptian music provides an exotic refrain, enhancing the surreal quality of the spoken narrative. The chanting has a ritualistic quality – the voices ascend in one bar and retrace their steps in the next, symmetrical and steadily repetitive. Their voices and the instrumental also seem here to link this tale to stories of the same kind told all over the world and representing the human condition. Here the generational and familial find parallels in this trio: all three members came from a famous clan of musicians – Egyptian MacCrimmons, if you like, called 'Musicians of the Nile'. This particular sample was from Al-ward Al-froll, on the album *Charcoal Gypsies,* also released by Real World records in 1996. Discovered in 1975 by Alan Weber, Musicians of the Nile toured extensively with their traditional Egyptian/Arabic sounds. Their music featured in a Martin Scorcese film *The Last Temptation of Christ* and they came to the attention of Real World through the accompanying album *Passion.* Martyn gives more weight to the rhythm of the sample, which is lighter and more syncopated in the original form, in the spirit of repackaging and remodelling to reach new and wider audiences. In so doing he ends *Grit* with his championed themes of resistance to loss, honouring the path taken by other cultures, and renewing the claim for equity for traditional music and culture from around the world.

This refinement reflects a new focus in Martyn's approach. The selectivity in choosing a song, or a section of a song for the heart of a track was key to producing a cogent and confident album. This mastery was something Martin Swan, longstanding collaborator, had noticed. Martyn remarked that Swan's album *Mouth Music* was 'the first stage in the deconstruction of the dark thing called dance music' and had influenced him hugely. In a conversation recorded between the two men for the *Grit* documentary, Martin Swan observed that '*Grit* is different' in that in previous albums he felt every track 'had the genesis of at least three great pieces of music' and that Martyn had not previously focused in on one of them, whether through impatience or a 'desire for complexity'. But in *Grit,* observed Swan, 'everything felt... comfortable with the essential notion of what that piece was.' Martyn commented in response that 'I've taken quite a few years to get to a stage where I can actually hear what it is that I need to get and all the other bits, I just get rid of them.' He added that *Hardland* had taught him this lesson, having remarked earlier that both Martin Swan and Martin Low had advised him to home in on one idea and focus on that. 'I'm a rubbish DJ. I use it (the deck) as a tool, as a starting block and I've seen really skilful usage of it.' Martyn commented that for a long time he felt that he was trying to show off technological prowess, with 'techno wanking', as he termed it, adding 'Ninety percent of the work that went into *Grit* was technological', involving many hours in front of the computer. For Martyn, this was a major shift in emphasis. He talked in several interviews of becoming 'a receiver' rather than a player, with comments such as 'This album is a way forward for me to become involved in other people's music.' The loss of connection with his own instrumental playing had been replaced with a new connection to the music of others, specifically traditional song. *Grit* unveiled an invigorating new way forward for Martyn. He talked enthusiastically about plans to work with Gaelic psalm precenting, taking it into areas of religious conflict around the world. In the process of making *Grit*, Martyn himself experienced a creative transformation. 'People just don't get it', he would say. 'If only they'd listen to the resonance between an Islamic chant and a Gaelic psalm, they'd realise that Muslims and Christians can live together in harmony, each with their own expression'.[6]

The track titles of the album also reflect his course. They are all simple, straightforward one or two-word monikers (in contrast to many traditional song titles). As such, the titles are more characteristic of cool dance culture, symbolising in their stark nudity that notion of finding one idea or musical phrase and building a track around that. Their order on the album, and the titles themselves, were swapped around by Martyn in the editing process, whether in collaboration with Real World or before final submission. An earlier iteration of his title notes has 'Liberation' as the second track, whereas in the final edit it was track 5, a kind of turning point in the album. 'Chanter' is track 8, appearing as track 3 in the album; 'Nae Regrets' is track 5 and had been pushed one forward to track 4; 'Rant' is called 'Black Cloud' and was initially placed as track 6, while 'Why' is called '1746–1946'. As he explains in notes, his intention was to tie together the experiences of war as felt by Highlanders two centuries apart, or more particularly, the experiences of the *after effects* of war. Why, then, would he change the name of the track to 'Why'? It is speculation, of course, but it seems yet another instance of Martyn's search for simplicity of expression. '1746–1946' is a clever title but Why? communicates the feeling of anguish of those who have survived. Calum Ruadh's simple question 'Why?' is asked by many a survivor as well as many a victim – why me? Why did I survive? Why did I get cancer? 'Why?' embraces Martyn's own war with that disease and thus his personal story in a way that the initial title does not. And when people used to say to him, 'why you?', he'd simply reply, 'why not me?'

The first and last tracks, 'Move' and 'Storyteller', seem to have been crystallised early in Martyn's creative process, at least in terms of title and position. What does this tell us about Martyn's personal journey in making *Grit*? It tells us simply that the album is a narrative, a story, and the tracks are akin to titles. Martyn uses the word 'story' several times in his album notes, which he describes as 'stories behind the music'. He commences with 'This is my story about triumph in the face of struggle. It is a story of the people and songs I grew up with, and most importantly, it is their voices, traditions and the inspiration they have given to be passed on to the next generation.' Therefore, while tradition-bearing was undoubtedly the main thrust of *Grit*, it was delivered as a story by Martyn, whose editorial choices were clearly informed by this overarching narrative.

Indeed, Martyn also seems to be experimenting with narrative forms in the music of the album itself. His album notes may explain the stories behind the music, however the stories aren't necessarily concealed but contained in, or embodied by the songs and tunes. 'Wedding', for example 'describes a fictitious but typical Highland wedding', yet it is also, according to Martyn, 'an abstract tone poem'. Tone poems are a classical construct of musical narration and emotional sequencing. An innovation of Romanticism, they had their heyday in the 19th century and fell into obsolescence in the 20th. Yet here is Martyn resurrecting a traditional (or at least forgotten) classical genre in an abstract, improvised musical setting.

The track 'Why?' muses upon the luck involved in survival and the effects of war on those left behind, linking a lament from Culloden to the famous bard Calum 'Ruadh' Nicholson from Skye (apparently a relative of Martyn) pondering that he is the only one left of his brothers. This was all the more poignant to Martyn because he knew that his own great-grandfather, John Stewart, had been one of four brothers, but was the only one of them to survive the Great War. The horrendous losses of that conflict were a huge factor in the drain from Gaeldom – the drain of blood, of language and of culture. The Calum Ruadh passage on the track is in the form of a 'narrative' called 'The Old Home' and recorded by the same field worker, Thorkild Knudsen, who recorded the female precentors of Psalm 118 used in 'Liberation'. In this track, Calum, a crofter, revisits the site of his old family home where there is a sound of running water in the background from a burn or stream. He speaks in English but sings his composition in Gaelic. Calum himself died in 1978. This is interwoven with a famous lament composed by

a woman, Christine Fergusson, for a lover killed at Culloden, 'Mo Ruin Geal Og'. The Battle of Culloden is also famous, perhaps one of the best-known stories in Scottish history, and here Martyn also works in contrast, this time between the iconic and the personal, global and individual.

The final track in *Grit*, 'Storyteller', is a direct setting of spoken narrative, uncensored and apparently unexpurgated. Its wordiness appears exaggerated, if anything, with the repetition of 'she/he says' almost forming a rhythmic accompaniment all by itself. Martyn originally included a far more detailed account of the allegory behind this story in an earlier version of his track notes, and one that is worth quoting here, as it provides a far clearer understanding of the song itself and of Martyn's personal interpretation of this piece.

> The story is an allegory about deceit, brutality, complicit victimisation and petty power struggles that go on in most families. The king (a control freak) throws out his daughter, Doris, for breaking his milk-pitcher, which is actually the fault of a deceitful, jealous stepmother. He then proceeds to remove her limbs and her ability to feed her baby using his sword (an allegory for complicit victimisation and cowardly brutality). He leaves her in a state of depression (she's bleeding to death) but before he goes the daughter curses him, saying that he will be sick one day and the only person who will cure him is her son (guilt). His daughter then meets an 'auld wise man' (I guess he would be a psychotherapist today) who points out that she is actually quite capable of managing and she goes on her way. Of course, she gets word many years later that the King is dying (of remorse I think) and she goes to see him with her now grown-up son. The son uses the very same sword to chop off the King's 'poisoned foot' (he confronts him with what he has done to his mother

Doris) and this cures him (of remorse and reconciles the King with his daughter). There is perhaps a twist here, in that the son takes the King's place – I take this to mean that all our faults and grievances are passed on from one generation to the next no matter how hard we try and forgive them.

As Martin Swan also pointed out in his conversation with Martyn Bennett, 'Storyteller' ends without music, as does the whole album, with the unassuming line: 'So I don't know very much more about it.' However, there is a sound effect running in the background until the last – it has the slightly eerie, exploratory and otherworldly hisses, breathing and tones of a submarine or deep-sea diver. *Grit* leaves us hanging, suspended below the surface.

There is dark humour to 'Storyteller' that is woven throughout the whole album. Indeed, one of the more natural and human moments in it is when the narrator admits, with a giggle, that he does not know exactly how the frog inserted into the king's bed heals his severed foot! Humour was integral to Martyn's personality. As his friend and Cuillin bandmate Rory observed, every moment there was room for humour, it was there. *Grit* is in fact peppered liberally with irony, funny twists and *double entendre*. Greg Lawson was still uncovering these as he was creating the music of the Grit Orchestra.

He remarked:

> He was a mischievous person... There are lots of funny parts to *Grit*. I mean like 'Chanter' – 'You play the melody on the chanter' – to have 'you play the melody on the chanter' coming in as this constant thing and then it's in B major. Pipes don't play in B major – they play in B flat. So you've got the one piece that has chanters on it, you can't play on the pipes!

Martyn hints further at the subversive spirit of this track. When discussing it for the *Grit* documentary, he finishes with the throwaway comment that a chanter 'is also a slang word for your willy.' The colloquial and bawdy are represented throughout in Martyn's usual ironic style. 'Nae Regrets' continues in the same slightly risqué vein, this time with Annie Watkins from Dundee who, as Martyn commented in the notes: 'was about 4′ 10″ with a voice, not of an angel, but the power of a small PA system.' 'Ale House', as Martyn recorded in his draft notes, 'talks about people getting blind drunk and having sex'. (Indeed you don't have to listen too attentively to catch highly suggestive voice samples of a woman enjoying herself a lot!) The backing track is pure electronica, contrasting even more starkly with the raw, organic intonation of Jeannie's rendition of 'The bonnie wee lassie who never says no', a very rhythmic and steady-paced 4/4 beat conjures up drunken copulation. Martyn has enhanced the sexual nature of the piece without over-exaggeration, allowing the lyrics and Jeannie to lead. In so doing he showcases a very old, strong, and vibrant tradition of bawdy entertainment in Scottish culture.

An older form of entertainment still, that of the gallows, is in evidence in the penultimate track, 'Rant'. This too had a different title in its original version, called 'Black Cloud'. Given the sampling of the term 'one rant' with a scratchy, rave-repetitive rhythm, the name change seems fair enough! The traditional song featured here is known as 'MacPherson's Lament' or 'Rant' and sung by a colourful character from Portsoy, Jimmy MacBeath. Although the song deals with an execution and was known as a 'lament' there is little about it musically to place it in a lamentation category. The melody is fairly jaunty, in C Major, and MacBeath's marvellously gnarled rendering has been considerably accelerated by Martyn. A fiddle plays a refrain in another cheerful ditty at intervals, the sound is dangerously dirty, teetering on the tune and only just holding it. So what is it all in aid of? Martyn elucidated the narrative of the song very well in his album notes:

> MacPherson of Kingussie was an infamous 'freebooter' (whisky smuggler) condemned to death at Banff in 1700 for robbing the rich and giving to the poor. The story goes that MacPherson was a fine fiddle player, and before he was hanged he broke his fiddle over the gallows and threw it into the crowd.

In speeding up to a jumping, thumping club beat, the song takes on a hedonistic entertaining pace. This is a pure dance track. Another tradition long forgotten and seemingly bizarre to us in the present was that of convicts sentenced to death dancing on the way to the gallows, watched by a crowd gathered for the spectacle. There is a nihilistic darkness to this song, as MacPherson is described dancing and playing a fiddle tune 'Below the gallows tree'. The ghoulish entertainment is given a rasping, mindless track with the scratchy original recording creating a sense of all this being long ago, one that sits in contrast to the techno beat and contemporary sound effects. Martyn weaves the rhythm and 'one rant' with MacBeath's solo in a way that carries forwards over time the incongruity and contrast of the condemned man and upbeat celebratory mood of the crowd. Martyn himself described Jimmy's voice as 'like a bunch of gravel being dragged along the ground, but that's appealing to me. I like lived-in voices.' He also described his own instrumental work on dance tracks in the past as 'a bit of a rabble-rousing thing' and here he appears to revive that atmosphere and motivation, drawing a striking parallel between gallows humour and the darkness of dance music to which Martyn frequently referred.

Grit was of course formed throughout Martyn's illness and a period in which he was contending with challenges that took him to very dark places emotionally. Is it an accident that Martyn included a song about a fiddler who smashed his fiddle before being hung on the gallows and threw it to the crowd? *Grit* may evince mischievousness and fun, but it also expresses the bittersweet and the anger and the turmoil of Martyn's fight for survival, and contention with loss, with things being cut away from him – body parts, the ability to connect with his instruments, the strength and fitness to escape to the mountains, or even enjoy the company of friends and family for extended periods without having to rest. Of the track 'Liberation', Martyn recorded in his notes: 'This piece "wrote itself" at the beginning and end of a most traumatic and life changing experience. I could not find any other way to express the profound feeling of losing faith, and the determination to find it again.'

Likewise, 'Wedding' is an intensely personal piece, with improvisation from Martyn on viola and Kirsten on piano, another musical inversion for two classically trained musicians, particularly Kirsten, who had never improvised before. It's a heartfelt, organic contribution to the track, lending it intimacy and authenticity but it is also deeply poignant in the context of all that this young couple were facing at the time. 'Storyteller' also invites direct comparisons with Martyn's own experiences; it is, after all, an allegory, designed to offer parallels with the personal and individual nature of experience. The physical brutality of cutting away limbs and breasts and thus the ability to nourish children is symbolic of psychological and spiritual inheritance in 'Storyteller' and yet ironically, for Martyn, cancer had visited a similar level of physical brutality on him, cutting away his spleen, leaving him mutilated by scars, removing not just his ability to provide for children, but to have any at all. As the King dismembers daughter Doris, the sound of a life support machine is introduced.

Martyn, in an interview promoting *Grit* with Ann Donald for *Scotland on Sunday*, responded when asked where he thought his self-avowed anger came from: 'I don't know. Maybe my genes,' he suggests, adding 'I just think certain catalysts happen in your life and set it off and you can't control it. For me it was going down that dark path of ambition'. In 'Storyteller', the dark aspects of the human ego are reiterated with every generation. Ambition and power are key components – the male protagonist is, after all, a King. The themes of ambition, anger, destruction, the darker human aspects of human nature, are all explored frankly and fearlessly in *Grit*, eddying around the tracks in the same way they had swirled through Martyn's life.

Real World

So much for the content and the meaning of the album. But there were very practical issues for Martyn to face. Who would release it? With the disappointing Rykodisc experience still fresh in his mind, and with strong memories of the slog involved in self-releasing, Martyn was keen to gain the support of a significant label. He turned to Real World, founded in 1989 by WOMAD along with the high-profile rock musician and producer, Peter Gabriel.[7] Martyn was aware of their solid reputation in the industry, and in particular the trust they had earned amongst their artists who were always given the space and freedom they needed to make the music they wanted, rather than the music they thought the market demanded, and so he sent them an early demo of *Grit*.

As it turned out, he was knocking on an open door, for those running the label were already well aware of him and his music. Amanda Jones has been managing the label since its inception, and had seen Martyn perform at WOMEX, a world music showcase event, and had been highly impressed. 'We were always aware of him – I can't remember how I was sent the music originally but he was very much on the radar. We received material for *Grit* – it was well formed by the time I listened to it. The concept was well on its way'.[8] Amanda sent the demo to Peter Gabriel as 'nothing is signed without his approval, understanding and enthusiasm. He was completely knocked out by it, and was sold on it immediately', she recalled. 'The response to Martyn was entirely instinctive – it was just music that turned us on when we listened to it. We respond where we feel there is fantastic quality, and authenticity and great skill in the music-making as well'. Peter Gabriel himself concurred: 'It was a delight when we first got *Grit* sent to us and I think we were quite surprised and excited by what we heard. It was a sort of mix that seemed very fresh and yet had all these traditional references.' In Real World, Martyn found his experimental approach and desire to explore new territory was both understood and warmly encouraged. Gabriel remarked 'I think we all get excited when we feel someone is pushing the boundaries and experimenting.' And so the deal was done. Martyn was delighted, but Amanda was realistic about what they were taking on:

> When we started working with Martyn we were sensitive to the fact that he was not well and that there would be limitations to what he would be able to do. That he wouldn't be able to perform live anymore – so the 'ambition' in a cold, commercial sense, is limited by that. That didn't worry us at all. But what I would say is that Martyn was utterly driven about the music – about making sure the music was as close to his vision as it could be. He was incredibly ambitious in driving the minute attention to detail that he wanted to achieve with this recorded work.

Amanda and her team were soon to discover exactly *how* much their new artist was driven by detail, for now that the release of the album was assured, he set about 'improving' it in every way he could think of. 'There was continual changing and tweaking', she remembered, 'and it was so difficult to pin him

BRAVE NEW MUSIC: THE MARTYN BENNETT STORY

With Rob Bozas at Real World.

down to saying it was finished. He even changed it after we'd mastered it, let's be honest!' Annie Reed, Rob Bozas and Sophie Beck from Amanda's team were all closely involved in the project, and have stayed close to Kirsten and the Trust ever since. Annie in particular was at the sharp end of Martyn's obsessive approach, and had the unenviable task of securing clearance for all of the samples he had used. That was no easy task!

For Martyn, emerging from radical cancer therapy and incarceration in hospital, meeting this creative challenge felt like a special calling: 'The *Grit* demos ended up in Real World when I was actually at my lowest ebb in three years' treatment', he explained on the *Grit* television documentary. 'Peter Gabriel then sent me a letter saying would you do a remix for my new album? Which was the first thing I did when I got out of hospital.' The remix was of a track called 'Sky Blue', elements of which had appeared on two of Gabriel's albums released in 2002, *Up* and *A Long Walk Home*, that featured his soundtrack for the Phillip Noyce film, *Rabbit-Proof Fence*. Martyn was very excited to have landed this commission: 'I'm not sure I'd ever seen him so happy', remarked BJ Stewart:

> Sky Blue was a very significant episode in Martyn's life and career. Martyn had just been released from hospital in Edinburgh after a pretty exhaustive stem cell transplant and weeks in isolation. He got out in record time. There was a new lease of life in Martyn due to Real World's enthusiasm for *Grit* but especially as he had been asked by Peter Gabriel to remix 'Sky Blue'. He moved into an absolutely derelict house with builders working all around him and set manically to work even though just days before he was seriously ill and also prone to catching any kind of infection. I remember him playing it to me before it was finished. He was like a child in a sweety shop. So enthusiastic and full of life. Rubbing his hands together in glee and laughing hysterically at the new massive, rasping fart noise he had come up with for the track. His mischievous tendencies were in full flow as he was aware that the noise and volume of it would raise eyebrows or perhaps even appal some people. I often wondered did he tone it down, or perhaps Peter Gabriel did, or perhaps it was the same as I heard that day in that dilapidated house studio.

Martyn later reflected that if it hadn't been for the Real World deal happening after the radical treatment he had just been receiving, he may possibly have given up creating or playing music completely. After remixing 'Sky Blue', he turned his attention with renewed enthusiasm to finalising *Grit*. It was a highly intensive process, as he set about remixing, tweaking, adding, subtracting, remixing again before eventually settling on its final iteration. It was as 'finished' as it was ever going to be. Having worked with hundreds of Real World artists over the years, Amanda Jones knew that albums are almost never actually finished in the minds of the musicians themselves, and so it was with Martyn: 'What we do is capture it in a moment of time. If Martyn had continued to work maybe *Grit* would have evolved into something different.' Real World were supportive, encouraging and fully invested in Martyn. And they were patient! It was an excellent fit and just what Martyn needed to restore confidence and direction after a long spell of seclusion and debility:

> … because they've given me an outlet it's been like someone coming along and saying 'Martyn you've got to do this. This is your life's work, y'know, this is what you're supposed to do, why you're here on this earth. You're supposed to be doing this type of music that brings together cultures, y'know, in a friendly way. God willing if I've got time left, that's what I really want to do.

In considering what might have been, had Martyn lived, Real World would almost certainly have been involved beyond that one album. Martyn's final live performance (pictured opposite) was supporting Peter Gabriel at a concert in Brighton in November 2003, and it was beautifully fitting that 'Blue Sky' was added as a bonus track along with 'Mackay's Memoirs' when *Grit* was re-released by Real World in 2014. And it was the success of Gabriel and Bennett's collaboration that inspired the Real World 'Scottish Showcase' at Celtic Connections in January 2007. Gabriel commented in an interview at the time with *The Scotsman*: 'At its heart it's a Martyn Bennett tribute… He was an enormously gifted, soulful, passionate, generous musician.'

Grit remains Martyn's last gift to us. As Greg Lawson has said:

> We need people like Martyn, to challenge our points of view, in an honest way, and give us a chance to see a different picture. And that was his role – and that is why he is important, still.

11

Blessed Warrior

I hope my relationship with cancer is like that of a knight and a dragon. You see, my real name is Martyn Bennett-Knight, which if you look in the old books about names means Blessed Warrior. Martyn Bennett

MARTYN'S ADULT LIFE commenced with a duel with testicular cancer, an assault on manhood just as it was beginning. It was diagnosed as he was graduating from college, treatment was successful, and he chalked it up to stress. It was a shock for everyone and a significant event in his life of course, yet apart from regular attendance at clinics, he came through it, was able to focus fully again on life and music and move on. However, it was during one of these check-ups years later that the spectre of cancer revisited him, confirmed in November 2000 by a diagnosis of Hodgkin's Lymphoma. A year of chemotherapy and radiotherapy followed, but the cancer crept back and in January 2002 a splenectomy launched a year of even more radical treatment involving both chemotherapy and a bone marrow transplant. As Martyn explained:

> I had a routine check. I had cancer when I was about 20 years of age just as I was finishing college. This time was a routine check and they found some bumps and things which I wasn't worried about – and I didn't actually expect anything to come from them but as it turned out

the diagnosis came back that I had another type of cancer unrelated to what I had before so, this was out of the blue, my career was kind of doing well and I was doing a lot of live music and working quite hard and I thought I was on my way to making something more of my music and my career and then I had to just stop and commit myself to probably quite a few years of treatment.[1]

While understandably, nobody close to Martyn wishes to dwell too much on his illness in their reflections on his journey, nor let it define his memory, there is no escaping the cruel fact that receiving treatment for cancer dominated the last years of his life. It curtailed band tours and bookings, reduced his ability to play his beloved instruments to his own standards, and led to protracted spells of confinement in hospital or at home. His studio went with him, however, and he continued to work through courses of treatment in Edinburgh and recuperation at home on Mull. *Glen Lyon* and *Grit* were both produced and released during this time, and he worked busily on several other projects too. In these long days and nights, his mind was also highly active, absorbing new narratives from books and films, researching remedies and nutritional approaches for improving his health, and applying himself to philosophical issues with which he had long been grappling. These he shared extensively in interviews, and in messages to his fans through his website, and they provide several points of direct insight into Martyn's experience of cancer and how it shaped his mind, his creativity, his identity and his plans for the future. As Kirsten would later reflect: 'For five years Martyn wasn't well and for five years he didn't get more and more ill: it wasn't a downward spiral, but that illness dominated his life and mine. The journey was incredible, really.' As we know, this journey ended in tragedy, claiming Martyn's life prematurely, and so exploring and to some extent retracing his path is crucial to a fuller understanding of his character and legacy – of the man he became, and of the last music he gifted to us.

The isolation of immunosuppression and other constraints imposed on him by treatment came to serve as what we might call an inverse inspiration for Martyn's music-making. In his own words: '*Grit* was an album for which I stumbled upon the music and it came about by accident – it was a means to keep my mind focused over the last few years because I was stuck in a room a lot of the time and didn't have any means of escape.' While labelling the songs he chose for *Grit* as 'powerful', he was nonetheless restricted in his choice of material by his circumstances: 'I couldn't go outside because of the fact that I was getting chemotherapy at the time, and so I had the records that were at my disposal, you know, from basically my mum's record collection, cos I was staying in Edinburgh at my mum's at the time.' This seclusion both informed and intensified Martyn's creativity but also imposed strictures:

> I realised it was going to take a year to do this course of treatment they had in mind, and I thought 'well I'd better do something with my time, so I brought some of my studio down and it fitted into a small cupboard that was

like 8 foot by 3 foot, it was really a narrow, totally tiny little thing. I was really just using my studio as an escape from emotional feelings and physical feelings.[2]

That escapism fed through into the art he created at this time, for the music of *Grit* is *big* music. It is *strong* music. From his boxroom emerged a soundscape that is expansive, airy, and without horizons. Its voices are bold, uplifting and joyous. The paradox was not lost on him, for he was aware that some classical composers also wrote music that was completely 'against the grain' of their circumstances at the time. Stravinsky's output was at its most cheerful, he noted, when his family was dying of tuberculosis and Martyn saw a direct parallel in *Grit* which emerged at least in part from his own 'darkest moments'.[3] The pain and frustration shaped his creativity, both emotionally and practically, imposing a distinct and new set of challenges with which to contend. And Martyn Bennett-Knight would prove himself to be a contender in every sense: by name and by nature.

Chief among these challenges, then, was physical limitation. This was particularly acute for the venturesome and highly active young man that Martyn had always been. This struggle with illness took him to extremities of physical endurance and suffering that were permanently debilitating and yet which also delivered fresh insights and inspiration to him as he adjusted his concept of himself as a man and musician. For someone whose identity was greatly invested in physicality – always adventurous, climbing mountains, cycling, extremely fit and agile, and whose music after all, was rooted in dancing – the principal psychological challenge of cancer therapy was arguably the loss of physical strength, agility and energy. This he resisted, often with remarkable results. He broke records in the speed of his physical recovery from bone marrow transplantation; he would often cycle to his chemo sessions *and* up Arthur's Seat!

When Martyn became ill, it goes without saying that it was a time of great pain for his loved ones. For Ian there were long years of hope that his son would be able to get clear of his illness, 'unhappily replaced by resignation' as the cancer took hold and the treatments began to fail. Yet Ian's accounts of their final days spent together are strikingly reminiscent of the early years, delighting in the simple pleasures of being outdoors and in touch with the rocks:

> I have some fond memories of trips with my partner, Ruth, to the Thomson home on Mull, of day trips to the islands of Staffa and Iona with him and Kirsten as well as frolicking on the beaches of southern Mull and Calgary and getting up to our ankles in cattle-churned mud in MacKinnon's cave where we found a precipitated limestone bowl with cave pearls; there was the odd walk up the hill in the early days of the illness when he was still strong and even out to the coast in the later stages when he was slowly losing weight and energy. It was a time of transition when it was possible to see the wiry fit lad of the days when he would show you his 100 one-arm push ups but when more often there was a gaunt look on his face that hid a troubled heart.

On Mull, Martyn threw himself into renovating three cottages that he and Kirsten had bought next to the home of her parents, Maggie and Brian Thomson. Kirsten's sister Julie remembered him in Mull being happiest when working with his hands, and that he was particularly good at carpentry; he made furniture for the three cottages. 'He made them very well', recalled Julie, adding 'He'd work for hours on them' and 'he was very accurate'. He would also work for hours on things that perhaps should have been left to specialists. On one famous occasion, he insisted on rewiring the middle property and was upstairs in the loft for hours, other tradesmen and family waiting on standby while he installed the ceiling lights. Suddenly, there was an almighty commotion and Martyn crashed through the ceiling landing in a heap on the floor

below, covered in fresh plaster, rubble and wires. 'Everything was wrecked, absolutely wrecked', laughed Julie, the event attracting a great deal of hilarity for the witnesses! Julie was a regular helper with the renovations: 'We were always doing work together. He always had a story when you were working away, or a latest healthy thing that he was going to try, or he'd make a tune out of things that he had to hand.'

His escapades throughout his illness were a source of regular amusement. His mother-in-law, Maggie, remembered Martyn popping out to the hen field one day and returning sometime later with 'a big basket' of magic mushrooms. On another occasion, they recalled him being stopped on his bicycle by Tobermory police, because he had no helmet and no hands on the handlebars. Martyn, according to Julie, had a firmly held belief that 'policemen didn't like him because he was wee!' Even when he became frailer, he would want to go walking as much as possible. Julie would often accompany him. He always went past any sign saying 'private', and he liked to go into rhododendron bushes: 'we'd sit like kids and just chat, in the rhododendrons, on the side of a hill!' Rory would also appear and go walking in the hills with Martyn. Julie remembered them listening to the landscape, discussing the music made by running water or trees. 'His ears were his sketchbook'. Even as he became extremely weak his desire to take to the hills was undiminished; on one memorable occasion, he persuaded Julie to take him out in a storm for just a few minutes in the dark and rain, and as she helped him up the side of the hill, a stag in rut was roaring and crashing about just below them.

Martyn needed and wanted to share his journey through his illness. In a public website letter to friends and followers after his bone marrow transplant, he expressed both elation at being alive after his release from hospital and the pragmatic business of contending with ongoing pain and reduced physical ability:

> Hello!!! I have some hair again, a bit of colour in my cheeks, and most of all I am alive. It is really a strange feeling to be totally fucked, yet feel alive. I don't think I can really explain what this feels like – this 'alive' feeling. To borrow the words of Milan Kundera, it is the 'unbearable lightness of being'. I want to dance yet I have no means of expression other than to sit and watch this beautiful world and hope that in time I will find eyes without pain. Perhaps I will learn to cry.

Martyn signs off this message in his new knightly character with the words 'blessed be'. This was a few months before the release of *Grit*, when he still had real hopes of recovering health. In his final statement when this had all but evaporated, he describes the 'Martyn on the cover-shot of *Grit*' being turned from 'indestructible young warrior' to 'a small, vulnerable, very frightened little boy, beaten down repeatedly over many years.' Even then, he is contriving some kind of rebirth or transcendence of the pain that has been accompanied by an equally strong 'compassion for every living thing' and 'a further determination to return to this beautiful planet.' It appears Martyn may have entertained ideas of some kind of afterlife in worldly nature, or reincarnation, or that he was striving for a physical recovery that would amount to the same. Regardless, his love of earthly existence seems to have intensified to a greater degree than the pain he suffered, and so he searched for a broader view of the landscape and he fought on with courage and optimism for life in all its possible expressions and manifestations.

Martyn's ever-evolving sense of identity was similarly informed by fantasy and escapism through his immersion in legendary tales. He developed an avid enthusiasm for the *Lord of the Rings* books and films, and for the Disney animation, *The Great Cimeron*, both charting epic journeys in which heroes reject and escape convention and capitalist consumerism. Kirsten:

> He was an avid reader of the same thing. He read *The Hobbit* about 25 times, *Lord of the Rings* 100 times, until he got unwell, then he embraced every single religious culture there is going – Krishna, Hinduism, Islam – I don't think he read them cover to cover, but he dabbled in finding something that would help him. It's interesting because he didn't go to church, *we* didn't. But then he wondered 'maybe I need some help, maybe there is a way'.[4]

For Martyn, the natural world and wilderness seemed to be redemptive, offering the promise of salvation. And so, in his last letter to fans and friends, he mixes symbolic references from film, Gaelic literature and the folklorist, poet and scholar Hamish Henderson to invoke the transcendental: 'Perhaps you are all my carrying stream. Combined you may be able to lead me to the white shores'. The source of creativity and musical ability were something that Martyn conceived as both external: a 'stream' or a 'current of energy', but also divine in that the loss of connection with this stream feels to him 'as if God has turned away from me'. It was this palpable sense of disconnection with his music, and instrumental performance in particular, that eventually led Martyn into the darkest hours of his life.

After he had returned from Edinburgh to Mull in 2003, following the bone marrow treatment and with the album *Grit* well underway, Martyn was alone one summer's day upstairs with his instruments in his studio at home. Suddenly he was in a rage, violently smashing up his precious instruments – an old and valuable violin, a set of pipes that had been through several wars, even his recording equipment and mixing desks. The incident left him in shock. Kirsten remembered that he could not speak about it, or indeed really speak at all in the aftermath. She called his friend, Chris MacLullich, and explained what had happened, putting Martyn on the phone. Chris recollected:

> It was the day when he broke all the instruments, I was up in Benbecula at the time, and I was doing the final writing of my PhD. Kirsten called me first and said 'Martyn wants to speak to you' and he told me what had happened and then we started talking about getting together and doing something. His idea on that day was that we should meet and hire a canoe and paddle down the Spey so we made this plan. It was quite shaky – it didn't have dates or anything, but it was just three days paddling down the Spey on an open canoe. And we talked about it for a long time, you know, what we would do, how we would do it, and it didn't happen in the end because he got too sick. He was in a state of shock and he was just saying that he'd done something he regretted, and he just felt dark. He was feeling low. He needed to have a change of scene, he needed to go and do something to cheer him up. He didn't go into detail. He

just wanted to go and do something different after. He felt upset about what had happened and wanted to go and get a break.

Greg Lawson also spent time with Martyn in the wake of this incident, finding as Chris had done that it was simply too raw a subject for Martyn at that time, and that it was diversion that their friend needed at this point:

> I went up to Mull with McFalls and I went to see him and Kirsten and I helped him sand his floor. And I said 'Marty, man, you're far too skinny to be holding that thing!' Because you have to hold your bodyweight against it and he'd lost a lot of weight. I said, 'You can't be running around with that. I've got a free day. Let's just do the floor together.' Which is still for me the best time I spent with him. I'm so aware of all the times I *didn't* spend with him. I didn't go walking in the mountains with him. I didn't sit and really talk about music at deep enough levels with him. I didn't just, like, hang out with him. All of those things were things I desired to do with Martyn but never got round to doing. So it was after we did the floor he showed me his box of instruments and he talked about that whole thing of breaking your instruments, and talked about I suppose – sound – cos I said to him: 'It's not the instruments; it's the fact that you've chosen not to make sound anymore.' If I couldn't make sound in this world then I don't know what I'd do, cos I love making sound. It's just why I play the violin, you know? And by breaking his instruments he'd actually severed the cord of tangibly making sound with an instrument. That for me is what he really cut. He was just very quiet. He hadn't released it. He'd broken instruments and he knew what that meant.

The destruction of his instruments was a pivotal moment for Martyn, and when he had come to some kind of acceptance and understanding of the incident, he would still evade engagement with suggestions that he might return to playing. When Martin Swan put this scenario to him, Martyn said that he might sing, giving a similar response to Mary Ann Kennedy when pressed on the possibility. As he entered the final years of his life, he seemed more engaged in a musical creativity that involved production rather than playing himself, as he explained to Mary Ann Kennedy, reflecting on recording the orchestral soundtrack for *Grit*: 'I was very nervous about it, because I was still sort of coming out of a third year of treatment, again, and eh, I'd lost a lot of confidence in who I was and what I was about.'⁵ Discussing the effect of bone marrow therapy on his instrument playing, he observed: 'The treatment affects you on a cellular level. I don't feel like the person I know I used to be. And the instruments were the front line of that experience.' In another interview for the TV documentary *Grit*, he also claimed that he thought the treatment affected him 'on a cellular level'. Recalling the afternoon when he destroyed all of his instruments he explained:

> It was out of extreme pain that it happened, a disconnection with who I am as a person. It was the worst experience I've ever had, you know, worse than having organs taken out. I've had quite a few organs taken out over the past few years but out of these ashes come other things. I'm a recipient now, I'm a receiver now. You can't regret what happens; it's life.

While Martyn's sense of connection with himself and his music became strained, his illness seemed only to strengthen his connection with Kirsten. In February 2002, the young couple were married in her parents' kitchen. The wedding followed a downturn in Martyn's health. Immediate family members were present: Margaret, Ian and his partner, Ruth, Kirsten's parents, Maggie and Brian Thomson; her sister Julie and partner, Colin. An assortment of fragments of the day seem to stand out in the memories of those present. The ceremony was conducted by both the local priest and the local presbyterian minister, by all accounts both marvellously eccentric and fascinating characters who were themselves great friends. Martyn was ill and in pain and had to go to bed for a while afterwards. BJ phoned from America to congratulate them but remembered mainly speaking to Kirsten that night. Martyn's father had composed a waltz on the fiddle with his partner Ruth, who had carefully arranged it in notation, and decided to call it 'Mull Wedding' in anticipation of the occasion. As he recalled:

> It was an evening spent in Newfoundland with friends and Ruth and myself. After supper we'd always go off to a piano in the other room – we would start playing tunes as we played in a small amateur group. We were just between tunes and I was just diddling on my fiddle and it started doing something or other and it suddenly turned into this waltz. So I kept on playing. And Bill on the guitar realised it was a tune probably worth recording – so he went off and came back with a tape recorder and we played it. Ruth was on the piano and she came up with a piano line and within half an hour it was done. At the time we had a tune and it sounded good, and worth keeping. So I think after playing it a few times and talking about it, we were trying to decide what to call it – by that time Martyn's wedding had been set in Mull and I was going to be travelling over within a week or so of that session. So I decided to call it 'Mull Wedding'. We gave it to Martyn with other gifts of pottery and all kinds of Indian teapots and so on and played the tape, which would have just been a cassette tape, and played it for him.

Ian remembered Martyn in kilt and waistcoat and hose, and that 'it was a nice occasion', although he felt Martyn 'was still mentally trying to deal with the idea that he was going to die'. Guests arrived in the evening to congratulate the newlyweds, including Gordon MacLean from An Tobar, and friends Kenny Fraser and partner, Petrea Cooney. However, the whole event had a poignancy that almost seems surreal in the recollections of those who were there. Maggie, Kirsten's mother reflected: 'We tried to make it as nice as we could but it was difficult', continuing, 'We put flowers everywhere' in an attempt to make the setting as special as

possible. Martyn had wanted to say vows in the nearby castle but was too unwell on the day, so the ceremony itself was relocated to the conservatory. Julie summed it up simply and emotionally: 'It was a very loving day. It was like everyone just made it happen and made the effort to make it beautiful and lovely and there was singing and lovely music and stories.'

Marriage, return to Mull and home renovation heralded a new phase in Martyn's life, one that also involved casting off material belongings of youth. In the postscript of an email not long beforehand, Martyn discussed the sale of the trappings of his life as a young, carefree, able-bodied bachelor: 'I thought about auctioning off a lot of my things – to make a fresh start, raise money for the Bethesda Trust as well as Kirsten and I (who are rather skint to be honest).' Among the items listed are 'a cherished pair of hiking boots which have climbed more mountains than I can remember and I can no longer use due to my ill health' and 'my cherished hand-built mountain bike'. All of this speaks of a man who is moving onto a new phase in life and apparently accepting greatly reduced mobility as a result of his illness. There is a palpable sense that they are both in this together, sharing the hardships of a life blighted by the toughest of conditions. However, the pain that was experienced and expressed in this process seems to have heralded a transition into a fresh phase, a passage into maturity. Martyn and Kirsten were clearly a unit practically and emotionally, and marriage sealed this legally and symbolically but also in a way that seemed to mark a transition for both to a new territory in every sense; making home in Mull, eschewing many of the material trappings and semi-nomadic lifestyle of their 20s, and dealing with the very grim challenges of permanent debilitation and disease. They were growing up together.

The seriousness of disease, of decision-making, of marital commitment and maturity was not matched, mercifully, with a loss of fun in Martyn's world. All of those who came into contact with Martyn in his final years, whether of acquaintance auld or new, remarked on his humour and uplifting company. Mary Ann Kennedy commented in her condolences: 'Martyn was a truly beautiful soul. He always sent me away uplifted when I came to see him – even when he was so ill, he made me feel like I'd been so lucky to share even a short time with him.' However, it was not all profound and philosophical around Martyn by any means: Rory, for example, remembered him ordering copies of *Hello* magazine, *the Sun* and *Viz* to offset the more esoteric and New Age material he also consumed in the hospice. Julie Thomson recollected that Martyn became somewhat addicted to eBay, and was always buying things for family and friends 'whether they wanted them or not!' He was known to halt important meetings with distinguished medical personnel all gathered around to discuss his treatment in order to place a bid, as she remembered, with great amusement! BJ recalled an experience of sledging with Martyn when he was ill, escaping with a dilapidated sledge and resulting in two broken toes for BJ, skinned legs and backside for Martyn! Many people visited at this time, including his cousins and his grandmother, Peigi. Deirdre meanwhile remembered Martyn accompanying herself and Kirsten out for a coffee very near the end, and he needing the support of walking sticks by then, but wanting to do something they always enjoyed together in times of health. Martyn preferred the café to the pub, their favourite in Edinburgh being Ndebele in Tollcross run by his friend, Jeni Ayris. Mike Cuthbert, the cameraman who filmed the documentary about *Grit* wrote in a letter to Kirsten after Martyn had died, remembering the 'joy and humour Martyn brought to the table' and concluding: 'I'm so happy that, though the film conveyed a sense of pain, what shone through was his impish sense of humour and infectious love of music. What you saw was what he was; a lovely, noble man.' It was his friend Chris MacLullich who perhaps said how his friends felt about Martyn most eloquently yet simply: 'He was just such a marvellous human being. You want other people to get a taste of the spark Martyn was.'

In the final months of his life Martyn was increasingly turning from music to thoughts of travel. Very near the end, he was asked by Mary Ann Kennedy about what he would like to do next and responded:

> My wings are beginning to spread. I need to go from
> Mull now… and go and see a bit of the world, I think.

It's funny... when you feel your time's running out... you suddenly think 'what would I really, *really* like to do? And you start to get quite selfish. I think you should be. You shouldn't worry about time scales. I think people put things off all the time, because they, y'know, they think they have more responsibilities or something to their job or whatever or to their families. And of course, we do have responsibilities but get out there and do what you want, when you want to do it, immediately, because you just don't know.

As Martyn entered his final days, he and Kirsten were confined to the Marie Curie Hospice in Edinburgh. Kirsten remembered this time as 'lonely' and Martyn being insistent that he was going to get better and go away somewhere without even her. 'I'm going to go to the West and be like an eagle and go and live in the mountains. That's what I'm going to do. I have to be alone to do it.' Music in many ways seemed long behind him, as Kirsten reflected: 'When someone dies, everyone focuses on the great thing that they did. But when you're there in it, that isn't what you're left with. When he did die I was totally shocked and it was the only thing Martyn had done without me, apart from say that he was going to go away. But at the last, he just slipped away. He just went really quietly in the end. It was strange, unbelievable,' his death still bewildering so many years on.

In Martyn's final hours, at his bedside were his beloved wife, Kirsten, his mother, Margaret and his father, Ian. Also present was Father Kevin Pearson, who gave him the last rites. Martyn died on 30 January 2005. He was 33.

THE LIST

1997/ISSUE 309/FORTNIGHTLY/£1.90

T IN THE PARK
FULL LINE-UP INSIDE

GLASGOW AND EDINBURGH
EVENTS GUIDE
MUSIC/THEATRE/CLUBS/ART/SPORT/TV

clubbers
...d for it

...GERALD
...ation with
...oman In White

...AGE
...CLUB
...test from
...orthern souls

...ost World,
...otta, Gary Jacobs,
...m Shatner

Piping Hot
music, the crack, the long summer nights
complete guide to Scotland's folk festivals

FOLK ROOTS MAGAZINE
MARCH 2001 No. 213
22nd ANNIVERSARY YEAR 2001
£3.20

fROOTS

Local Music From Out There

MARTYN BENNETT
Highland Hardbeat

BEN MANDELSON
That Mustapha Bloke

Sainkho Namtchylak
While & Matthews
Ethiopiques
Timor Tales
Papa Noel
John Hiatt
Safarini
Da Lata
more!
WIN! An Chang Project CDs!

12

Passing On

THAT WEEK, TUDOR MORRIS, Director of the City of Edinburgh Music School at Broughton, had taken the current generation of his pupils into Cava Studios in Glasgow to make a full recording of 'Mackay's Memoirs', the magnificent pibroch-centred piece Martyn had created for the school's centenary a few years earlier. Martin Swan had been asked to produce this new recording, and had been actively discussing the score and arrangement with Martyn in the hospice only days beforehand. Tudor and others were present in the studio to help out and to oversee the whole project. As he recounted:

> It was the last day of recording when we got the news that Martyn had died. We were there in the recording room and it was a case of 'What the hell do I do'? So I didn't tell the performers, I thought no it just wouldn't be the right thing to do. So we finished the recording and it was a pretty grim day for us up in the control booth – there were a number of us there, and you've got to be smiling and encouraging and it was just that feeling of getting it finished and then the next day, we'll have to tell everyone. It was very moving. Martyn was very aware of the recording and was very supportive and so we wanted to get it done and done properly. And we think it was.

With Broughton High School Students.

Even while Martyn himself was passing on, the music he had given us was in the air, clear and vital, assuming new form, played with pleasure and pride by another generation of fresh young talent. As the days since his death have unfolded into weeks, months, years, and now decades, his musical presence has stayed with us, celebrated and treasured by those who knew and loved him, and by those who simply loved his music. Martyn Bennett's following is still growing, his music still pulses with vitality and challenge and inventiveness. His work continues to inspire, to be passed on: he led, others have followed.

Martyn must have had at least a taste of the potential of his own musical legacy, a sense of his place in the cultural soundscape of Scotland beyond his time here. However, he was nervous about how he might be remembered. 'Don't let them make me into a trophy' he implored his friend and agent, Lisa Whytock. The 'they', presumably, is all of *us*. Yet while it is beyond the scope of this biography to evaluate his legacy, it is, I think, important to acknowledge the remarkable human being he was, and above all to offer an appreciation of Martyn's great gift to us all: his 'brave new music'.

The starting point, perhaps, is to remember that we are dealing with a very short career here. There are dozens of major artists who have been mentioned in this book, and they nearly all shared the luxury of a long life in which to achieve great things. In contrast, Martyn's professional career lasted little more than a single decade, and he fought serious illness for half of it. And yet, for me at least, his name does genuinely belong in the pantheon of men and women whose creativity graces the pages of our cultural history books, or whose faces adorn the walls of our galleries. The carrying stream of Scotland's music was rapidly transforming as it entered the next millennium and a new era of digitisation and globalisation. Martyn Bennett was one of its chief navigators, shifting our perceptions from within Scotland, showing us what our music could be, joyfully revealing all its glorious possibilities – to the world, and to ourselves.

The list of musicians who have cited Martyn Bennett as one of their key influences is a long one. Early converts were the members of the band, Croft Number 5, several of whom had met at school in Inverness in the 1990s, and who were all part of what band member John Somerville referred to as 'that beautiful resurgence in Highland music that started with the Feis movement and moved into bands like Wolfstone and Capercaillie'.[1] The Feis system, founded in Barra in 1981, provides short, intensive courses on a range of instruments for young people across the Highlands. The 'passing on' of the tradition was, and remains, at the core of its mission, and many of its tutors have themselves come through the system in their younger day before going on to develop careers in music. John's brother, Misha, recalled that alongside the Feis there was a kind of 'dirty music scene going on too – whether it was Wolfstone playing at the Kirkhill village hall or the Railway Club in Inverness – there was a whole series of bands in that scene.' So there was the Feis on one hand and that 'grotty music scene' on the other.

Hungry for a bit of 'grot', they discovered the music of Martyn Bennett! 'We were fan boys without a doubt', admitted guitarist Spad Reid. 'Total fan boys'! Still in their mid-teens, they travelled across the Highlands and beyond to take in his gigs. The first time they witnessed Martyn playing live was when they and half a dozen others took a bus from Inverness to Aberdeen in 1998 to see Cuillin play at the Lemon Tree. The music they encountered there was a step away from anything else around at the time. 'There were great bands around at the time like Wolfstone, The Old Blind Dogs, Drop the Box, Shooglenifty, Rock, Salt and Nails but Martyn took that to the next level by replacing that with electronics – that was the progress' John concluded. And for Misha: 'It was leaving behind the folk-rock thing – that was a bit of a revolution for people – people began to realise that folk didn't just have to go with that rock sound. Not that I'm knocking that, but for us, listening to Martyn, listening to Shooglenifty, or Drop the Box – we realised it doesn't have to be that big anthemic rock thing'. And as the band's fiddler, Adam Sutherland, concluded:

> I think all of us again, back to the grounding of the village halls, and being around the older standard bearers of the tradition and even just the local crofter who played in the village halls – being around these people did teach you that healthy respect. And Martyn always had that – I think that was one of the big things of his personality – that he had that respect for what had come before. Martyn had one foot in the past and one foot stepping forward – that is what he seemed to have, and that is what we tried to do as well.

Croft Number 5 formed officially in 1998, taking the ideas they had been drinking in from the scene all around them and from

Coda Music, Edinburgh: shop window 2018.

PASSING ON

Martyn in particular, and adding in plenty of their own, developing their art and taking the music off in their own direction. Martyn admired what they were doing and offered his support, suggesting at one point that he might work with them as a producer for their first recording, although in the event that didn't happen. The band itself has become an important reference point for those who have emerged since: they too have 'passed it on'. It isn't hard to trace those threads of influence down to the present day, leading fairly directly to bands who are now taking their blend of 'Celtic Fusion' to festivals across Scotland and well beyond, such as Niteworks, An Dannsa Dub and Yoko Pwno. As one music journalist recently concluded, 'Speak to any artist at the electronic end of the Celtic fusion spectrum, and Martyn Bennett's name is almost certain to crop up'.[2]

In the piping world specifically, virtually all those who have been 'pushing the boundaries' in one way or another cite Martyn as a core influence, along with his contemporary, the late Gordon Duncan. Having been broadcasting on piping for over 20 years myself, those are without doubt the two names that have been mentioned consistently and frequently in my broadcast interviews over those two decades. One of the most prolific and ubiquitous of them is multi-instrumentalist and composer, Ross Ainslie, who is unequivocal about the debt he personally owes to Martyn and his music:

> It's not often, when listening to music that it changes your world. Well it happened to me when first listening to Martyn Bennett's self-titled debut album. I'll always remember it, it's set in stone in my head – pipes are cool is what I thought! I followed Martyn's journey, eagerly anticipating his latest offerings. He was a consummate musician who had an understanding of music way ahead of his piping peers. Each album release was a growth and adventure which was a joy to listen too. I only met

Martyn twice, the first was after a concert I played at Celtic Connections in the piping centre, I think it was called 'young pipers of Scotland' or something similar. Martyn was in the audience watching (I had no idea), and after the gig I headed to the Central Hotel for the usual madness and Patsy Seddon (harp player and singer) came up to me and said 'Have you seen Martyn yet? He wants to meet you!' As you can imagine my excitement levels grew – I'm going to meet one of my heroes! I never managed to say what I wanted to say to Martyn as I was very star struck. He was quite ill and frail when we met, and he said he was looking for someone to play pipes for him on some recordings he was doing as he wasn't up to it himself health wise. It was a huge honour to be asked but unfortunately, he deteriorated not long after. Since then I've been lucky to play at a few tribute concerts for Martyn: the first was a night in the Fruitmarket in Glasgow – I guess it was 2006 – myself, Rory Campbell and Fraser Fifield shared the piping duties. Then more recently on some amazing gigs along with the Grit Orchestra. Martyn's music is ingrained in Scottish culture, a figure who showed no fear and had a forward-looking approach that I can only have admiration for. The body of work he achieved in his short life is commendable and I have the upmost respect for the man![3]

Stuart Cassells, a former winner of the BBC Radio Scotland Young Traditional Musician of the Year contest and a founder of the global phenomenon that is the Red Hot Chilli Pipers, had a similar story to tell. He was introduced to Martyn's debut album in his teens while attending a festival in Brittany with the Vale of Atholl Pipe Band:

> Martyn was all I listened to for a couple of years. When *Bothy Culture* came out I was Pipe Major of Royal

Burgh of Stirling and we had the band at the Lorient festival that year and that album was the soundtrack of the festival in the dorms that year. I never met Martyn personally unfortunately, but he made an incredible impact on my music and on the Red Hot Chilli Pipers.

John Mulhearn is the current Head of Piping Studies on the degree course run jointly by the Royal Conservatoire of Scotland and the National Piping Centre, and is a prolific composer and performer in his own right:

As a teenager when I first became aware of Martyn, his music bridged what felt to me like foreign and unrelated lands. I vividly remember walking along Great Western Road in Glasgow, with *Grit* playing on my Discman and having the feeling of a new musical world opening up – one where my developing interest in electronic and 'alternative' music could meet the traditional music I had grown up learning, and doing it in a wholly convincing and compelling way. It demonstrated that the contemporary world of technologically facilitated music was part of a natural continuum and process. That revelation continues to inform my whole outlook on music, art and education. Influential beyond words. It's honestly hard to imagine me doing what I do today without his work as a formative influence.

The new generation of top pipers continue to recognise Martyn's importance, and many are drawn to his music. In the very week in which I'm writing this I have had the pleasure of serving as the external examiner for the 4th Year final recitals on the piping degree course run by the Royal Conservatoire of Scotland and the National Piping Centre in Glasgow. One student, Bede Patterson from Australia, treated us to his interpretation of

Martyn's composition, 'Karabach'. With Ewan Johnston on piano and Dean Garrity on soprano saxophone, it was a beautiful and highly moving rendition of a piece Martyn wrote as his response to the humanitarian crisis in Armenia due to the Nagorno–Karabakh conflict that had been raging since the early 1990s. Martyn had seen footage of a child singing in the midst of the blood spilling and hate, and its simplicity and innocence had moved him greatly. The original involved Martyn playing along with jazz guru, Tommy Smith, and appears on an album, *Ceol Tacsi*, featuring tracks recorded on the BBC Alba television programme of that name. With fellow musicians Jim Sutherland, Donald Shaw, James Mackintosh and Manus Lunny in tow, it is a stunning piece of music that drips with both anger and hope. As James recalled, they wanted the pipes to fade out towards the end, rather than stop abruptly. That would normally be achieved by the engineer using a fader slide on the sound desk, but Martyn came up with a rather more natural solution: he kept playing, but wandered out of the studio and along the corridor! The tune has had a new lease of life in recent years too – it is regularly played by the Grit Orchestra and in 2024 it featured in the live set of the National Youth Pipe Band of Scotland.

Of course, piping is only one part of Martyn's story, and as I was drawing the research for this book to its conclusion, I was keen to sit down with someone who might help to 'take stock' and offer an informed view of his body of work and its impact on what has come since. Anna-Wendy Stevenson spent many years as the course leader on an Applied Music degree within the University of the Highlands and Islands, and so is very well placed to gauge Martyn's ongoing influence on today's emerging musicians. 'He set a ball rolling' she concluded:

> And we haven't met anyone yet who has matched Martyn. Because his writing of music is like a very well referenced essay. And I say that to students. Because if you listen to something like *Grit*, he has made a

symphonic work using samples – but they're not just like, 'Oh I like the sound of that sample' – they're ethnographic samples. He is trying to stimulate us in every way – in a really visceral kind of way to do with the music, but also to try to stimulate us to think as an internationalist. I think he tried to stimulate people to think about what unites us rather than what separates us, but with the deepest respect. But also to ask hard questions, like what do we do to each other?

As the grand-daughter of a significant Scottish composer, the late Ronald Stevenson, (whose work Martyn greatly admired) and as a classically trained violinist turned trad fiddler herself, Anna-Wendy recognises the essence of what lies at the heart of great works of music. 'What is the idea or the concept that they are presenting in that work? I think that is a really big thing actually. It was huge in my grandad's work, and it was huge to Martyn's work.' She highlights the importance to Martyn of what she terms 'encounters' – an open engagement from early in his life with all manner of interesting people. She knew from their long teenage chats that they were both privileged to have been brought up within homes 'with an open house mentality – we weren't sheltered from adult conversations. We weren't banished to bedrooms at all. In fact, we were expected to be part of it.' Martyn maintained that open attitude in all of his dealings with everyone, and that honesty and questioning pervades his work at every turn, she believes. 'He didn't do small talk, but would chat about everything in a deep way, especially his feelings'. And that depth was carried over to the work he produced:

> The whole thing does remind me of a really good art portfolio – artists or sculptors – they're first of all starting off with 'let's understand the form with pencil and really practise that'. In a way that's what the first

album was – bringing a few techniques together but honing the skill and understanding of the melody. It was still relatively conventional forms. But making sure there's expertise in that. 'Mackay's Memoirs' was music written to a brief. I think it's brilliantly delivered and it also is like a mini sketch going into the portfolio, of demonstrating solid orchestration techniques with a really limited palette in terms of the melodies – it's all pentatonic melodies. But he's using the techniques really nicely to make a really pleasant piece of music. And there's nothing wrong with that. In fact it was great – very melodic, really nice subtle, very small counter-melodies. And he gave the different musicians the chance to shine at different points. It's a little miniature basically. That's what I think of 'Mackay's Memoirs'. With *Grit*, I see it as a symphony. I talk about it using that term. It's got an arc. It is so crafted. *So* crafted. He thinks about harmonic dynamics, not just loud and soft dynamics. There is a deep understanding of textures, and a real deep understanding of these classical forms as well. And there would have been a progression after the symphony of *Grit*. It would have been really interesting, but not predictable, I think!

These seem to me to be astute observations from a close friend of Martyn, and who is also an experienced educator and highly respected musician in her own right. I concur fully with her assertion that there is a marked progression in his portfolio of work that deepened significantly as his career progressed. And it is tempting, of course, to pick up on her final point above and to join with her in wondering where it might all have led, had he lived. 'What if' history is a dangerous game to play, and yet the clues as to where he might have gone next were there when he was still with us for sure. 'He just loved sound', Kirsten had pointed out in an earlier chat – 'that was so important to him. It was all about the quality of sound'. Production, sound design, film score composing – these may have been the paths Martyn would have followed, but we can only guess of course, and perhaps trying to do so is a futile exercise in any case. I do think Anna-Wendy was right though – it would have been interesting and unpredictable!

Much has been done by way of tribute to Martyn since his passing. The Martyn Bennett Trust was established in 2005 by some of his close friends and family 'to reflect Martyn's vision of music through supporting performances, commissions, new recordings and educational projects'. The organisation has certainly done that, and for two decades now it has been the driving force behind many such projects, and has collaborated with others on several more. Just three months after Martyn died, dozens of musicians who had worked with him gathered to perform at a memorial concert in Edinburgh's Queen's Hall, raising thousands of pounds for the Marie Curie hospice in which he had spent his last days. It was an occasion of high emotion, of course, but the mood was largely one of celebration rather than mourning. As *The Herald* reported:

> Rarely can an audience have radiated such affection for an absent star. As performance after performance was greeted with rapturous applause and heartfelt cheers, it was as if the audience were trying consciously to communicate approval and – there's no other word for it – love through those onstage to the man who presided over events from the screen behind them.[4]

The line-up gave us a sonic snapshot of Martyn's journey in music. Pupils from the music school at Broughton performed 'Mackay's Memoirs' to a standing ovation, Sheila Stewart and Flora MacNeil, two of the iconic voices of *Grit*, sang in Scots and Gaelic respectively, reminding us of the deep roots of so much of his art.

Croft Number 5 re-lived the night the crofter spotted the Shputnik in Glenshiel while jazzers Tom and Phil Bancroft along with Kevin MacKenzie played a new piece in tribute to their late friend, 'The Missing Martian'. Capercaillie members, Donald Shaw and Karen Matheson contributed beautifully, as did Rory Pierce who sang and Gillian Thompson who danced to 'Nae Regrets'. Fred Morrison moved between fiery reels and an exquisite rendition of the tune he had played at Martyn's graveside, 'Lament for the Children'. Peter Gabriel 'sang without great fanfare before taking his seat in the auditorium' while Kirsten took to the keyboards joining Mouth Music on stage. And Margaret led us to Glen Lyon with her moving personal tribute to her son, voiced through 'the only song I could have sung for him' – 'Griogal Chridhe'.

Margaret has celebrated Martyn's life in her own ways too. 'It's not the time you have, it's what you do with what you've got' Martyn reflected when his illness began to take a firm hold, a proclamation that inspired the title of her collection of tributes. It was published in 2006 as *It's Not the Time You Have: Notes and Memories of Music-making with Martyn Bennett*. It is a warm, sincere and eclectic gathering of interviews, anecdotes and reminiscences revealing both the breadth and depth of respect and love in which Martyn was held. This was followed by the release of a three-track CD, *Love and Loss: Remembering Martyn in Scotland's Music*, the proceeds of which helped to endow the Martyn Bennett Memorial Scholarship at the Royal Conservatoire of Scotland. And Margaret has continued to share her unique insights through public talks and lectures as well as through presentations to the next generation of students who know his music but who never knew the man.

In the summer of 2005 Martyn was awarded the degree of Doctor of Music (honoris causa) by the RSAMD, the first honorary doctorate ever awarded posthumously by that institution. Further recognition came in 2012 when he was inducted into the Scottish Traditional Music Hall of Fame, taking his place alongside many of

the great artists whose music, songs and voices he had championed in his own work. Recognition of another kind was bestowed on him in 2014 when his life became the subject of a stage play written by Kieran Hurley and directed by Cora Bissett, with Sandy Grierson playing the role of Martyn. Described as 'An ambitious cross-form, Scots-Canadian site-specific production based on the inspiring life and music of one of Scotland's most innovative, pioneering and influential musicians',[5] it was a high energy piece of immersive theatre that brought together aerial acrobatics, circus artists, dancers, actors, folk singers and both traditional and classical instrumentalists, as well as plenty of Martyn's own dance music. Martyn never did anything by halves, and neither does Cora Bissett! The play opened at the Tramway in Glasgow to generally positive reviews, and moved on to Mull for a short run thereafter, but the wider tour that Cora and the production team had hoped for never materialised.

After the first concert in April 2005, many other fundraising events followed and the money raised by the Trust over almost two decades has supported a variety of projects across Scotland and well beyond, including in Argentina and Columbia. It has commissioned new music, funded educational trips, hosted workshops and maintained a website that continues to be a vital resource for fans, students and researchers (including this biographer!). From the start it also aimed to maintain Martyn's profile and ensure his music continued to reach as wide an audience as possible by releasing or supporting new products.

Birds and Beasts was released in 2010 on the Delphian label and featured Mr McFall's Chamber performing new arrangements of some of Martyn's music, along with Fraser Fifield who also contributed two of his own compositions. It includes the only recording we have of his 'Piece for String Quartet, Percussion and Scottish Smallpipes' that had caused all those problems back in 1995, which James Mackintosh had described as 'a really complex piece of music' and which Tom Bancroft had rather more candidly called 'really fucking hard'! We can certainly hear where they were coming from, the time signatures and rhythms weaving, crossing, clashing and resolving in a marvellously eccentric middle passage that defies description.

As I sit here now with it playing in my headphones, I'm thinking circus clowns, rush hour traffic and bar room gossip, but with the frenetic cacophony interrupted now and then with a pause to take in a gentle summer sunset. It is truly magnificent, and without doubt one of the most sophisticated pieces of music incorporating smallpipes yet to emerge in 40 years of the instrument's revival.

Two years later, the Trust released *Aye* in partnership with Long Tale Recordings run by Rob Bozas, who as a member of the Real World team had previously worked on *Grit*. Richard England, of Cadiz Music Distribution also came on board with the raising of funding for the album. *Aye* is a 'greatest hits' compilation featuring eight tracks drawn from *Martyn Bennett*, *Bothy Culture*, *Hardland* and *Grit*, plus the *Sky Blue Remix* and two tracks which had never

been released, 'Crackcorn' and 'Paisley Spin'. The first of these had been created on Mull in 1999, and features Martyn himself on vocals, singing an American folk song, 'Jimmy Crack Corn' along with his friend, Ian Fraser. The second new track emerged from a commission to compose the music for a collaborative dance project for the Spin Festival in 2001, celebrating the heritage of Paisley in Renfrewshire. As a fan of Gerry Rafferty who hailed from the town, Martyn opted to build the piece around samples of three tracks from Rafferty's 1971 debut album, *Can I Have My Money Back?* Sadly, Martyn was unable to complete the full project due to his illness, but this 'affectionately irreverent' track is something of a triumph and is one of the few in which Martyn drew on the voice of a mainstream artist. In fact, the original intention had been to include 'Paisley Spin' on *Grit*, but difficulties in securing

clearance meant that it was left off, and only timely interventions by Martha Rafferty, John Byrne and Rab Noakes ensured that permission was gained to include the track on *Aye*. Its use by the Grit Orchestra as the final encore piece in their live shows is poignant to say the least. As the lyrics say, 'To each and every one of you, I say goodbye farewell adieu'. Overall, the *Aye* CD was very well received, critics welcoming it as a reminder of Martyn Bennett's timeless appeal and unique contribution to the music of Scotland. The tracks, for reviewer Rob Adams, 'both exhilarate and make you wonder just what fantastic musical sorcery might have followed had Bennett's creativity been allowed to continue'.[6]

Perhaps unexpected recognition of an aspect of Martyn's work came from the organisers of the 400th anniversary celebrations of the publication of the 'authorised version' of the King James Bible, that took place in the presence of Queen Elizabeth at Westminster Abbey in November 2011. A roll call had been compiled of those artists who had made use of it since its publication in 1611. Having quoted from Psalm 121 in 'Mackay's Memoirs' and Psalm 118 in 'Liberation' on *Grit*, Martyn was in there along with the likes of Tallis, Handel, Elgar, Purcell and Vaughan Williams – exalted company indeed!

And so we return full circle to the man in black, baton in hand, epitome of cool, conducting the most ambitious series of celebrations of Martyn's music yet to appear. Greg Lawson has led his Grit Orchestra on several occasions now at Celtic Connections, The Edinburgh International Festival and WOMAD, giving the full treatment to *Bothy Culture* as well as *Grit* and several other tracks along the way. They have all been truly momentous occasions, the 2018 Celtic Connections event at the SSE Hydro Arena in Glasgow serving up a spectacular mix of aerial acrobatics and dance from All or Nothing, and stunt cycling from Danny MacAskill (albeit tamed somewhat by a broken knee!). 'Like Bennett's music, and as a slice of modern Scottish culture' concluded Kate Molleson in *The Guardian*, 'the whole night was a weird fusion of the deep-rooted

Grit Orchestra.

and the brazenly off-kilter. Somehow it worked.'

Yes, somehow the music of the Grit Orchestra *does* work. It works because Greg Lawson and his 80 or so colleagues manage to capture the essence of Martyn Bennett and his music. It is deep, quirky, ambitious, unique and joyous.

Perhaps the final major task of the Martyn Bennett Trust has been to commission this biography. I hope it too has captured something of the essence of Martyn Bennett and his music. Now go listen to it. Loudly.

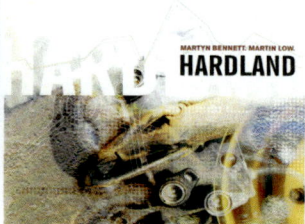

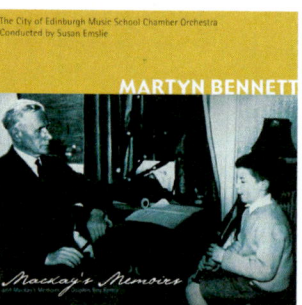

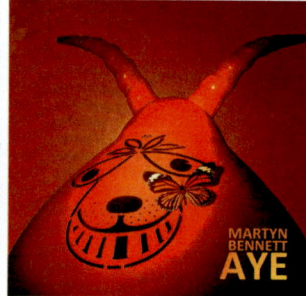

13

Liberation

THE ROAD TO Calgary Bay on Mull's north-western coast is a single track, twisting across an ever-changing landscape towards the sea. If unfamiliar with its contours and turns, you can't afford to be in a hurry. Locals have no such qualms! On the final descent towards the bay, the land and sky seem to relax and expand into a vista of vivid green *machair* and aquamarine sea, while the white shell sands beyond sweep a semi-circle of cinematic scale.

Set back from the road, surrounded by fields and backed by old and wise-looking trees is a rectangular graveyard, enclosed by a neat limestone wall. The path on one side is rutted and trickling with mini tributaries from recent rainfall. A sign on the way in says that it is private ground, but cheerfully ignoring such a warning seems fitting for this visit! Wandering around the enclosure it becomes apparent that it is an ancient site clad with a relatively new exterior: old cross slabs mark the way to the deep past, hinting at the earliest Columban adventurers who first brought Christianity to the shores of Iona, a few miles to the south. The sea carried people here and the sea took them away. The nearby ruins of a cleared village are an etching on the grass, telling the tale of traumatic evictions and departures for the New World from Calgary pier. It is an achingly beautiful final resting place for the Scottish-Canadian and adopted Muileach, Martyn Bennett.

It is a place to remember, to reflect, to contemplate. And many do. I know of one young man who has travelled here with his family every year since the age of 12 to play a tune on his pipes. It is quite simply something he wanted to do since first hearing Martyn's music and his story.[1] And there are many more who are drawn to this spot to pay quiet tribute in their own way.

Martyn had maintained such fervent hope of recovery that his last wishes were somewhat impractical, as he wanted to be sent out to the western sea in a burning birlinn, like a Norse-Gael warrior! That couldn't happen, of course, but Kirsten was determined to honour her husband's wishes as closely as possible, accepting the offer of a lair from her brother-in-law, in the family burial ground. Martyn's headstone is hard to find at first, but reveals itself in the far corner. In line with an old gnarled sycamore, it is a striking, asymmetrical Ballachulish slate that Kirsten had found in Oban. Although almost too slender to carve, sculptor Ian Newton went to work on it. The artistry is bold, the inscription brief.

> Martyn
> Bennett
> Knight
> 1971
> 2005
> Liberation

Martyn Bennett-Knight liberated our music and scoffed at boundaries. He gave us vast, colourful soundscapes and finely detailed musical miniatures. He brought new life and vigour to the traditions he inherited, and passed them on with sparkling energy and fresh meaning. His artistic horizons were wide, distant, and he was constantly searching for what might lie beyond. He was intrigued by humankind's need to create wonderful sounds and he celebrated cultural difference wherever he found it. He invited us to come with him to explore, to dance, to laugh, to sing. And it was all laced with adventure, irreverence and fun. He opened up new possibilities and dared us to follow, gifting us startling insights through his music. Brave, new music.

Timeline

1971   Martyn Bennett born 17 January 1971 at St John's, Newfoundland, Canada.

1976   Moves to Scotland.

1979   Settles in Kingussie where he starts piping lessons with David Taylor.

1986–89   Moves to Edinburgh, attends Broughton Music School.

1990–93   Studies performance in violin and piano at RSAMD, Glasgow, where he meets his future wife, Kirsten.

1993   Moves back to Edinburgh to relearn the 'fiddle'; collaborates and gigs with multiple cross-genre musicians.

1994   Plays support to Mouth Music at inaugural Celtic Connections. Embraces club culture and dives deeper into electronic music.

1995   Record deal with Eclectic. Records first album, *Martyn Bennett*.

1996   First album released. Performs at *Braveheart* premier and to a crowd of 50,000 at Hogmanay.

1997   Secures deal with American label, Rykodisc. Records *Bothy Culture*, released in UK in October. Forms the band Cuillin to tour Europe and North America.

1998   *Bothy Culture* gets worldwide release. Tours with Cuillin to USA, Canada, UK and Europe. Main stage at T-in the Park; infamous Paris gig at Buddha Bar.

1999   Moves to Mull with Kirsten and starts recording *Hardland* which has its debut at the Millennium concert at Edinburgh Castle. His epic 'Mackay's Memoirs' written and performed for the opening of the new Scottish Parliament.

2000	Performs at Celtic Connections. Further tours of UK and Europe. Blows away crowds at the Cambridge Folk Festival. Diagnosed with cancer in October and starts treatment, pulling all engagements.
2001	Further hospitalisation and major surgery. Continues to work on *Glen Lyon* and the early seeds that will become *Grit*.
2002	*Glen Lyon* released in March on Foot Stompin' Records. Martyn is asked to remix Peter Gabriel's 'Sky Blue'. Record deal with Real World. Martyn and Kirsten are married on Mull.
2003	*Grit* released in October. Martyn performs for Peter Gabriel in November. It is to be his last public performance. BBC *Grit* documentary televised.
2005	Martyn dies on 30 January at Marie Curie Hospice, Edinburgh. 'Mackay's Memoirs' is finally recorded the following day.
	The Martyn Bennett Trust is set up to promote and protect Martyn's music and legacy.
	The Trust holds a tribute concert at the Queens Hall in Edinburgh featuring a whole host of musicians including friends and family. Peter Gabriel performs too.
	In the summer of 2005 Martyn is awarded the degree of Doctor of Music (honoris causa) by the RSAMD, the first honorary doctorate ever awarded posthumously by that institution
2006	Margaret Bennett releases *It's Not the Time You Have... Notes and Memories of Music Making with Martyn Bennett*
2006–09	The Trust holds several large tribute concerts in honour of Martyn Bennett in Edinburgh and Glasgow.

TIMELINE

2010   *Birds and Beasts*, an album of newly arranged Martyn Bennett tunes – a collaboration between the Trust, Delphian, McFalls Chamber Orchestra and Fraser Fifield – released on Delphian Records.

2012   The Martyn Bennett Trust releases the compilation *Aye* with Long Tale Recordings, featuring two unreleased tracks, 'Paisley Spin' and 'Crackcorn'.

Martyn is inducted in to the Scottish Traditional Music Hall of Fame.

2014   Real World release *Grit – Gold Edition*, adding the additional tracks 'Sky Blue' and 'Mackay's Memoirs'.

Cora Bissett and Kieran Hurley's award-winning stage production of *GRIT* performed in Glasgow and Mull.

2015–25   The Grit Orchestra is formed and hold its first gig at Celtic Connections, performing Greg Lawson's orchestral arrangement of the full *Grit* album. Many more high-profile concerts are held, including at Womad Festival, the Hydro in Glasgow and both opening and closing concerts at the Edinburgh International Festival.

2017   Real World release *Grit* on vinyl.

2024   *Grit* is awarded 'Modern Scottish Classic Album' at the Scottish Album of the Year Awards.

2025   The Grit Orchestra perform in Glasgow at Celtic Connections to mark the 20th anniversary of Martyn's death. The release of the biography, *Brave New Music: the Martyn Bennett Story* from Luath Press.

Author Acknowledgements

MANY PEOPLE HAVE contributed to this biography in many different ways. Martyn's family, friends, colleagues and collaborators have given generously of their time in interviews, chats, emails, letters, phone calls and on social media. Without that crucial input this book would simply not exist. Some of them are quoted and acknowledged in the text, while many are not. But collectively, a significant proportion of all those who have been involved in Scotland's music scene during Martyn's lifetime and since his passing have contributed through casual chats, brief asides, stories and anecdotes – the folk process in action!

I am especially grateful to Martyn's immediate family – Kirsten Bennett, Margaret Bennett and Ian Knight. I appreciate that sharing their treasured memories of Martyn as a husband or son must have been a deeply emotional, and at times, very painful, thing to do. Each of them has taken the time to read through earlier drafts of the text, and I have gratefully taken on board their comments and suggestions in producing this final version.

I would also like to thank all at the Martyn Bennett Trust, and especially BJ Stewart who has served as my contact and collaborator throughout. I thank him for his interviewing, encouragement, his endurance and most of all, his patience! For various reasons it has taken me at least twice as long to finish this book as I had originally envisaged (actually maybe even four times as long), and a lesser man would have given up on me long ago.

My thanks also go to Gavin MacDougall, Jennie Renton and all at Luath Press for sticking with us after a rather long wait!

My family give me their constant support, and thanks especially to my wife, Wendy West, for help with admin and organisation of the extensive Martyn Bennett archive of press cuttings, interviews and reviews.

Thanks also go to Gillian Cook for help with some interview transcriptions. James Robertson generously offered to read the first draft of the text: to have one of Scotland's finest writers offer his thoughts and advice so enthusiastically and candidly has been a great boost, and his input has been invaluable and gratefully received.

I am also hugely indebted to Georgie Farron, whose informal job title may have been 'research assistant' but whose job description (if there had been one!) would actually include a great deal more besides: chief editor, and at times even co-author, would be more accurate titles, given the scale of her commitment and the breadth, depth and quality of her input. As an emerging scholar, she has so much to give and I look forward to reading

ACKNOWLEDGEMENTS

her own contributions to the study of Scotland's culture in the months and years to come.

Finally, my own heartfelt thanks go to Martyn himself. He may not be here to pass comment, but I did spend enough time in his company when he was still with us to get to know something of his character, his talent, his humour and his infectious zest for life. It has been an honour and great privilege to have had license to peer deeply into that life, and I can only hope that he would not have been too disappointed with the result. Martyn, I thank you and I salute you.

The one thing that would have made him happy for sure is for you to go and listen to his music. So please do.

The Martyn Bennett Trust Acknowledgements

THE MARTYN BENNETT TRUST, which has commissioned this biography, would like to thank the following people and organisations who have all helped enormously in making this project become a reality:
Ross Ainslie, Alasdair Baird, Tom Bancroft, Aly Barr, BBC Scotland, Kenny Bean, Nicola Benedetti, Margaret Bennett, Ian Benton, Alan Bett, Cora Bissett, Kerry Black, Garry Boyle, Rob Bozas, Julie Bull, John Byrne, Stuart Cassells, Jamie Chambers, Duncan Chisholm, Gillian Cook, Don Coutts, Mike Cuthbert, Sadie Dayton, Gary Doak, Georgie Farron, Peter Gabriel, Barbara Gordon, Brian Gordon, Jamie Hale, Mhairi Hall, Lorraine Hammond, David Harrower, David Hayman, Sam Heughan, James Holm, Kieran Hurley, Colin Hynd, Amanda Jones, Susan Morgan Jones, Albert Jordan, Phill Jupitus, Richard Kellett, Neil Kempsell, Mary Ann Kennedy, Ian Knight, Greg Lawson, Su-a Lee, Andy Levy, Liz Lochhead, Chris MacDonald, Kenny MacDonald, Calum Angus Mackay, Leslie MacKenzie, Talitha MacKenzie, James Mackintosh, Gordon Maclean, Màiri MacLean, Dolina MacLennan, Chris MacLeod, Donald MacLeod, Leòdhas Macleòd, Uisdean MacLeod, Christopher MacLullich, Colin MacLellan, Colin MacPherson, Seumas Mactaggart, Mac TV, Simon Manfield, Karl Mariner, Marc Marnie, Sam Maynard, Neil McFadyen, Robert McFall, Mary McGookin, Gwen McGinty, MG ALBA, Pauline McLuskie, David Moir, Fin Moore, Hamish Moore, Tudor Morris, Ann Morrison, Deirdre Morrison, Fred Morrison, John Mulhearn, Hamish Munro, John D Niles, Tina Norris, Matt Osborne, Dave Peabody, Rory Pierce, Penny Precious, Ruaridh Pringle, Jane-Ann Purdy, David Rae, Real World Records, Annie Reed, Barry Reid, Jamie MacDonald Reid, Lesley Riddoch, Douglas Robertson, Gary Robertson, Gloria Rosson, Manon Rousso, Matt Seattle, Damian Shields, Ian Smith, Mairi Smith, John Somerville, Misha Somerville, Adam Sutherland, Jim Sutherland, Anna Wendy Stevenson, Gordon Stevenson, Martin Swan, David Taylor, *The List* magazine, *The Scotsman* newspaper, Cat Thomson, Julie Thomson, Maggie Thomson, York Tillyer, Dan Tuffs, Lisa Whytock, Sue Wilson.

A heartfelt thank you to everyone at Celtic Connections, especially Donald Shaw and Lesley Shaw, for their incredible generosity and unwavering support. Special thanks to Lesley Anderson and James Robertson for their expertise and kindness, Creative Scotland for the funding that made this all possible and for their guidance and patience. Thanks also to Gavin MacDougall, Jennie Renton, Amy Turnbull and all at Luath Press for believing in this project. And finally, huge thanks to Gary West, Kirsten Bennett and Rachel Baker, for everything.

Photo Credits

BJ Stewart and Karl Mariner: 217, 333
BJ Stewart: 8, 111, 126–127, 152, 169, 170, 183, 198, 207, 209, 214, 246–247, 248, 251, 252, 262–263, 269, 272, 274, 281, 286, 300, 308, 311, 320–321, 332, 335, 336, 339, 340
Colin MacPherson courtesy of *The Scotsman*: 123
Colin Turner: 176
Daily Record: 92
Dan Tuffs: 148–149
Dave Peabody: 234–235, 258
David Harrower: 97
David Moir courtesy of *The Scotsman*: 157
Donald MacLeod courtesy of *The Scotsman*: 114
Duncan Chisholm: 95
Gary Robertson and BJ Stewart: 177
Gary Robertson: 178
Gwen McGinty: 340
Ian Knight: 49, 59
Ian MacKenzie courtesy of Talitha MacKenzie: 63, 68, 81
James Holm: 37, 111, 120, 154
Jamie Hale: 227
John Niles: 138
Kenny Bean: 108
Kenny MacDonald: 201
Kirsten Bennett: 27, 35, 57, 73, 83, 141, 142, 158, 237, 294, 303, 330
Leodhas MacLeod: 242
Manon Rousso: 12
Marc Marnie: 75
Martin Honeysett courtesy of Penny Precious: 111
Martyn Bennett: 15, 17, 21
Martyn Bennett and BJ Stewart: 220–221
Ruaridh Pringle: 150
Sadie Dayton: 130, 162
Scotsman Publications: 47, 317
Susan Morgan Jones: 145
The List and *fRoots*: 315
Tina Norris: 105
York Tillyer: 297

Endnotes

Overture
1. Personal communication, June 2024.

Chapter 1 Beginnings
1. Margaret's research was published in her book *The Last Stronghold: Scottish Gaelic Traditions in Newfoundland (Canada's Atlantic Folklore-folklife series)*. Canongate Books Ltd, Breakwater Books Ltd, 1989.
2. Interview recording (out-take) for *Grit* television documentary, filmed by MacTV for BBC Scotland Arthouse, first broadcast 7 December 2003. Producer Calum Angus Mackay; Director David Rea.
3. Frank R. Shaw, 2005 'A Chat with Margaret Bennett' <online article> https://www.electricscotland.com/familytree/magazine/junjul2005/story29.htm.
4. Ian reflected on those years too: 'In the summer of 1973 Martyn was with both of us when we travelled about western Newfoundland using a camper and staying with the MacArthurs when I began a regional study of Carboniferous rocks from the Valley to northern east shores of the Great Northern Peninsula. I then spent two years on a regional geological study and so in '74 and '75 he was principally with me when I mapped the Codroy and Anguille Mountain area. During the three years in the valley I cultivated a vegetable garden, got to know many of the MacArthurs and Cormiers, and talked about their life, farming traditions, berry picking, hunting and fishing, as well as chatted with them about music.
5. Personal correspondence, August 2024.
6. Margaret Bennett, 2006, *It's Not the Time You Have: Notes and Memories of Music-making with Martyn Bennett*, Grace Note Publications p.3 and note 5.
7. Frank Blackwood, 2004, *MinFo* Vol 10, No 2, Fall 2004, https://www.gov.nl.ca/iet/files/mines-production-mrip-vol10no2.pdf
8. Personal communication, June 2018.
9. Television documentary *Grit*, 2003.
10. RCS lecture, May 2023.
11. Personal communication, June 2018.
12. This is a traditional song popular in Tennessee, Virginia and North Carolina, and first recorded in 1927. It was included on the Folkways Records highly influential album *Anthology of American Folk Music* released in 1952, and thereafter widely covered and recorded although not, it seems, by Woody Guthrie. The version Martyn knew was recorded by Joe Hickerson who included it on his 1970 album *With a Gathering of Friends*. It was one of Martyn's favourites from the age of two.
13. The song is 'Henry my Son'. Martyn knew it from a Pete Seeger album of his mother's.
14. Sean Connery recorded a version of the narrative, along with the Royal Philharmonic Orchestra, for Decca in 1966.
15. *Grit* television documentary, 2003.
16. Interview with Mary Ann Kennedy, BBC Radio Scotland, 2003.
17. In Margaret Bennett, 2006, 7.
18. Contained in a draft entry for his website.
19. In conversation with Sue Wilson.
20. *Scotland on Sunday*, 7 December 2003.
21. David Taylor, quoted in Margaret Bennett, 2006, 7.
22. Personal communication 2024.
23. Personal communication 2024.
24. Margaret Bennett, 2006, 3.
25. Interview with Mary Ann Kennedy BBC Radio Scotland, 2003. The TMSA is the Traditional Music and Song Association of Scotland, founded in 1966.

Chapter 2 The Music Apprentice
1. Interview, March 2018.
2. *Grit* television documentary 2003.
3. Although Martyn was due to begin his career at Broughton in 3rd Year, Margaret requested that he repeat 2nd Year, as his reading was rather slow, and he was beginning his new instruments from a standing start. This was granted.

4. For an in-depth interview with Colin MacLellan about his father, see the website piperspersuasion.com
5. Bunty MacLellan, interview with Margaret Bennett, January 2006, and quoted in Margaret Bennett, 2006, 21-22.
6. Interview, March 2024.
7. Interview for *Pipeline*, BBC Radio Scotland, February 2019.
8. Personal communication, March 2024.
9. As pointed out, for instance, in his obituary in *The Scotsman*, 28 October, 2004.
10. Margaret remembered her father bringing home a stereogram when she was around 12, a huge advance on record players. 'It had two speakers placed strategically and had a demo record where you could actually hear the instruments spread out across the room'. The machine is now in the archives of the Royal Conservatoire of Scotland along with George's 4-track reel to reel recorder, Martyn's wind-up gramophone and their collection of 78 RPM records.
11. Quoted in Sue Wilson, 'Breath of Fresh Airs', *The Scotsman*, 2 April, 1996.
12. Interview, February 2019.
13. Venuti and Lang also provided much inspiration for another stalwart of the folk scene, Shetland guitarist, Peerie Willie Johnson. See James Robertson, *Michael Marra: Arrest this Moment*, Big Skye Press, 2017, 144.
14. Hugh MacDiarmid also hugely admired him, referring to 'Heifetz in tartan' in his major poem, 'A Drunk Man Looks at the Thistle'.

Chapter 3 Making a Name

1. Lorraine Hammond, personal communication to Margaret Bennett. Martyn was later to compose a tune for Lorraine and Bennett Hammond, entitled 'Blessings Counted', and on several visits to the USA he spent many hours playing music with Bennett in particular.
2. Ty Burr, *Entertainment Weekly*, 8 February 1991.
3. 'Piping Hot Martyn Reels Them in', *The Evening News*, 1 November, 1995.
4. These were *Mo-Di* (1993), *Move On* (EP, 1994), *Shorelife* (1995), *Seafaring Man* (2001), *The Scrape* (2003) and *The Order of Things* (2005).
5. 17 January 1994, *The Scotsman*.
6. 1 August 1994, *Daily Record*.
7. Personal Interview, October 2022.
8. Personal interview, May 2024.
9. Personal correspondence.
10. January 3 1995, *The Herald*.
11. https://bocan.tv/en/topic/the_scottish_urisk
12. https://www.delphianrecords.com/products/dcd34085
13. All Tom Bancroft quotes from Interview, February 2019.
14. Interview, February 2019.
15. 27 December 1993, *The Scotsman*.

Chapter 4 First Born

1. Quoted in Sue Wilson, 'Breath of Fresh Airs', *The Scotsman*, 2 April, 1996. It is unclear, however, to which review he was referring.
2. Lori H Watson, 'The New Traditional School in Scotland: Innovation, Beyond-Tune Composition and a Traditional Musician's Creative Practice', Unpublished PhD, Royal Conservatoire of Scotland and University of St Andrews, 2013.
3. http://martynbennett.com/Album_MartynBennett.html
4. http://martynbennett.com/Album_MartynBennett.html
5. Special Correspondent' [Hugh MacDiarmid], 'Scottish People and Scotch Comedians', *Stewartry Observer*, 23 August 1928, in *The Raucle Tongue*, vol. 2, 113–15 (114-15).
6. David Goldie, 'Hugh MacDiarmid, Harry Lauder and Scottish Popular Culture', in *International Journal of Scottish Literature*, Issue One, Autumn 2006.
7. Margaret Bennett, 'Hamish Henderson and Martyn Bennett – Conversations and Collaborations', in E. Bort, ed. *Anent Hamish Henderson: Essays, Poems, Interviews*, Grace Note Publications, Comrie, 2015.
8. Ibid, 176–77.

Chapter 5 Bellows Boy
1. Matt Seattle, 1995 & 2011 *The Master Piper: Nine Notes That Shook the World*, Dragonfly Music.
2. If you are interested in exploring this history in much more depth, a good place to start is the website of the Lowland and Border Pipers' Society (LBPS) at https://lbps.net For published histories, see Pete Stewart 2005, *The Day it Dawes: the Lowland Scots Bagpipe and its Music, 1400–1715* Ashby, White House Tune Books, and Pete Stewart, *Welcome Home my Dearie: Piping in the Scottish Lowlands, 1690–1900*.
3. Interview, February 2019.
4. Margaret Bennett, 2006, 102. The sketch is also included in that book on page 8.
5. Iain MacInnes 'Taking Stock: Lowland and Border Piping in a Highland World' in J Dickson, ed. *The Highland Bagpipe: Music, History, Tradition* Ashgate Publishing, 2009, 170–89: 170.
6. Margaret Bennett, 2006, 102.
7. *Grand Concert of Scottish Piping*, Greentrax Recordings, CDTRAX110, 1996.
8. One of the standard and oft-quoted blueprints was suggested by the ethnomusicologist, Tamara Livingston, in her article, 'Music Revivals: Towards a General Theory' in *Ethnomusicology* 43, 1999, (Winter), 66–85.
9. Livingston, 1999.
10. Recorded by Gary West, School of Scottish Studies Archives, SA.1999.21.

Chapter 6 Bothy Culture
1. Personal communication, May 2024.
2. Mairi McFadyen 'Bothy Culture and Beyond: a Live Lasting Culture' in *Bella Caledonia*, February 2018
3. John MacInnes, 'Sorley MacLean's Hallaig: a note' in Michael Newton (ed) *Dùthchas Nan Gàidheal: Selected Essays of John MacInnes*, 2006.
4. In his teens, Martyn had appeared in an earlier film of Tim Neat's, 'Journey to a Kingdom' and they had been friends since then. Tim allowed Martyn free access to hours of recording he made with Sorley, and Martyn also visited Sorley in Skye.
5. http://www.martynbennett.com/Album_BothyCulture-20-Years.html

Chapter 7 Cuillin
1. Personal interview, May 2024.

Chapter 8 Home
1. The piper, whistle player, saxophonist and composer, Fraser Fifield, was later to compose a piece of music celebrating that daily commute, entitled 'Kilchoan Ferry'. It appeared on the album *Birds & Beasts*.
2. Sue Wilson, *Songlines*, 2012.

Chapter 9 Glen Lyon
1. Margaret Bennett 2006, 74.
2. Ibid.
3. RCS Lecture 2023.
4. Liner notes for *Glen Lyon*, 2001. Margaret gave a powerful account of the significance of the songs in this album to their family: 'The choice of songs emerged from stories Martyn had heard as long as he could remember. His great-great grandfather, Peter Stewart, opens the album, a crofter-fisherman, the only one of four brothers to have died on land – the other three and their father drowned at sea. His son, Martyn's great grandfather, whom he called 'Seanair', was also one of four brothers, the only one alive at the end of the First World War: one slaughtered at the Somme, one at Mons, and one missing, presumed dead (after whom Martyn was named). His grandmother too had seen heartache, one sister recruited as a nurse in the Second World War died of tuberculosis at 21 and the second sister in the army died at 33. The Gael has always expressed emotion through song while life seemed like relentless hard work. Austerity aside, 'You'll have a dram, a tune, a song, a yarn.' Uig bard Nicolson referred to John Stewart's house as a 'taigh ceilidh' while his grandchildren remember Seanair's great sense of fun, the dancing in the kitchen on Saturday nights, songs and rhymes, and board games too. You can hear the roll of the dice in one of the songs.' Personal correspondence, 2024.

ENDNOTES

5. Martyn chose the photographs and commissioned a company called 16K design to make the cover. They chose the font.
6. Dai Woosnam (2001) available from www.livingtradition.co.uk
7. After Martyn's death, Margaret re-issued the album under both of their names, with the sub-title altered to 'A Family Song Cycle' and with a reworked cover. All of the commentary in this chapter, however, relates to the original 2002 release.
8. Artwork Notes, NVA, 2000, Available online http://nva.org.uk/artwork/path/
9. The photographer was Alan McAteer.
10. Interview for BBC Scotland *Artworks* documentary: *Grit*, 2003.
11. Margaret Bennett 2006, 75.
12. MacGregor, M. '"Surely one of the greatest poems ever made in Britain": The Lament for Griogair Ruadh MacGreror of Glen Strae and its Historical Background' (114–53) in Edward J Cowan & Douglas Gifford, *The Polar Twins* (1999) Edinburgh.
13. Interview for BBC Scotland *Artworks* documentary: *Grit*, 2003.
14. Captured from a BBC report of that same massacre.
15. Waulking songs were sung by women while fulling their woven cloth, a heavy job requiring team work to beat the cloth into its finished form. Singing in this context allowed for exploration of themes and issues important to them, and also typically included non-lexical vocables, or 'mouth music' in the chorus. The verse may be sung by a lead soloist and the choral refrains by the group.

Chapter 10 Grit

1. BBC Radio Scotland, 2003.
2. Robert McFall, liner notes to *Mr McFall's Chamber, Birds & Beasts*: Music by Martyn Bennett and Fraser Fifield, CD, Delphian.
3. Interviewed by Sue Wilson, 2016.
4. Personal correspondence, 2023.
5. The same thing happened in Margaret's grandparents' home where her grandfather would always read, but when he was away at the fishing his wife would take on these duties.
6. Margaret Bennett, private correspondence, 2024.
7. The World of Music, Arts and Dance festival founded in 1982.
8. Interview, May 2017.

Chapter 11 Blessed Warrior

1. Interview for *Grit* television documentary, 2003.
2. The 'cupboard' is perhaps more accurately described as a boxroom. He later moved his computer into a larger bedroom in his mother's flat.
3. Martyn was very familiar with some of Stravinsky's music which he considered 'fiendishly difficult to play'. He had direct experience of just how difficult, having been the solo violinist for a performance of *The Soldier's Tale*.
4. Margaret points out that Martyn did have a bible by his bed, and in Lewis had been given a book of Free Church sermons.
5. Interview with Mary Ann Kennedy BBC Radio Scotland 2003.

Chapter 12 Passing On

1. Interview with members of Croft Number 5 – John Somerville, Misha Somerville, Barry 'Spad' Reid and Adam Sutherland, January 2018.
2. Becca Inglis, 'Celtic Fusion: Where Bass Meets Bagpipes', *Bandcamp Daily*, February 2024.
3. Personal communication, March 2024.
4. 18 April 2005, *The Herald*.
5. https://www.corabissett.co.uk/work/grit
6. Rob Adams, *The Herald*, March 2012.

Chapter 13 Liberation

1. Callum Smith from Midlothian.

Luath Press Limited

committed to publishing well written books worth reading

LUATH PRESS takes its name from Robert Burns, whose little collie Luath (*Gael.*, swift or nimble) tripped up Jean Armour at a wedding and gave him the chance to speak to the woman who was to be his wife and the abiding love of his life. Burns called one of the 'Twa Dogs' Luath after Cuchullin's hunting dog in Ossian's *Fingal*. Luath Press was established in 1981 in the heart of Burns country, and is now based a few steps up the road from Burns' first lodgings on Edinburgh's Royal Mile. Luath offers you distinctive writing with a hint of unexpected pleasures.
Most bookshops in the UK, the US, Canada, Australia, New Zealand and parts of Europe, either carry our books in stock or can order them for you. To order direct from us, please send a £sterling cheque, postal order, international money order or your credit card details (number, address of cardholder and expiry date) to us at the address below. Please add post and packing as follows: UK – £1.00 per delivery address; overseas surface mail – £2.50 per delivery address; overseas airmail – £3.50 for the first book to each delivery address, plus £1.00 for each additional book by airmail to the same address. If your order is a gift, we will happily enclose your card or message at no extra charge.

Luath Press Limited
543/2 Castlehill
The Royal Mile
Edinburgh EH1 2ND
Scotland
Telephone: 0131 225 4326 (24 hours)
Email: sales@luath.co.uk
Website: www.luath.co.uk